Regional Development and the European Community
A Canadian Perspective

Ian McAllister

The Institute for Research on Public Policy
L'Institut de recherches politiques
Montreal

Printed in Canada
Legal Deposit Second Quarter
Bibliothèque nationale du Québec

Canadian Cataloguing in Publication Data
McAllister, Ian, 1937-
   Regional development and the European Community

Bibliography: p.
ISBN 0-920380-59-X

1. Regional planning — European Economic Community countries.
2. European Economic Community countries — Economic conditions.
3. European Economic Community countries — Social conditions.
4. Regional planning — Canada. 5. Canada — Economic conditions —
1971- * 6. Canada — Social conditions — 1965- * I. Institute for
Research on Public Policy. II. Title.

HT395.E82M32   338.94   C82-090041-9

The Institute for Research on Public Policy/L'Institut de recherches politiques
2149 Mackay Street, Montreal, Quebec H3G 2J2

Table of Contents

Foreword

A major problem in Canada for many years has been the disparity in the levels of prosperity and in the rates of economic growth among the regions of this country. It is a problem by no means unique to Canada. Most of the advanced, industrialized countries face it in varying degrees. However, such disparities take on a political as well as a social and an economic quality in a federation. States or provinces, identifiable as political units and also responsible as governing authorities for major services under a federal constitution, become rich or poor and effective or constrained in their provision of services to people and institutions.

Fiscal arrangements to effect a degree of redistribution of government income can do much to offset the most serious differences in the capacity of governments, but they are only a palliative. They still leave enormous differences in 'fiscal capacity'. For the individual citizen, the consequences of the differences are seen in differing levels of taxes for services: higher in the provinces or states where the citizens are poorer. The underlying disparities in levels of economic activity and rates of growth are seen in differing rates of employment and unemployment; in widely different opportunities to achieve a satisfactory level of well-being without moving to another part of the country; and in the whole atmosphere of a province or region. Canadian regional disparities appear to be much greater than those in the most comparable federation, Australia. They seem to be not dissimilar in degree from those in the United States. Governments in Canada have made it a policy to try to reduce the differences. Programmes to stimulate development in slow-growth areas have been a feature of our system for many years, with debatable degrees of effectiveness and success.

Two important steps have been taken recently that will affect this important area of government action. The Constitution Act, 1982, for the first time gives constitutional sanction to a commitment to promote "equal opportunities for the well-being of Canadians" and to further "economic development to reduce disparity in opportunities" — all under the general description of "Equalization and Regional

Disparities." It is probably not a provision that will be enforceable in the courts, but both Parliament and legislatures will be constitutionally committed. That commitment is bound to involve some degree of obligation and, presumably, of action. The traditional approaches to regional development and the political pressures to demonstrate some measure of success are bound to be affected.

At the ministerial and administrative level, a major change was announced in the organization of the federal departments involved in economic development and in the allocation of responsibilities to them. The Department of Regional Economic Expansion has disappeared. There is now a Ministry of State for Economic and Regional Development and a Department of Regional Industrial Expansion. The ministry is to co-ordinate policy; the department is to implement programmes, with a more general mandate than that of "DREE."

As federal and provincial governments adjust their regional policies and programmes to these new circumstances, it is appropriate to consider how other nations have approached regional development. This study examines the experiences of the European Economic Community. While there are many obvious differences from Canada, a main one being that the ten provincial governments do not neatly equate with the ten member states of the EEC, one nevertheless is impressed by the similarity of many of the regional issues facing the EEC and Canada. Of particular interest is the manner in which the European Community has sought to balance the development banking role of the European Investment Bank with the broader co-ordinating and aid-granting role of the European Regional Development Fund. Of equal interest are the efforts to sensitize sectoral programmes to regional considerations — not an easy task, as witness the record of the Common Agricultural Policy.

As might be expected, no panaceas emerge from this review, but the book raises many questions that will have surprising familiarity to the Canadian reader and cites different solutions that are provocative.

Gordon Robertson
President

Avant-propos

Depuis nombre d'années, l'écart entre les niveaux de prospérité et entre les taux de croissance économique des différentes régions a constitué un problème d'importance pour le Canada. Ce problème est loin d'être exclusif au Canada : la plupart des pays industrialisés avancés y font face dans une certaine mesure. Dans une fédération, cependant, de telles disparités revêtent des dimensions tant politiques que sociales et économiques. Les États ou les provinces, identifiables comme entités politiques et responsables aussi, en tant que pouvoirs gouvernants, des principaux services aux termes d'une constitution fédérale, deviennent riches ou pauvres, efficaces ou embarrassés dans le cadre de cette prestation de services à la population et aux institutions.

Les dispositions fiscales visant à permettre une certaine redistribution des recettes de l'État peuvent aider énormément à contrebalancer les différences les plus marquées dans les capacités des gouvernements; elles demeurent cependant un palliatif. Il reste toujours d'importantes différences dans la « capacité fiscale ». Pour le citoyen, ces différences se traduisent par divers niveaux d'imposition pour les mêmes services : des impôts plus élevés dans les provinces ou les États aux citoyens les plus pauvres. Les différents taux d'emploi et de chômage, les écarts prononcés entre les possibilités d'atteindre un niveau de vie suffisant sans avoir à déménager dans une autre région et l'atmosphère d'une province ou d'une région témoignent des disparités sous-jacentes des niveaux d'activité économique et des taux de croissance. Les disparités régionales semblent être beaucoup plus prononcées au Canada que dans la fédération qui lui est la plus apparentée, soit l'Australie. Elles semblent à première vue assez comparables, en termes de degré, à celles des États-Unis. Les gouvernements canadiens ont eu comme politique de tenter de combler ces différences. Depuis de nombreuses années, notre régime se distingue par des programmes, au succès et à l'efficacité contestables, destinés à stimuler l'expansion dans les régions à faible croissance.

On a récemment pris deux mesures qui affecteront cet important secteur d'activité gouvernementale. La Loi sur la constitution de 1982 consacre pour la première fois dans la constitution l'engagement de « promouvoir l'égalité des chances de tous les Canadiens dans la recherche de leur bien-être » et de « favoriser le développement économique pour réduire l'inégalité des chances » — cela sous le titre général : « Péréquation et inégalités régionales ». Il ne s'agit probablement pas d'une disposition que les tribunaux pourront faire oberver; mais les législatures et le Parlement seront quand même engagés à la respecter. Cet engagement entraînera sûrement une certaine obligation et, vraisemblablement, certaines actions. On risque fort de voir se modifier les approches classiques du développement régional et augmenter les pressions politiques en vue d'afficher certains succès.

Aux échelons ministériels et administratifs, on a annoncé un changement d'envergure dans l'organisation des ministères fédéraux intéressés au développement économique et dans leurs responsabilités. On a aboli le ministère de l'Expansion économique régionale. Il y a maintenant un ministère d'État canadien au Développement économique régional et un ministère d'Expansion régionale industrielle. Le premier doit coordonner les politiques, tandis que le deuxième, dont le mandat est plus vaste que celui de l'ancien MEER, doit mettre les programmes à exécution.

Pendant que les gouvernements fédéral et provinciaux adaptent leurs politiques et leurs programmes régionaux à ce nouveau contexte, il convient d'examiner comment d'autres pays abordent le développement régional. Cette étude porte sur les expériences de la Communauté économique européenne. Malgré les différences évidentes (dont le fait que les dix gouvernements provinciaux ne sont pas le parfait équivalent des dix États membres de la CEE), on ne peut manquer d'être impressionné par les ressemblances entre de nombreux problèmes régionaux de part et d'autre. La façon dont la CEE a cherché à équilibrer le rôle de banque de développement de la Banque européenne d'investissement et le rôle plus global de subvention et de coordination du Fonds européen de développement régional est particulièrement intéressant. Sont également intéressants les efforts en vue de sensibiliser les programmes sectoriels aux considérations régionales — ce qui n'est certes pas facile, comme en témoigne le dossier de la politique agricole commune.

Comme on peut s'y attendre, cette étude n'offre aucune panacée; elle soulève cependant de nombreuses questions, que le lecteur canadien sera surpris de reconnaître, et offre diverses solutions captivantes.

Le président,
Gordon Robertson

Acknowledgements

I am indebted to Dr. Michael Kirby and Mr. Gordon Robertson, past and present Presidents of The Institute for Research on Public Policy, for their encouragement and support of this work. I am also most grateful to Dalhousie University for enabling me to spend a half-year on sabbatical leave in Europe.

Rector J. Lukaszewski is to be thanked for making me feel welcome at the College of Europe at Brugge, while a particular note of gratitude is due to Mr. Leon Paklon, the chief librarian at the college, and his staff, for being most helpful and hospitable.

To Professor Paul Romus of the University of Brussels, I am most grateful for his great encouragement and for sharing insights that are the result of his many years of experience with the European Commission.

To many members of the European Commission and its agencies in Brussels, and of the European Investment Bank in Luxembourg, I am most appreciative of their assistance, as well as to representatives of national delegations of the member governments and officials on development projects in various parts of the Community. The assistance of many members of the Mission of Canada to the European Communities, in Brussels, was consistently conscientious and cordial.

The encouragement and ideas of the Honourable Pierre de Bané, recently Minister of Regional Economic Expansion, were appreciated. His interest in regional development long preceded his role as minister.

Many people from the various EEC agencies under review have read drafts of the various chapters. Their comments were always constructive.

I am indebted to Mr. Ian MacBain, Deputy Minister of Finance for New Brunswick, to the staff of the Ambassador to the EEC Delegation in Ottawa, to Dean Tom Kent, Faculty of Administrative Studies at Dalhousie, and last alphabetically, but not least, to Dr. E.P. Weeks, all of whom kindly commented on evolving drafts.

Finally a special word of gratitude to Ms. Noreen Marshall, who spent many days commenting on and tightening the chapters in the final period of the work, prior to it reaching Ms. Ann McCoomb. Her editorial work was very greatly appreciated. The typing was done by Ms. Chris Gall, Ms. Jean Pottie, Ms. Ena Morris, and Ms. Constance Cole — always rapidly and with painstaking care.

Ian McAllister

Preface

Since the Treaty of Rome was signed, on 27 March 1957, the European Economic Community (EEC) has sought to tackle its regional development problems through a number of approaches. Prior to the oil crisis of 1973, the same year that saw the enlargement of the Community from six member nations to nine, regional development programming was viewed largely as the responsibility of the national governments. The main exception was the European Investment Bank, a Community instrument that raised its funds on the capital markets and invested the larger proportion in regions that were identified, according to a variety of criteria, as less prosperous.

Since 1973, increased initiatives have been taken, at the European Community level, to help tackle the more extreme regional problems within the EEC. Thus, a new fund was established in 1975 (the European Regional Development Fund), and instructions were given periodically so that the other Community instruments should be more responsive to regional problems.

Much of the onus for 'balanced' regional development still remains, nevertheless, with the national governments. The philosophy of the new European Regional Development Fund, for example, has been to supplement (largely by grants) the regional programmes of the national governments — not to run its own programmes. Such assistance has not, however, been given indiscriminately; the Fund has established frameworks and increasingly lucid criteria in order to generate a more harmonized approach to regional development across the Community. A fine balance has been sought between national-level initiatives, in genuine response to particular regional problems, and national programmes that could compete with each other and serve to balkanize the Community. The intended thrust of all EEC policies has been on integration and harmonization.

In terms of regional policy results, the record appears mixed. Some narrowing of disparities (quite broadly measured) can be argued for the 1960–1970 period, but the last decade has failed to show such progress — indeed conventional measures have tended to reveal somewhat wider discrepancies. Comparative data, however, remain really quite patchy between member countries, even though strides have been made to harmonize many of the regional statistical series.

It is clear that in many of the less prosperous areas, absolute gains can be identified — for example, in infrastructure such as school buildings, roads, and water systems. It is also clear that simply implanting infrastructure does not guarantee subsequent economic development.

The fact that, in overall terms, the record is mixed does not tell one what would have occurred had the various regional measures not been in place. With the downturn of the European economy, the regional situation could quite possibly have been far more serious.

Much the same kind of debate has occurred in Canada, regarding the effectiveness of federal and provincial regional policies. Indeed, it was because Canadian regional policies appear to be approaching a watershed period, dominated by uncertainty over both constitutional arrangements and the economic situation, that this review of the European Economic Community's regional policies was embarked upon. No panacea was expected nor discovered. Many common problems were noted, as well as similar policy and programme approaches. However, in sifting through the EEC experiences, a variety of conclusions and ideas were identified. These are presented in the hope they might provide comparative perspective of practical value to the reappraisal of Canadian regional policy options and their implications that is now gathering momentum.

Periodically throughout the review, Canadian comparisons are made and suggestions offered for Canadian application. In the process, the approach has been to document, in often substantial detail, the approaches of the key EEC regional instruments, so that the material will stand in its own right, regardless of some of the subsequent recommendations or comparative ideas.

The review falls into three main sections and a concluding chapter. Chapter One begins with an outline of the economic pattern of the European Economic Community, from pre–Treaty of Rome days to 1980. The regional distribution of production and employment is documented. The chapter then identifies the main regional problems, as perceived from a number of vantage points in the Community. The delineation of these problems does not tidily flow from the preceding data — albeit the data do serve to provide a backcloth. As in Canada, regional problems are the product of a wide mix of circumstances and often competing perceptions.

The second chapter seeks to identify the main thrusts of the national-level regional policies and programmes. A smorgasbord of regional policies and programmes is in evidence, and it is often by no means 'cut and dried' where a regional policy or programme begins or finishes, as distinct from broader macro or sectoral policies and programmes. Thus, the determination of what really constitutes a regional policy or programme is somewhat arbitrary. The second chapter draws heavily on a number of reviews of national-level regional policies, supplemented by observations from site visits, interviews, and supplementary data. As with the first chapter, it provides background to the main body of the work, which focuses on the EEC instruments.

Chapters Three to Seven concentrate on the European Economic Community and its main regional policy instruments and experiences. Chapter Three provides background on the institutions and general framework of the EEC. Chapter Four examines the first of the Community's regional development instruments — the European Investment Bank. Chapter Five reviews the record and experiences of the European Regional Development Fund. Chapters Six and Seven examine, respectively, the European Social Fund and the Common Agricultural Policy, in so far as they touch upon regional development policy.

Finally, Chapter Eight draws together some of the main experiences and conclusions with reference particularly to Canadian regional policy consideration.

List of Figures, Maps, and Tables

The European Community and Regional Development

1

Introduction

This chapter provides a general introduction to the ten-member European Economic Community.

The first section indicates the population changes since the Treaty of Rome came into effect on 1 January 1958,[1] and goes on to outline the broad pattern of the Community's economic performance, broken into three main phases — the immediate post-war decade, 1960–1972, and 1973–1980. Production and employment data are summarized, including their regional distribution. The growth in unemployment is documented.

The second section focuses on the main regional problems in the European Community, as perceived from a number of vantage points. It is primarily to tackle these problems that the instruments of national and European Community regional policies have been shaped. They form the subject of much of the rest of the review.

I. Population, Production, Employment, and Regional Distribution

Population

In 1958, the six founding member countries of the European Community had a population approaching 170 million. By 1972 this had increased to 190 million. With the entry of the United Kingdom, Denmark, and the Republic of Ireland in January 1973, the Community's population rose to 257 million. In 1981, including Greece as the tenth member, the Community contained some 270 million people.

Since the beginning of the 1960s, there has been a decline in the national rates of increase in the Community — attributable to falling birth rates (partly a reflection of the population age structure and partly due to the tendency to have fewer children). In the latter half of the 1970s, there has been a significant drop in net immigration, as the Community has sought to contain problems of growing unemployment.

Map 1.1
REGIONAL MAP OF THE EUROPEAN COMMUNITY

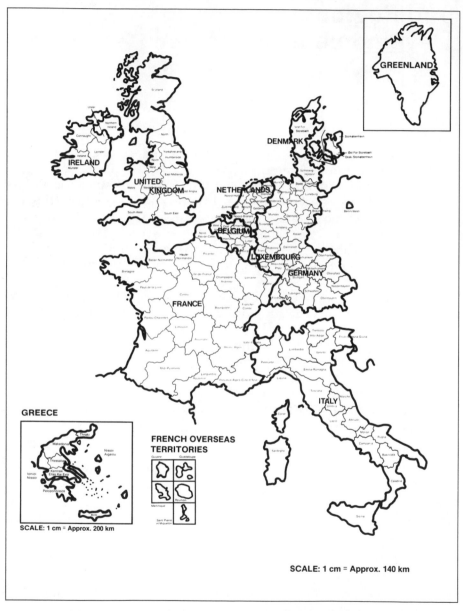

Source: Commission of the European Communities, *Regional Development Atlas 1979* (Brussels: 1979).

Table 1.1
POPULATION PROJECTIONS 1958–1985

	Estimated Total Population[a] (millions)		Proportions of Population by Age[b]							
			0–14		15–50		60+		75+	
	1958	1980	1975	1985	1975	1985	1975	1985	1975	1985
G	54.3	61.3	21.7	15.9	58.2	64.5	20.0	19.6	4.7	6.3
F	44.8	53.7	24.1	21.9	57.5	60.4	18.4	17.8	5.1	6.1
I	49.5	57.1	24.2	21.1	58.4	60.7	17.5	18.1	4.1	5.2
NL	11.2	14.1	25.6	20.5	59.3	63.1	15.1	16.4	4.0	4.8
B	9.0	9.8	22.6	18.8	58.2	62.2	19.2	19.1	5.0	6.0
L	0.3	0.4	20.2	17.5	61.4	64.7	18.5	17.8	:	:
UK	51.9	55.9	23.3	19.8	57.0	59.8	19.7	20.3	5.0	6.1
IRL	2.8	3.4	31.8	30.3	55.3	55.2	15.4	14.5	4.1	3.9
DK	4.5	5.1	22.8	14.7	58.8	60.3	18.7	20.1	5.0	6.2
EUR 9	228.3	260.9	23.9	20.6	58.0	61.2	18.0	18.2	4.6	5.6
G	8.3	9.4								

Sources: [a] Eurostat
          [b] Commission of the European Communities, *The Regions of Europe* (Brussels: January 1981), p. 9.

Table 1.1 shows the population for 1980, by member country, and projections to 1985, indicating a likely growth in the proportion of the population in the labour-force age group and also in the number aged 60 and over.

Population Density

The Community's population is far from evenly distributed. Some 25 per cent of the population live on about 6 per cent of the land area, and some 50 per cent live on approximately 20 per cent of the territory. Map 1.2 illustrates the population density in 1978. Despite substantial internal migration over the past two decades, the relative pattern of population density has not changed markedly. Thus, the ten regions of lowest density accounted, in 1961, for 5.3 per cent of the total population (of the nine) and covered 18.2 per cent of the territory; in 1977, they still accounted for 5.3 per cent of the population. Conversely, in 1961, the ten most densely populated regions (covering 3.9 per cent of the Community land area) contained 18.4 per cent of the population; in 1970, this was 18.2 per cent; and in 1977, it was 17.8 per cent of the total population.[2]

Map 1.2
POPULATION DENSITY IN 1978

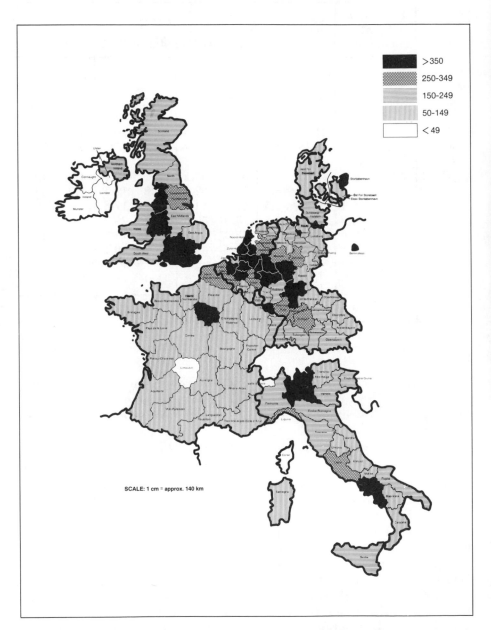

SCALE: 1 cm = approx. 140 km

Source: Commission of the European Communities, *The Regions of Europe* (Brussels: January 1981), p. 129.

Map 1.3
URBAN POPULATION CHANGE BY REGION 1960–1970

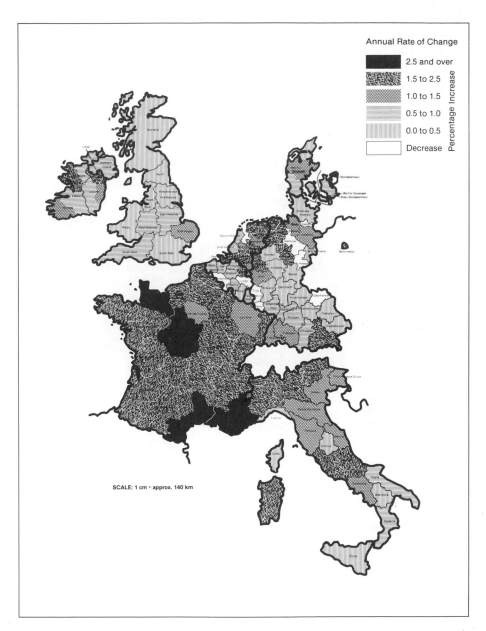

Source: Commission of the European Communities, *The Regions of Europe* (Brussels: January 1981), p. 21.

The Netherlands and Belgium remained the most densely populated member countries throughout the 1960s and 1970s, while Ireland and France were the least densely populated. All member countries with the exception of the Netherlands experienced increased population density, in some regions, over the period. France had the greatest proportional increase during the 1960s, but Ireland took the lead in the 1970s.[3]

Urbanization

France, Italy, and Ireland have had quite substantial increases in the proportion of population in major urban areas over the past two decades; Denmark's increases were far more modest. Conversely, Germany, the United Kingdom, the Netherlands, Luxembourg, and Belgium experienced a modest decline in the proportion of population in major urban areas over the same period.[4] Maps 1.3 and 1.4 show urban population change by region for the periods 1960–70 and 1970–80.

In France, the greatest increases in urbanization have occurred in the provinces bordering on the Mediterranean and in the areas south and west of Paris, although all regions experienced greater than average increases in urbanization, especially in the 1960s. Northern and central Italy and Sardenga experienced rapid urbanization in the 1960s whereas Abruzzi, Molise, Puglia, and Sardegna had the greatest increases in the 1970s. Rapid urbanization in Ireland has been concentrated in the Mayo and Galway areas as well as the regions on the southern border of Northern Ireland and down to Dublin. The Storkobenhavn region of Denmark has also had a high annual rate of increase in urbanization throughout the period.

Germany experienced decreases in urbanization in the western regions bordering on Luxembourg as well as the Schleswig-Holstein area in the north and some regions bordering East Germany. Most regions of Belgium with the exception of Limburg experienced very minor increases or even decreases in urbanization. The Drenthe area of Holland had the greatest urbanization throughout the period with the Zeeland area experiencing a decrease in the 1970s. The north and northwest regions of the United Kingdom, as well as the southwest, had decreases in urbanization in the 1970s.

Caution has to be exercised in generalizations about urbanization, particularly given the relatively congested nature of much of Europe. While narrowly defined urban areas may be experiencing slower growth or some outflow of population, frequently (as in the United Kingdom) the people are spreading into the surrounding hinterlands and along the transport routes. Extreme land use and environmental pressures are apparent across much of Europe in the countryside surrounding middle- and larger-sized towns.

Map 1.4
URBAN POPULATION CHANGE BY REGION 1970–1980

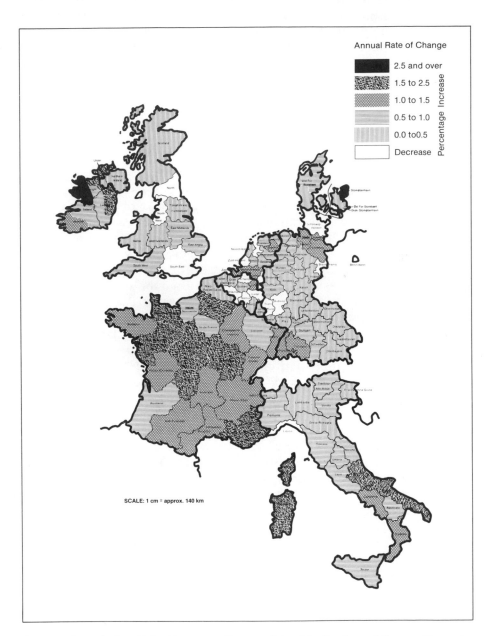

Source: Commission of the European Communities, *The Regions of Europe* (Brussels: January 1981), p. 22.

A 'Damming Up' of Poorer Areas

During the 1970s, a 'damming up' process seemed to have been occurring in poorer areas such as southern Italy. Thus, whereas in the 1960s, 51 of the regions of the Community (of a predominately rural category) saw net out-migration, for the 1970s this had been reduced to 34, and for 12 of these the rate had slowed.[5] The less favourable employment climate, in the more central/northern regions to which workers formerly migrated, was the main cause for such a change.

Production and Employment

Production

In overall terms, the European (nine) Community's economic performance, since 1945, can be broken into three phases. The immediate post-war decade featured reconstruction of industrial plant, agricultural capacity, and urban transport/energy infrastructure. Then, from the mid-1950s, followed an era, running to 1973, of general economic prosperity and the development of a 'consumer society', with access to automobiles, a wide variety of services, credit cards, and television sets. The prosperity was far from evenly distributed, but absolute gains were widespread.[6] Then followed the post-1973 era. This was a period of faltering economic adjustments in conjunction with periodic oil price hikes.[7] An overall impression of the last two phases is captured in Table 1.2.

Four features might be highlighted from Table 1.2. First, the period of rapid expansion was followed (from 1974 on) by chequered growth in Gross Domestic Product (GDP). Secondly, productivity growth also faltered. Thirdly, unemployment rates — after tight conditions throughout the 1960–1973 period — steadily worsened. Fourthly, the rise in consumer prices, after more than a decade of relative stability at a low level, moved to substantially higher plateaux.

As measured in aggregates such as GDP, economic growth was far from uniform among the individual member countries. This is indicated in Table 1.3.[8]

In 1958, Germany and France can be seen to have ranked somewhat behind the United Kingdom. By 1973, Germany had established a commanding lead over France, with the United Kingdom trailing behind and only just ahead of Italy. The picture, in 1980, has remained the same as in 1973, so far as GDP 'placings' are concerned.

In terms of the average annual growth rate of GDP, France had the best overall record followed closely by Italy and then Germany. The United Kingdom trailed badly in all three periods. All member countries had slower rates of GDP growth after 1973, particularly in 1975, when all but Ireland and France suffered negative growth in real terms (Table 1.4).

Table 1.2

THE COMMUNITY ECONOMY 1960–1981

	GDP volume growth	Productivity growth	Rise in consumer prices	Compensation per employee	Current account balance of payments	General government financial deficits	Savings ratio of households	Monetary supply growth M2/M3	Unemployed in labour force
	$\%^b$	$\%^c$	$\%^b$	$\%^b$	% GDP	% GDP	%	$\%^b$	%
1960-1972	4.8	4.6	4.0	9.3	0.5	-0.3	:	11.3	2.2
1973	5.9	4.8	8.2	14.3	0.1	-0.7	18.1	17.5	2.5
1974	1.7	1.6	12.7	16.9	-0.0	-1.7	18.6	12.4	2.9
1975	-1.4	-0.1	12.5	16.5	0.0	-5.6	19.4	13.2	4.3
1976	5.0	5.2	10.3	12.4	-0.5	-3.8	18.0	12.7	4.9
1977	2.3	2.0	9.8	10.1	0.2	-3.3	16.8	12.7	5.3
1978	3.0	2.6	7.3	9.7	0.8	-4.0	16.8	13.5	5.5
1979	3.4	2.6	8.6	10.6	-0.5	-3.6	17.1	12.2	5.6
1980	1.3	1.2	12.0	13.1	-1.5	-3.5	16.6	10.6	6.0
1981^a	0.6	0.9	9.7	10.3	-1.2	-3.9	16.9	9.0	6.8

Source: Commission of the European Communities, *European Economy Annual Economic Report 1980–81* (Brussels: November 1980), p. 12.

Notes: ^a Forecasts of the Commission services on the basis of present or anticipated policies.
^b % change over previous period.
^c Per occupied person, whole economy.

Table 1.3
GDP 1958–1980, '000 MILLION ECU,* AT CURRENT PRICES AND EXCHANGE RATES

	DK	G	F	IRL	I	NL	B	L	UK	EC
1958	4.6	53.5	53.0	1.4	29.3	8.4	9.2	0.4	58.2	218.1
1968	12.2	130.0	121.0	2.9	78.7	24.1	19.9	0.8	101.1	490.6
1973	23.5	280.4	203.4	5.3	125.3	49.0	36.7	1.6	144.6	870.2
1980	47.3	593.0	593.0	12.7	281.3	116.5	83.4	3.2	360.3	1966.7

Source: Commission of the European Communities, *European Economy Annual Economic Report 1980–81* (Brussels: November 1980), p. 137, Table 5.
Note: * See the Glossary for an explanation of the currency units of the Community.

Table 1.4
GDP VOLUME GROWTH 1958–1980 ANNUAL AVERAGE PER CENT CHANGES

	DK	G	F	IRL	I	NL	B	L	UK	EC
1958–67	5.0	4.8	5.2	3.4	5.7	4.5	4.0	3.3	2.9	4.5
1968–73	4.5	5.3	5.6	5.1	5.0	5.5	5.2	5.9	3.5	5.0
1974–80	1.6	2.4	2.9	3.1	2.8	2.3	2.1	1.1	0.6	2.2

Source: Commission of the European Communities, *European Economy Annual Economic Report 1980–81* (Brussels: November 1980), p. 138, Table 7.

Table 1.5
GDP PER CAPITA 1958–1980, ECU, AT CURRENT PRICES AND EXCHANGE RATES

	DK	G	F	IRL	I	NL	B	L	UK	EC
1958	1008	986	1183	499	592	751	1024	1337	1122	955
1968	2506	2184	2424	997	1485	1895	2072	2371	1832	1978
1973	4689	4524	3910	1733	2281	3649	3767	4484	2583	3391
1980	9229	9674	8735	3713	4923	8259	8462	8791	6445	7538

Source: Commission of the European Communities, *European Economy Annual Economic Report 1980–81* (Brussels: November 1980), p. 137, Table 6.

Table 1.5 shows per capita GDP for the member states. In 1958, Luxembourg had the highest per capita GDP followed by France and the United Kingdom. By 1968, Denmark had assumed the lead with France again in second place, and the United Kingdom had dropped to seventh place ahead of Italy and Ireland. Germany replaced France in the number-two position by 1973 and had the highest per capita GDP in 1980.

Table 1.6
GDP PER CAPITA GROWTH 1960–1978 ANNUAL
AVERAGE PER CENT CHANGES

	DK	G	F	IRL	I	NL	B	L	UK	EC
1960–67[a]	4.0	2.9	4.3	*	4.9	4.1***	3.9	1.9	2.2	3.4
1968–73[b]	3.8	4.6	4.7	3.1**	4.2	4.4	4.9	5.0	3.2	4.3
1974–78[b]	1.4	2.2	2.6	2.3	1.5	1.8	2.0	0.5	1.2	1.9

Sources: [a] Calculated from Eurostat, *National Accounts ESA — Aggregates* (Luxembourg: Statistical Office of the European Communities, 1977), p. 8.
  [b] Calculated from Eurostat, *National Accounts ESA — Aggregates* (Luxembourg: Statistical Office of the European Communities, 1980), p. 160.
Notes: * Information not available.
       ** 1971–73.
       *** 1964–68.

Table 1.6 shows again the drop in growth rates after 1973. In 1975, only Ireland showed a positive per capita GDP growth rate. France again had the best growth record over the period.

Distribution: Gross Domestic Product Per Head by Region

A recent EEC study (COM(80)816 Final) concluded, when breaking down GDP on a smaller-region basis, that after a slight contraction of regional disparities during the 1960s, as measured by GDP per head (valued at current market prices and exchange rates), the gap had widened somewhat in the 1970s. Thus, the study found that the relative gap between the ten strongest and ten weakest regions rose from 2.9:1 in 1970 to 4.0:1 in 1977. Two reasons were viewed to be important for this reversal. First, the different performance records of the member-state economies and, secondly, the 1960s had seen emigration from the peripheral (largely weaker regions) to the central areas of the Community, whereas the 1970s had seen a stemming, and sometimes even reversal, of such a process.

   The regions where GDP per head was below the Community average (of the ten), for 1977, are shown in Map 1.5. The addition of Greece increases the number of regions that have less than 50 per cent of the Community average level of GDP per head from nine to sixteen. It also means a widening of the relative gap between the ten richest and ten poorest regions from a ratio of 4:1 to 5:1 (on the basis of 1977 data).[9]

   The regions where GDP per head is significantly below the Community average (i.e., less than 75 per cent of the average) are in Greece; the Mezzogiorno, central, and northeastern regions of Italy; the United Kingdom regions other than the London-dominated South East; Ireland; Greenland; and the French Overseas Department.

   Apart from variations in factor endowments, the two main reasons for the regional discrepancies are differences in employment rates and

Map 1.5
GDP PER CAPITA SITUATION IN 1977 FOR THE
COMMUNITY OF TEN*

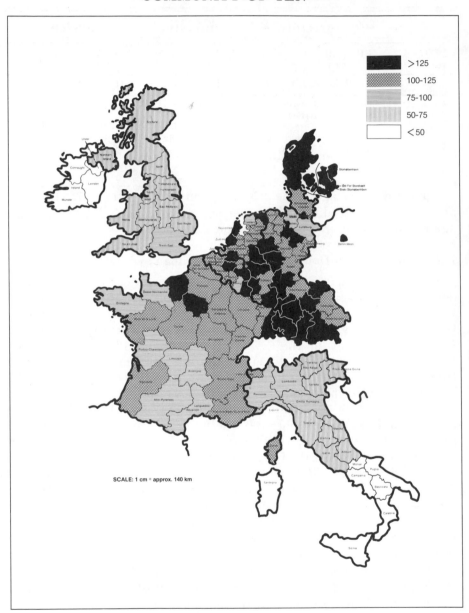

Source: Commission of the European Communities, *The Regions of Europe* (Brussels:
January 1981), p. 105.
Note: * French Overseas Departments and Greenland not included in calculations.
Greece was included and fell <50 except in the regions including Athens and
Thessaloniki (50−75 range).

Table 1.7
PERCENTAGE OF TOTAL WORK-FORCE IN THREE MAIN-SECTOR GROUPINGS

	Agriculture		Industry		Services	
	1950	1971	1950	1971	1950	1971
Belgium	13	4	49	44	38	50
Luxembourg	26	10	40	47	34	43
France	28	13	37	40	35	45
Germany	22	8	45	49	33	42
Italy	44	19	30	43	27	35
Netherlands	13	7	40	38	45	54
EEC (Six)	29	12	38	43	33	45

Source: Hugh Clout, *The Regional Problem in Western Europe* (Cambridge: Cambridge University Press, 1976), p. 8.
Note: The post-1973 experience can be seen in Table 1.8.

in productivity. The latter is viewed as of greater significance in the recent assessment by the European Commission.[10]

Employment Distribution by Sector

The European Community (of six) faced the 1973 enlargement, and oil price increases, after a period of sweeping structural transformation that had begun long before the signing of the Treaty of Rome. Table 1.7 illustrates the scale of change. The proportion of the work-force in agriculture was radically reduced, the growth sector being services heavily oriented to an urban life-style. Modest expansion had occurred in the manufacturing sector.

    After 1973, employment in agriculture continued to decline, reflecting productivity gains as more 'modern' production systems continued to be applied; the service sector continued to absorb some additional labour (see Table 1.8). The major difference was that the manufacturing sector reversed its trend of the 1960s, now also reducing its labour requirements. In the Canadian situation, it can be noted that the proportions were not the same, but the trends were (albeit there was a modest increase in the absolute numbers employed in manufacturing).

Regional Employment by Sector

In Maps 1.6 to 1.8, agricultural, industrial, and tertiary employment are shown, by region, as a proportion of total employment in the nine

Table 1.8
CIVILIAN EMPLOYMENT BY SECTOR
(in thousands)

	Agriculture			Industry			Services		
	1971	1974	1978	1971	1974	1978	1971	1974	1978
Belgium	162	140	123*	1,581	1,565	1,213*	1,961	2,096	2,181*
Luxembourg	11	10	9*	66	72	66*	61	68	72*
France	2,683	2,236	1,907	8,102	8,287	7,764	9,653	10,435	11,250
Germany	2,144	1,882	1,608	12,611	12,158	11,124	11,470	11,648	11,947
Italy	3,875	3,412	3,090	7,617	7,639	7,633	7,603	8,358	9,209
Netherlands	320	304	289*	1,743	1,629	1,513	2,549	2,645	2,753
Denmark	256	227	219*	869	761	735*	1,213	1,367	1,460*
Ireland	273	254	236*	323	331	310*	451	470	476*
UK	736	683	654	10,547	10,457	9,774	12,748	13,575	14,183
EEC (Nine)	10,460	9,148	8,372*	43,459	42,899	40,520*	47,709	50,662	52,835*
EEC (Nine) (per cent)	10.3	8.9	8.2*	42.8	41.8	39.8	46.9	49.3	51.9
EEC (Six) (per cent)	12.3	10.7	9.5	42.7	42.0	39.7	44.8	47.3	50.9
Canada	607	579	573	2,470	2,784	2,864	5,027	5,762	6,535
Canada (per cent)	7.5	6.3	5.7	30.5	30.5	28.7	62.0	63.1	65.5

Source: For 1971, 1974, and 1977 data — compiled from O.E.C.D., *Labour Force Statistics 1966–1977* (Paris: 1979), Table 7.
For 1978 data — compiled from O.E.C.D., *Labour Force Statistics* (November 1979, Quarterly Supplement).

Note: * 1977 not 1978 data.

Map 1.6
AGRICULTURAL EMPLOYMENT IN 1977
(Employment in Agriculture as a Proportion
of Total Employment)

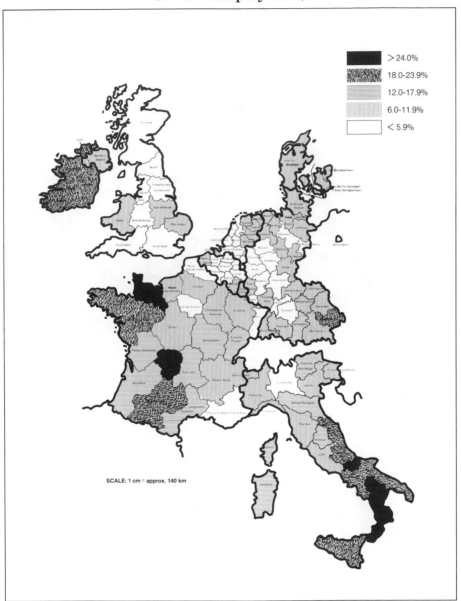

> 24.0%

18.0-23.9%

12.0-17.9%

6.0-11.9%

< 5.9%

SCALE: 1 cm = approx. 140 km

Source: Commission of the European Communities, *Regional Development Atlas 1979*
(Brussels: 1979).

Map 1.7
INDUSTRIAL EMPLOYMENT IN 1977
(Employment in Industry as a Proportion of Total Employment)

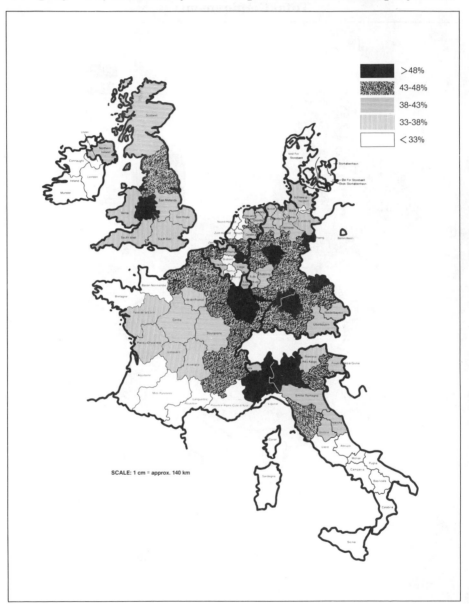

Source: Commission of the European Communities, *The Regions of Europe* (Brussels: January 1981), p. 77.

Map 1.8
TERTIARY EMPLOYMENT IN 1977
(Employment in the Services as a Proportion of
Total Employment)

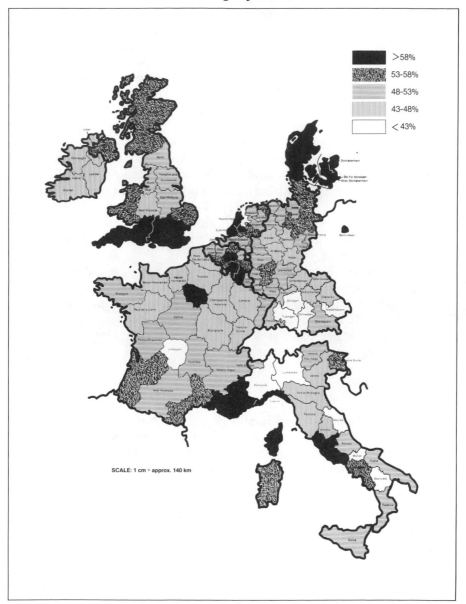

Source: Commission of the European Communities, *The Regions of Europe* (Brussels:
January 1981), p. 82.

members of the community for 1977. In general, high percentages of the labour force employed in agriculture are associated with regions with low GDP per head, and further studies suggest considerable underemployment[11] in agriculture, particularly in Italy, the southeast regions of France, and Brittany.[12] Conversely, the highest agricultural incomes are to be found in the north and centre of the Community, based on generally large farms (producing cereals and sugar beet particularly) in East Anglia and the Paris Basin, mixed farming (much of North Germany), or small but intensive holdings for livestock or market gardening (the Netherlands). In each case, productivity is high, and a relatively small proportion of the labour force is so employed.

In Map 1.7, industrial employment can be seen to be concentrated in the centre of the Community, especially in Germany, Belgium, the Netherlands, much of north and northeastern France, the Midlands and more northern parts of England, and northwestern Italy (especially the Milano−Torino triangle). Table 1.9 gives a very broad picture of the regions specializing in slower-growing sectors (such as textiles), and faster-growing sectors (such as market services and transport equipment).

Finally, tertiary employment is shown to have reached its highest proportions around the capitals and largest cities (Map 1.8). The public sector, it might be noted, accounts for over 45 per cent of the Community's GDP and tends to be concentrated in the capitals, although all member countries have fostered programmes of decentralization over the past two decades.[13]

Unemployment Rates by Region

As the overall unemployment rates for the 1970s indicate (Table 1.10), the structural changes failed to absorb the numbers seeking work and, overall, relatively higher unemployment rates prevailed. As will be emphasized in later chapters, this scenario has substantially coloured regional development policy formulation in the latter half of the 1970s.

A broad pattern of unemployment rates, based on 1979 data, can be gleaned from Map 1.9. The Italian Mezzogiorno, Ireland, Northern Ireland, and Scotland reflect a long-standing pattern of high unemployment rates, but the spread of higher unemployment to a number of regions in France, Belgium, and broader areas of the United Kingdom can also be seen. Map 1.10, based on 1977 data, provides a view of the more serious aspects of unemployment — the longer-term rates (i.e., unemployment lasting six months or more). Much of southern and central Italy, Limburg, Hainaut and Liège in Belgium, Corsica in France, and Ireland are shown to be so affected.

Map 1.9
UNEMPLOYMENT RATES IN 1979
(EEC 9 = 100)

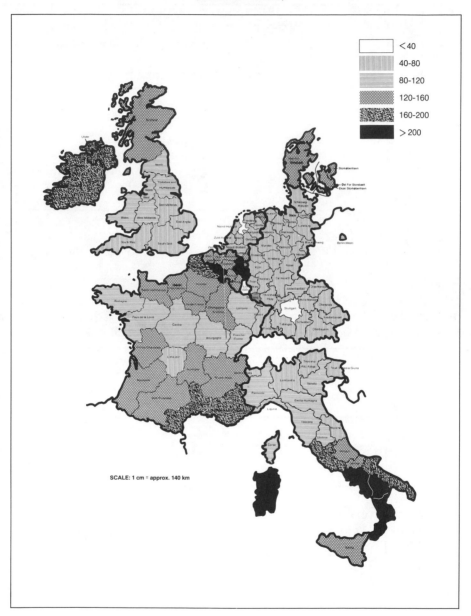

Source: Commission of the European Communities, *The Regions of Europe* (Brussels: January 1981), p. 25.

Table 1.9
REGIONS WITH HIGH SPECIALIZATION IN SLOWER-GROWING AND FASTER-GROWING SECTORS 1970–1977[a]

	Slower-Growing Sectors					Faster-Growing Sectors			
	Agriculture, Forestry, and Fishing	Ores, Ferrous and Non-Ferrous Metals*	Textiles, Leather, and Clothing*	Food, Beverages, and Tobacco*	Minerals and Non-Metallic Products*	Transport Equipment*	Non-Market Services	Other Market Services	Credit Insurance
	31 Regions	*16 Regions*	*13 Regions*	*8 Regions*	*8 Regions*	*9 Regions*	*1 Region*	*3 Regions*	*9 Regions*
	Calabria Puglia Basilicata Abruzzi Molise Emilia-Romagna Sicilia Campania Veneto Marche Sardegna Umbria Trentino-Alto Adige	Valle d'Aosta Umbria Liguria Sardegna Piemonte Trentino-Alto Adige Lombardia	Toscana Marche Lombardia Veneto Umbria		Emilia-Romagna Abruzzi Toscana Veneto Umbria	Piemonte			Lazio Lombardia Liguria
	Champagne-Ardenne Languedoc-Roussillon Bretagne Bourgogne Basse-Normandie Picardie Limousin Auvergne Centre Midi-Pyrénées Poitou-Charentes Pays de la Loire Aquitaine	Lorraine Nord-Pas-De-Calais Basse-Normandie	Nord-Pas-De-Calais Alsace Champagne-Ardenne	Alsace Aquitaine	Alsace Picardie	Franche-Comté Haute-Normandie Pays de la Loire Picardie Ile de France		Ile de France Provence-Alpes-Côte d'Azur-Corse	Ile de France
	Schleswig-Holstein Niedersachsen							Hessen	
	Ireland			Ireland Northern Ireland Scotland South West East Anglia					
	East Anglia	Wales Yorkshire and Humberside North West Midlands	East Midlands Northern Ireland Yorkshire and Humberside North West			West Midlands North West South West		South East	South East
	East Netherlands								West Netherlands
		Luxembourg (G.D.)							Luxembourg (G.D.)
		Region Wallon		Denmark*	Region Wallon		Brussels Region		Brussels Region

Source: Commission of the European Communities, *The Regions of Europe* (Brussels: January 1981), p. 85.

Notes: * Regional data not available for Germany or Denmark

Map 1.10
UNEMPLOYMENT LASTING SIX MONTHS AND OVER AS A PROPORTION OF LABOUR FORCE, 1977

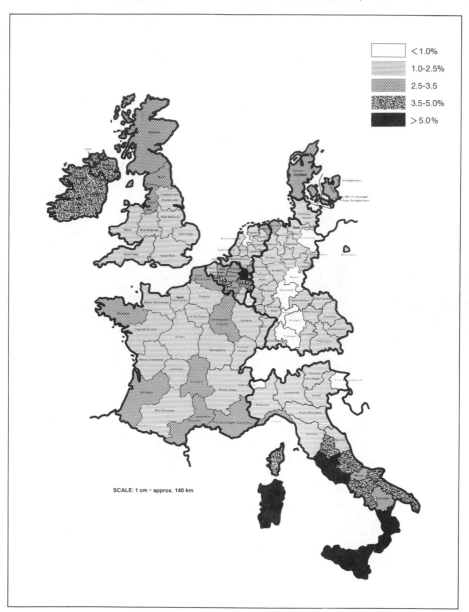

SCALE: 1 cm = approx. 140 km

Legend:
- <1.0%
- 1.0-2.5%
- 2.5-3.5
- 3.5-5.0%
- >5.0%

Source: Commission of the European Communities, *The Regions of Europe* (Brussels: January 1981), p. 31.

Table 1.10
NUMBERS UNEMPLOYED, 1970–1980, AS A
PERCENTAGE OF CIVIL ACTIVE POPULATION

	DK	G	F	IRL	I	NL	B	L	UK	EC
1970	1.0	0.6	1.3	5.3	4.4	1.0	2.2	0.0	2.5	2.0
1971	1.2	0.7	1.6	5.2	5.1	1.3	2.2	0.0	3.2	2.5
1972	1.2	0.9	1.8	6.0	5.2	2.3	2.8	0.0	3.5	2.7
1973	0.7	1.0	1.8	5.6	4.9	2.3	2.9	0.0	2.5	2.5
1974	2.0	2.2	2.3	6.0	4.8	2.8	3.2	0.0	2.4	1.9
1975	4.6	4.2	3.9	8.5	5.3	4.0	5.3	0.2	3.8	4.3
1976	4.7	4.1	4.3	9.5	5.6	4.3	6.8	0.3	5.3	4.9
1977	5.8	4.0	4.8	9.4	6.4	4.1	7.8	0.5	5.7	5.3
1978	6.5	3.9	5.2	8.7	7.1	4.1	8.4	0.7	5.7	5.5
1979	5.3	3.4	6.0	7.9	7.5	4.1	8.8	0.7	5.3	5.6
(1980)	5.8	3.5	6.5	8.7	7.5	4.8	9.2	0.6	6.5	6.0

Source: Commission of the European Communities, *European Economy Annual Economic Report 1980–81* (Brussels: November 1980), p. 136.

Further refinements of the labour-force data reveal a growing number of young people reaching working age and a substantial increase in the female participation rates (and unemployment rates of both categories). Maps 1.11 and 1.12 illustrate these points.

II. Perceptions of Regional Problems in the European Community

Broad Issues
Since 1973, broad economic and security issues have dominated development policy formulation in the European Community.[14] The overall problems have been viewed in terms of the following:

- Energy saving and the development of new sources

- The containment of inflation with minimal social upheaval

- The improvement of the Community's overall competitiveness in the face of increased competition (from countries such as Japan and South Korea) and rising costs that were not associated only with the energy situation

- The maintenance of a viable international monetary system

- Rising levels of unemployment across much of the Community

- International security, with particular concern being expressed about reliable access to oil supplies, the developments in Afghanis-

Map 1.11
SHARE OF YOUTH UNEMPLOYMENT IN
TOTAL UNEMPLOYMENT, 1977

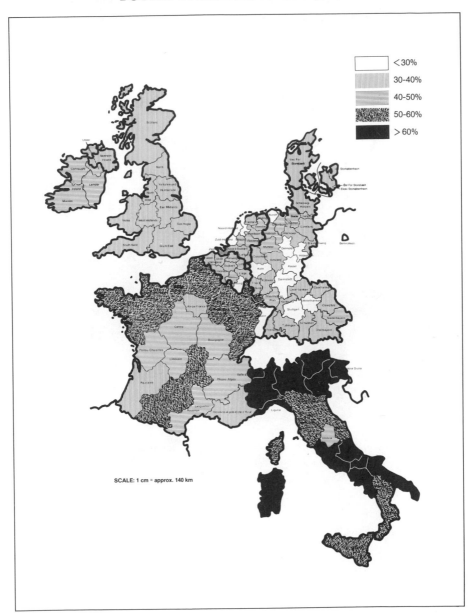

Source: Commission of the European Communities, *The Regions of Europe* (Brussels:
January 1981), p. 33.

Map 1.12
FEMALE LONG-TERM UNEMPLOYMENT AS PER CENT
OF TOTAL LONG-TERM UNEMPLOYMENT, 1977

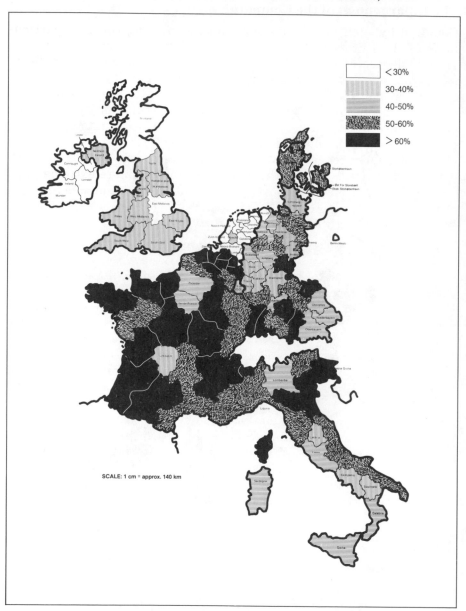

Source: Commission of the European Communities, *The Regions of Europe* (Brussels: January 1981), p. 34.

tan, Poland, Iran and, most recently, the United States government under President Reagan.

The Enlargement of the Community

Coloured by such broad considerations, a growing concern (particularly at the European Community level) has been how to achieve a greater degree of regional balance across the Community. In large part, this reflects the recognition that the Community, as a whole, is only as strong as the sum of its parts; in part, it is because the somewhat deep-rooted nature of many of the regional problems is now better appreciated, after two decades of substantial public expenditures. This concern is heightened because the list of future applicants (and indeed Greece as newest member) comprises countries with extreme disparities within their borders, and yet more extreme gaps when contrasted with the majority of the more affluent members.

What Are the Regional Development Problems?

The data in the earlier part of this chapter illustrate, in sweeping terms, the context in which the regional issues are set. Over the past few years, in particular since the formation of the European Regional Development Fund, there have been efforts to identify and compare, in far more explicit terms than hitherto, the character and scale of regional problems across the Community as a whole. Such work is far from complete in any definitive sense. The very delineation of regions is a somewhat arbitrary process. For example, for many statistical purposes, the nine member countries have been broken into European Community Regions, of which there are 52, and also into Basic administrative units, of which there are 112.[15] Such divisions may appear tidy statistical frameworks, but they often fail to reflect economic realities, as well as social and political perceptions of what are appropriate regions. Moreover, some territorial areas — which cross two or more of the 'statistical' regions — are far more homogeneous (or alternatively complementary) on the basis of political, cultural, or economic criteria than is shown by the regional demarcation lines or even by national boundaries.

From the painstaking work on both economic and social statistics, to date, two broad conclusions can be drawn:

1. The statistical information, on which much regional problem and policy analysis is based, is still far from homogeneous between countries — or comprehensive within countries. The state of the art is far from advanced, although substantial progress has been made in the past few years.[16]

2. Public perceptions are particularly focused on regional problems and issues at the member-state level, rather than at the Community level at large. Two points will illustrate. (a) A recent survey, based on 8,892 interviews, found that the principle of assisting less-favoured regions is accepted by public opinion in the Community, but people have greater reservations when it comes to devoting part of taxes paid to the development of such areas in other Community countries.[17] This is reinforced, at the political level, each time the Community budget is prepared and member governments clash swords over their net national contributions. (b) In the overall spectrum of regional disparities and balance, Germany (particularly but not exclusively) really does not have regional disparity problems of anything like the dimensions of Italy or Greece. Yet, quite understandably from the vantage point of their own national balance, German politicians are concerned about achieving more balanced growth and income distribution in Germany. Indeed, the countries that already enjoy the greater degree of balanced regional economic development appear, in many ways, the most concerned about further improving the regional balance in their countries (e.g., Germany and the Netherlands). The merits of balance are perhaps best appreciated by those who have more nearly achieved it.

The broad delineation of regional problems and issues, in the European Community, is thus — just as in Canada and most other countries — a product of political consensus and compromise, social perception and agitation, supported (and sometimes contradicted) by growing use of economic and social statistics.[18]

Seven Main Categories of Regional Problems

Out of such a process, it is possible to identify some broad level of consensus as to what are the main regional problems of the Community today. The problems fall into the following categories:

1. *Peripheral areas of the Community*, most of which have a far higher proportion of the labour force in agriculture (than the average) and yet have relatively low productivity measures for agriculture. They tend to be characterized by low income levels, high unemployment, underemployment, and low-quality infrastructure. The Italian Mezzogiorno, much of rural Greece and Ireland, and large areas in the west of France fall into this category.

2. *Old, industrial areas* that have failed to adjust, or are in the very slow throes of adjusting, to sweeping structural and technological changes. These include areas built on the basis of shipyards, such as Genova in Italy and the Clyde and Tyneside in the United Kingdom; areas dominated by older coal and steel complexes such as Charleroi in Belgium, the south of Luxembourg and Saarland, Wales, and the northern United Kingdom; and textile areas such as Lancashire that are facing competition from Third World countries. Among the alarming features about these regions, in addition to the high

unemployment levels and run-down character of much of the industrial plant, is the degree of the general environmental degradation
and the poor quality of social infrastructure.

3. *Urban growth problems*, where the cities are dominating very broad
areas, yet have failed to digest effectively the influx of people
including commuters from outlying communities. In turn, many of
these communities have themselves become caught in the urban
sprawl. Milano, London, and Paris are extreme cases in point, but
large numbers of other cities that have exceeded the one million mark
(a rough indicator) show signs of serious strain.

4. *Environmental degradation*, although not so widely commented on
in the literature, is clearly a problem of major proportions and one that
member countries are treating in radically different ways. On the one
hand, Germany, France, and the Netherlands appear to be integrating
environmental guide-lines with their regional development planning
in a serious (and often most effective) manner. On the other hand,
Italy in particular and Belgium to a lesser degree (largely in the
coastal zone around Zeebrugge) appear to be negligent.

5. *Frontier regions* are the areas abutting the East European bloc
countries. West Germany has developed incentives to encourage
greater development along these borders.

6. *Mountain village areas*, particularly in Italy and Greece, where
inadequate infrastructure (including roads, power, and irrigation) has
compounded the problems of isolation and terrain.

7. *Ethnic divisions* that are linked, in varying degrees, to economic
circumstances. One of the continuing challenges to EEC regional
policy has been the appropriate treatment of groups that may not
perceive themselves as having the ear of their national government,
but that believe themselves — according to not unreasonable criteria
— to be eligible for additional, regional development aid and improved
representation.

It is in response to such a mix of problems that the national
governments have evolved the very wide range of regional development instruments, discussed in Chapter Two. It is because of the view
that yet broader and more comprehensive approaches to regional
policy and balance are required that the European Economic Community has developed Community-wide policies and instruments to
address regional development. These are the subject of Chapters Four
through Seven.

APPENDIX 1.1

The Regions of Europe

The Community Statistical Office defines two types of territorial units: the European Community Regions (RCE) and the Basic administration units (Uab). There were 52 RCEs and 112 Uabs including Greenland and the French Overseas Departments in the EEC before Greece joined on 1 January 1981.[19] In the following list comprising both, the RCEs are numbered.

GERMANY
1 Schleswig-Holstein
2 Hamburg
3 Niedersachsen
    Braunschweig
    Hannover
    Lüneburg
    Weser-Ems
4 Bremen
5 Nordrhein-Westfalen
    Düsseldorf
    Koln
    Münster
    Detmold
    Arnsberg
6 Hessen
    Darmstadt
    Kassel
7 Rheinland-Pfalz
    Koblenz
    Trier
    Rheinhessen-Pfalz
8 Baden Württemberg
    Stuttgart
    Karlsruhe
    Freiburg
    Tübingen
9 Bayern
    Oberbayern
    Niederbayern
    Oberpfalz
    Oberfranken
    Mittelfranken
    Unterfranken
    Schwaben

10 Saarland
11 Berlin (West)

FRANCE
12 Île de France
13 Bassin Parisien
    Champagne-Ardenne
    Picardie
    Haute-Normandie
    Centre
    Basse-Normandie
    Bourgogne
14 Nord-Pas-De-Calais
15 Est
    Lorraine
    Alsace
    Franche-Comté
16 Ouest
    Pays de la Loire
    Bretagne
    Poitou-Charentes
17 Sud-Ouest
    Aquitaine
    Midi-Pyrénées
    Limousin
18 Centre-Est
    Rhône-Alpes
    Auvergne
19 Meditérranée
    Languedoc-Roussillon
    Provence-Alpes-Côte
      d'Azur
    Corse
    France D'Outre Mer

ITALY

20 Nord Ouest
    Piemonte
    Valle d'Aosta
    Liguria
21 Lombardia
22 Nord Est
    Trentino-Alto Adige
    Veneto
    Friuli-Venezia Giulia
23 Emilia-Romagna
24 Centro
    Toscana
    Umbria
    Marche
25 Lazio
26 Campania
27 Abruzzi-Molise
    Abruzzi
    Molise
28 Sud
    Puglia
    Basilicata
    Calabria
29 Sicilia
30 Sardegna

NETHERLANDS

31 Noord-Nederland
    Groningen
    Friesland
    Drenthe
32 Oost-Nederland
    Overijssel
    Gelderland
33 West-Nederland
    Utrecht
    Noord-Holland
    Zuid-Holland
34 Zuidwest-Nederland
    Zeeland
35 Zuid-Nederland
    Noord-Brabant
    Limburg

BELGIUM

36 Brussel
37 Vlaanderen
    Antwerpen
    Brabant
    Limburg
    Oost-Vlaanderen
    West-Vlaanderen
38 Wallonie
    Brabant
    Hainaut
    Liège
    Luxembourg
    Namur

LUXEMBOURG

39 Luxembourg

UNITED KINGDOM

40 North
41 Yorkshire and Humberside
42 East Midlands
43 East Anglia
44 South East
45 South West
46 West Midlands
47 North West
48 Wales
49 Scotland
50 Northern Ireland

IRELAND

51 Ireland

DENMARK

52 Denmark
    Storkobenhavn
    Ost for Storebaelt
    Vest for Storebaelt
    Ekski Skorkobenhavn
    Grønland

**GREECE: Preliminary
          Breakdown
          by Planning
          Regions**[20]
Iónioi Níssoi
Ípiros
Kentriki Ellás Kaí Évia
Kríti
Makedonía
Níssoi Aigaíou
Pelopónnissos
Thessalía
Thráki

APPENDIX 1.2

Trade Integration and Adjustment

The impact of the trade integration process of the 1958–1972 era, followed by the adjustment to radically new energy prices of the post-1973 period, on regional development in the Community is far from obvious. Certainly it seems to have been less traumatic than gloomier forecasters might have anticipated, in large part because of the general economic buoyancy of the pre-1973 era. The substantial degree of migration within and between Community members (especially in the 1960s) provided either something of a safety valve, or postponed a day of reckoning, depending on how well the migrants will continue to adjust and how strong the poorer regions might become over the decades ahead.

Relatively higher unemployment levels in the Community as a whole, and signs that the disparities might be widening between the richer and poorer regions (over the 1970–1980 period), provide good reason for the additional interest, at the European Community level, in more balanced regional development.

In this appendix, a brief overview of the trade patterns of the EEC members is given.

In 1958, EEC exports between the six member countries accounted for some 30 per cent of total EEC member-country exports. By 1972, intra-export trade, between the six member countries, had reached some 50 per cent of their total exports.[21]

The entry of the three additional member countries, in January 1973, broadened the internal Community market at the very time that oil prices were raised so dramatically by members of the Organization of Petroleum Exporting Countries (OPEC). Thus, not only did the EEC face the complexities of adjusting to its internal expansion, an alternate structure had to be developed for competitively priced energy and a reassessment of economic life-styles. This was in an international trading environment beset by uncertainties and harassed by speculative forces.

The data in Table 1.11 illustrate the manner in which the value of oil imports from OPEC countries escalated as a proportion of all imports to EEC countries, between 1958 and 1980, with the exceptions of France and the United Kingdom. In the case of both the latter, however, OPEC oil had accounted for a substantially smaller proportion of imports at the time of the first OPEC price escalation in 1973 (some 9 per cent in 1973). The data also indicate that EEC exports to OPEC members grew in relative importance as well (again France being the exception); this was mostly in the form of machinery and transport equipment.

Table 1.11
FOREIGN TRADE: GEOGRAPHICAL STRUCTURE OF THE COMMUNITY COUNTRIES' EXPORTS AND IMPORTS

A. Structure of EEC Exports by Country and Region, 1958 and 1980, Percentages of Total[a]

Exports of / to	BLEU 1958	BLEU 1980	DK 1958	DK 1980	D 1958	D 1980	GR 1958	GR 1980	F 1958	F 1980	IRL 1958	IRL 1980	I 1958	I 1980	NL 1958	NL 1980	UK 1958	UK 1980	EEC 1958	EEC 1980
BLEU	—	—	1.24	1.96	6.64	7.84	1.03	1.83	6.34	9.34	0.80	5.04	2.27	3.33	14.97	15.06	1.93	5.31	4.85	6.93
DK	1.63	1.19	—	—	2.96	1.90	0.18	0.88	0.75	0.70	0.05	0.74	0.77	0.69	2.63	1.88	2.37	2.10	2.00	1.45
D	11.56	21.27	20.05	19.19	—	—	20.46	17.89	10.40	16.02	2.22	9.79	14.29	18.30	18.98	29.93	4.20	10.37	7.40	12.74
GR	0.67	0.43	0.36	0.54	1.43	1.08	—	—	0.66	1.06	0.05	0.38	2.12	1.53	0.92	0.66	0.66	0.46	0.97	0.63
F	10.60	19.41	2.97	5.31	7.58	13.31	12.85	7.39	—	—	0.79	7.74	5.31	15.14	4.87	10.56	2.42	7.43	4.56	10.25
IRL	0.35	0.30	0.30	0.52	0.25	0.38	0.36	0.10	0.16	0.48	—	—	0.13	0.27	0.45	0.42	3.50	5.41	1.14	1.24
I	2.27	5.52	5.31	5.06	5.02	8.55	6.01	9.71	3.37	12.50	0.43	3.11	—	—	2.74	5.77	2.11	3.86	3.06	6.65
NL	20.70	15.20	2.19	3.83	8.10	9.50	1.96	5.68	2.03	4.87	0.51	5.46	2.05	3.69	—	—	3.14	7.81	5.37	7.03
UK	5.71	8.48	25.91	14.12	3.95	6.54	7.64	4.13	4.89	6.97	78.76	42.61	6.83	6.09	11.90	7.90	—	—	5.53	6.41
Total intra-Community trade	53.49	71.80	58.33	50.53	35.93	49.10	50.49	47.61	28.60	51.94	83.61	74.87	33.77	49.04	57.46	72.18	20.33	42.75	34.88	53.33
Other European OECD countries	10.39	9.75	17.22	27.81	23.73	17.91	6.72	3.25	10.52	13.43	1.80	5.27	16.58	14.79	12.26	8.96	9.62	18.21	16.36	16.42
USA	9.42	3.35	9.34	4.66	7.31	6.13	13.61	5.65	5.93	4.42	5.85	5.25	9.71	5.31	5.64	2.58	8.83	9.44	7.83	5.59
Canada	1.13	0.28	0.68	0.61	1.19	0.62	0.27	0.44	0.83	0.61	0.67	1.29	1.19	0.62	0.79	0.27	5.77	1.54	2.33	0.71
Japan	0.60	0.49	0.20	1.74	0.95	1.13	1.36	0.48	0.32	1.00	0.05	0.48	0.32	0.91	0.41	0.45	0.61	1.21	0.59	0.96
Australia	0.55	0.23	0.26	0.43	1.02	0.60	0.09	0.36	0.42	0.27	0.08	0.59	0.99	0.59	0.68	0.28	7.11	1.66	2.48	0.65
Developing countries of which:	18.80	11.09	9.65	11.51	22.30	14.71	7.19	28.15	48.38	23.32	1.57	9.54	27.86	23.33	18.14	11.02	33.81	22.16	27.88	17.64
OPEC	3.34	4.63	2.33	4.19	4.78	6.51	0.10	15.38	21.27	8.85	0.27	4.37	7.49	12.67	4.48	5.45	7.03	9.20	7.76	7.77
Other developing countries	15.46	6.46	7.32	7.32	17.57	8.20	7.09	12.77	27.11	14.47	1.30	5.17	20.37	10.66	13.66	5.57	26.78	12.96	20.12	9.87
Centrally planned economies	3.75	2.26	3.80	2.71	5.00	5.60	16.25	11.14	3.70	4.75	0.21	1.57	4.69	4.01	1.98	2.21	3.09	2.74	3.86	4.00
Rest of world and unspecified	1.87	0.75	0.52	0.00	2.57	4.20	4.02	2.32	1.30	0.26	6.16	1.14	5.09	1.40	2.64	2.12	10.83	0.29	3.79	0.70
World (excl. EEC)	46.51	28.20	41.67	49.47	64.07	50.90	49.51	52.39	71.40	48.06	16.39	25.13	66.23	50.96	42.54	27.82	79.67	57.25	65.12	46.67
World (incl. EEC)	100	100	100	100	100	100	100	100	100	100	100	100	100	100	100	100	100	100	100	100

B. Structure of EEC Imports by Country and Region, 1958 and 1980, Percentages of Total[b]

Imports of from	BLEU 1958	BLEU 1980	DK 1958	DK 1980	D 1958	D 1980	GR 1958	GR 1980	F 1958	F 1980	IRL 1958	IRL 1980	I 1958	I 1980	NL 1958	NL 1980	UK 1958	UK 1980	EEC 1958	EEC 1980
BLEU	—	—	3.81	3.57	4.53	7.37	3.28	1.96	5.37	8.36	1.83	2.01	2.02	3.56	17.85	11.65	1.61	4.72	4.39	6.05
DK	0.53	0.46	—	—	3.35	1.72	0.73	0.60	0.63	0.64	0.70	0.65	2.19	0.88	0.67	0.88	3.07	2.11	2.00	1.18
D	17.16	19.66	19.84	18.75	—	—	20.31	13.94	11.64	16.18	4.00	6.08	12.13	16.60	19.48	22.21	3.60	10.75	8.21	12.06
GR	0.08	0.15	0.03	0.19	1.71	0.80	—	—	0.58	0.34	0.17	0.08	0.48	0.49	0.14	0.39	0.19	0.24	0.36	0.34
F	11.60	14.45	3.43	4.00	7.59	10.75	5.43	6.19	—	—	1.60	4.95	4.86	13.88	2.79	6.70	2.67	7.34	4.22	8.24
IRL	0.10	0.37	0.01	0.29	0.10	0.44	0.03	0.36	0.05	0.56	—	—	0.05	0.26	0.05	0.52	2.90	3.38	0.88	0.91
I	2.15	3.59	1.70	2.73	5.46	7.92	8.83	8.19	2.35	9.39	0.85	1.97	—	—	1.77	3.15	2.04	4.48	2.53	5.40
NL	15.72	16.37	7.34	7.74	8.03	12.00	4.77	3.87	2.53	5.42	2.86	3.57	2.58	4.17	—	—	4.22	5.63	6.40	7.49
UK	7.40	8.07	22.82	11.97	4.38	6.77	9.89	4.57	3.59	5.40	56.41	55.21	5.50	4.43	7.39	8.17	—	—	4.97	6.22
Total intra-Community trade	54.74	63.12	58.98	49.24	35.15	47.77	53.27	39.68	26.74	46.29	68.42	74.52	29.81	44.27	50.14	53.66	20.30	38.65	33.96	47.89
Other European OECD countries	8.11	7.83	19.48	26.44	15.84	15.44	9.45	7.11	7.97	10.43	4.26	4.79	12.02	11.05	7.70	7.72	13.92	17.69	12.01	12.87
USA	9.92	7.66	9.10	6.48	13.57	7.19	13.71	4.60	10.04	7.96	6.98	7.24	16.23	6.96	11.31	8.79	9.34	13.35	11.42	8.47
Canada	1.42	0.74	0.25	0.48	3.10	1.04	0.78	0.74	1.02	0.77	2.97	1.09	1.44	1.02	1.48	0.75	8.17	2.64	3.73	1.17
Japan	0.63	2.00	1.48	2.11	0.61	2.94	1.97	11.06	0.18	2.06	1.07	2.26	0.41	1.31	0.82	1.90	0.94	3.49	0.72	2.53
Australia	1.73	0.31	0.03	0.15	1.21	0.37	0.30	0.17	2.42	0.43	1.21	0.07	3.01	0.58	0.20	0.24	5.40	0.95	2.72	0.47
Developing countries of which:	19.50	15.69	6.06	9.57	24.43	20.08	9.56	27.89	46.71	27.14	9.67	7.48	31.18	28.89	25.02	23.50	34.98	20.12	30.32	22.16
OPEC	5.91	9.19	0.30	3.04	6.71	10.94	1.72	11.25	19.68	18.63	0.72	4.37	13.87	17.82	11.48	15.06	11.26	8.95	10.90	12.93
Other developing countries	13.79	6.50	5.76	6.53	17.72	9.14	7.84	16.67	27.03	8.51	8.95	3.11	17.31	11.07	13.54	8.44	23.72	11.17	19.42	9.23
Centrally planned economies	2.01	2.58	4.59	5.53	5.31	5.10	8.07	6.18	3.30	4.31	1.24	1.37	3.60	5.89	2.61	3.44	3.19	2.92	3.51	4.26
Rest of world and unspecified	1.94	0.07	0.03	0.00	0.78	0.07	2.89	2.57	1.62	0.61	4.18	0.58	2.30	0.03	0.77	0.00	3.76	0.19	1.54	0.18
World (excl. EEC)	45.26	36.88	41.02	50.76	64.85	52.23	46.73	60.32	73.26	53.71	31.58	25.48	70.19	55.73	49.86	46.34	79.70	61.35	66.04	52.11
World (incl. EEC)	100	100	100	100	100	100	100	100	100	100	100	100	100	100	100	100	100	100	100	100

Source: [a] Commission of the European Communities, *European Economy: Annual Economic Report 1981–82* (Luxembourg: November 1981), p. 175, Annex Table 30.
[b] *Ibid.*, p. 176, Annex Table 31.

Table 1.12
TRENDS IN THE STRUCTURE OF EECa EXTERNAL TRADE BY PRODUCT GROUP
1970, 1973, 1979

Product Group[b] as percentage of total	Intra-EEC trade			Extra-EEC trade					
				Imports			Exports		
	1970	1973	1979	1970	1973	1979	1970	1973	1979
Food, beverages, tobacco	13.3	14.4	12.9	18.4	17.4	11.3	7.2	7.7	6.8
Fuel products	4.4	4.7	8.7	16.6	19.0	28.5	2.9	3.1	5.3
Raw materials	5.8	5.5	4.5	20.1	18.1	12.5	2.7	2.8	2.4
Machinery and transport equipment	30.1	29.2	28.6	13.4	14.5	15.5	41.6	41.1	39.6
Chemicals	9.4	10.0	11.7	5.0	4.5	5.0	11.2	11.4	12.1
Intermediate manufactured products	25.3	24.7	}32.4	20.1	18.2	}24.6	22.9	23.0	}31.3
Manufactured products in final demand	10.3	10.6		5.2	7.2		9.8	9.3	
Miscellaneous	1.4	0.9	1.2	1.2	1.1	2.6	1.7	1.6	2.5
Total	100.0	100.0	100.0	100.0	100.0	100.0	100.0	100.0	100.0
Share of external trade[c] (for information)	48.9	51.7	50.4	51.1	48.3	49.6	48.0	46.7	44.2

Source: Eurostat, *Monthly External Trade Bulletin*, Special Number 1958–79 (Luxembourg: Statistical Office of the European Communities, June 1980), pp. 46–48.

Notes: [a] Nine member countries.
[b] SITC — Standard International Trade Classification — nomenclature.
[c] Intra- and extra-EEC imports.

The heavy dependence on EEC member-country markets was particularly noticeable in the cases of the Netherlands, Belgium/Luxembourg, and Ireland (all over 70 per cent in 1980). Despite the strengthening of its links from some 32 per cent of the value of its exports in 1973 to some 39 per cent by 1980, the United Kingdom is considerably less integrated, as a trading partner, than the other members (with the exception of the newest member, Greece).

One recent assessment concluded that the EEC member states had reacted to the post-1973 trading situation in essentially one (or more) of three ways:[22]

1. A number of countries had sought to improve their competitiveness by allowing their currencies to float downwards.

2. Most countries gave priority to securing productivity gains rather than sustaining employment, particularly in industry. Success was concluded to have "depended primarily on the situation existing at the outset: the countries with the highest productivity levels improved their positions while the others (Italy, United Kingdom) saw theirs deteriorate. . . ."[23]

3. Productivity increases were generally quite concentrated: for example, in agriculture in Denmark; energy in France, the Benelux countries, and the United Kingdom; intermediate products in Germany and Belgium; food products in France and the Benelux countries; current consumption products in Germany and the Netherlands; and services in France and the Netherlands.

The assessment continued to be somewhat negative about the United Kingdom record (despite North Sea oil) and to note the lagging productivity record in post-1970 Italy.

In Tables 1.12 and 1.13, additional details are given on trade patterns and composition by main product categories, while Table 1.14 indicates the main trading links by country.

Table 1.13

TRENDS IN THE STRUCTURE OF EEC^a EXTERNAL TRADE BY PRODUCTS, 1970, 1973, 1977

Products	FR of Germany			France			Italy			United Kingdom		
	1970	1973	1977	1970	1973	1977	1970	1973	1977	1970	1973	1977
Imports												
Food, beverages, tobacco	16.6	16.5	14.0	13.0	12.4	12.5	16.7	20.1	15.6	22.8	19.5	16.3
Fuel products	8.8	11.3	17.0	12.1	12.4	21.4	14.0	14.1	25.3	10.5	10.9	14.2
Raw materials	13.4	11.9	9.5	11.7	10.4	7.9	17.2	16.3	12.7	15.1	12.4	9.8
Machinery and transport equipment	18.9	17.9	19.1	25.2	25.8	22.6	20.3	19.8	18.3	16.6	20.8	22.8
Chemicals	6.3	6.5	7.4	8.1	8.4	8.4	7.9	8.1	7.9	6.0	5.7	6.6
Intermediate manufactured products	24.3	22.5	18.5	21.9	21.7	17.8	19.4	16.9	14.0	21.8	21.3	20.5
Manufactured products in final demand	8.8	11.1	11.5	8.0	8.7	9.0	4.0	4.5	4.0	6.4	8.5	8.3
Miscellaneous	2.9	2.3	3.0	—	0.2	0.4	0.5	0.2	2.2	0.8	0.9	1.5
Total	100.0	100.0	100.0	100.0	100.0	100.0	100.0	100.0	100.0	100.0	100.0	100.0
Exports												
Food, beverages, tobacco	3.1	4.0	4.4	15.3	18.4	14.0	8.3	8.1	7.5	6.4	7.0	6.6
Fuel products	3.0	2.5	2.6	2.1	2.1	3.0	5.1	5.7	5.6	2.6	3.0	6.3
Raw materials	2.7	2.8	2.5	5.7	5.7	4.5	2.4	2.3	1.7	3.4	3.5	2.8
Machinery and transport equipment	46.5	46.8	47.8	33.1	32.3	37.3	36.9	34.7	33.8	41.1	38.3	37.5
Chemicals	12.0	11.8	12.1	9.2	9.2	10.3	6.9	7.4	7.2	9.8	10.2	11.8
Intermediate manufactured products	21.9	21.9	19.4	24.7	21.9	21.0	20.6	22.7	23.3	24.8	26.2	22.7
Manufactured products in final demand	9.0	9.0	9.1	8.8	9.6	8.7	19.6	18.9	20.2	9.1	9.2	9.5
Miscellaneous	1.5	1.2	2.1	1.1	0.8	1.2	0.2	0.2	0.7	2.8	2.6	2.8
Total	100.0	100.0	100.0	100.0	100.0	100.0	100.0	100.0	100.0	100.0	100.0	100.0

Products	Netherlands			BLEU			Denmark			Ireland		
	1970	1973	1977	1970	1973	1977	1970	1973	1977	1970	1973	1977
Imports												
Food, beverages, tobacco	12.6	14.2	13.7	12.0	12.1	11.9	9.3	10.5	11.2	13.0	12.7	12.8
Fuel products	10.9	12.9	18.4	9.1	8.6	14.0	10.5	10.7	16.8	7.9	6.8	12.6
Raw materials	9.6	8.9	7.9	12.5	10.2	7.6	7.8	7.1	6.2	6.4	7.3	4.9
Machinery and transport equipment	25.5	23.3	23.0	26.2	27.0	25.3	27.6	28.8	26.8	26.2	27.0	26.8
Chemicals	7.8	8.0	8.0	7.3	7.6	8.3	9.0	8.8	8.6	9.1	10.9	11.3
Intermediate manufactured products	21.6	20.7	16.8	25.4	24.9	22.3	26.1	24.7	19.9	21.3	22.3	15.3
Manufactured products in final demand	10.7	11.2	11.4	7.5	8.5	9.3	9.5	9.2	9.9	8.4	9.3	9.7
Miscellaneous	1.3	0.8	0.8	—	1.1	1.3	0.2	0.2	0.6	7.7	3.7	6.6
Total	100.0	100.0	100.0	100.0	100.0	100.0	100.0	100.0	100.0	100.0	100.0	100.0
Exports												
Food, beverages, tobacco	23.3	22.0	20.6	7.1	9.2	9.2	35.5	35.3	32.4	43.5	43.3	39.7
Fuel products	10.7	12.1	18.1	2.7	2.8	5.4	2.5	2.2	3.2	1.3	0.7	0.7
Raw materials	7.7	7.3	6.2	4.6	4.0	3.6	7.4	7.2	7.1	7.4	6.2	4.2
Machinery and transport equipment	20.0	18.8	18.7	21.3	21.4	24.2	26.8	26.8	26.4	6.2	9.9	15.3
Chemicals	12.9	14.2	14.5	8.5	10.4	12.3	6.7	6.2	7.3	3.9	6.8	9.8
Intermediate manufactured products	18.0	17.8	15.0	45.0	41.8	34.0	10.4	8.6	11.7	12.5	16.9	15.0
Manufactured products in final demand	7.2	7.2	6.4	8.0	8.4	7.6	10.3	11.3	11.6	9.9	2.7	10.2
Miscellaneous	0.2	0.6	0.5	2.8	2.0	3.7	0.4	2.4	0.3	15.3	13.5	5.1
Total	100.0	100.0	100.0	100.0	100.0	100.0	100.0	100.0	100.0	100.0	100.0	100.0

Source: Compiled from Eurostat, *Monthly Trade Bulletin*, Special Number 1958–77.
Note: [a] Nine member countries.

Table 1.14
EEC PATTERNS OF TRADE,* 1977 AND 1978

TRADE WITH	IMPORTS (c.i.f.)		EXPORTS (f.o.b.)	
	1977	1978	1977	1978
WORLD	32244.5	38368.1	31635.0	38212.8
OECD COUNTRIES	23261.0	28737.0	23544.8	28567.6
Canada	418.5	424.8	291.2	339.1
United States	2458.4	2948.9	1956.6	2465.7
Japan	730.1	921.7	294.3	394.8
Australia	223.1	225.9	256.9	305.0
New Zealand	90.8	107.8	62.5	71.9
OECD-EUROPE	19340.1	24108.0	20683.3	24981.1
EEC	15912.4	19579.6	16029.4	19761.8
Austria	412.4	538.9	781.8	894.4
Belgium-Luxembourg	2107.0	2540.5	2264.9	2819.3
Denmark	380.9	491.2	535.4	622.0
Finland	262.8	316.7	203.5	219.9
France	2788.2	3453.8	3099.2	3767.6
Germany (Fed. Rep.)	4196.7	5177.6	3949.2	4836.8
Greece	144.6	185.2	274.9	332.0
Iceland	14.4	19.1	24.5	27.5
Ireland	286.3	394.5	325.5	444.7
Italy	1842.8	2354.3	1725.7	2122.9
Netherlands	2629.3	3038.8	2287.1	2755.8
Norway	364.2	569.7	454.3	411.7
Portugal	95.5	124.8	185.5	204.0
Spain	471.5	590.4	535.0	561.1
Sweden	766.9	911.3	842.4	872.0
Switzerland	817.1	1183.6	1147.0	1530.3
Turkey	78.2	88.8	204.9	166.4
United Kingdom	1681.2	2130.9	1842.5	2392.7
NON-OECD COUNTRIES	8951.3	9582.7	7884.8	9444.6
DEVELOPING COUNTRIES	7351.2	7722.2	6265.1	7486.7
Europe	207.5	197.5	396.9	448.3
Yugoslavia	149.0	174.3	338.6	394.8
Africa	1884.7	1986.6	2176.9	2451.3
Morocco	80.2	91.0	145.3	142.5
Algeria	198.8	212.8	349.4	386.0
Tunisia	54.2	61.3	92.9	118.7
Lybia	366.1	347.7	245.0	279.1
Egypt	67.7	105.4	160.0	193.4
Sudan	20.6	22.8	45.6	51.1
Senegal	33.5	23.0	37.7	39.5
Liberia	34.7	41.2	75.2	35.8
Ivory Coast	141.6	146.4	80.9	105.1
Ghana	44.1	44.6	39.2	44.6
Nigeria	332.0	359.0	438.9	496.4
Cameroun	50.4	63.8	40.6	51.5
Equatorial Customs Union	62.5	67.2	69.3	55.6
Zaire	102.3	116.4	42.4	41.5
Angola	5.3	14.0	22.4	27.6
Kenya	56.0	47.1	42.6	66.0
Mozambique	11.1	5.8	10.8	10.6
Madagascar	16.1	12.5	14.2	16.5
Zambia	43.1	32.0	23.0	22.2
Other countries	164.3	172.6	201.5	267.5

America	1046.0	1145.1	1016.7	1168.6
Latin America	943.4	1014.5	846.0	971.4
Mexico	41.3	41.5	76.2	136.1
Cuba	10.5	13.4	32.6	25.8
Jamaica	12.3	16.7	8.9	11.9
Panama	12.4	11.2	22.9	27.8
French Antilles	16.7	20.3	43.7	53.5
British Territories n.e.s.	34.4	48.0	48.0	46.4
Colombia	67.6	86.2	41.4	46.4
Venezuela	48.7	62.4	200.2	198.0
Trinidad and Tobago	10.2	11.3	19.1	25.2
Netherlands Antilles and Surinam	19.8	22.1	32.8	38.9
Ecuador	17.7	18.2	30.8	35.4
Peru	28.6	28.2	27.9	27.1
Brazil	328.3	325.4	208.6	224.7
Chile	62.6	77.4	28.8	36.9
Argentina	174.8	212.5	95.7	116.6
Other countries	160.1	150.3	99.1	117.9
Far East	1048.5	1237.7	805.4	1104.5
Pakistan	26.3	31.0	63.3	68.1
India	157.5	169.8	132.8	197.9
Ceylon	15.8	15.4	11.1	20.9
Thailand	72.3	98.9	50.9	58.9
Malaysia	125.0	136.9	56.9	81.6
Indonesia	80.4	90.1	101.6	99.4
Singapore	63.6	72.2	87.3	112.5
Korea (South)	121.4	151.0	62.8	106.7
China (Taiwan)	102.4	128.8	47.2	70.8
Hong Kong	192.7	241.3	111.1	175.2
Philippines	52.5	62.0	41.9	57.7
Other countries	38.6	40.4	38.4	54.7
Middle East	3137.5	3133.4	1846.3	2286.1
Lebanon	4.0	3.8	56.6	64.4
Israel	95.8	128.7	139.8	171.0
Iraq	388.3	481.0	167.6	203.4
Saudi Arabia	1217.2	1061.7	433.5	601.0
Kuwait	256.9	303.8	117.6	138.2
Bahrain	295.6	274.9	175.0	203.4
Iran	711.3	696.9	511.5	628.3
Other countries	88.6	102.8	208.6	238.7
Oceania	27.0	21.9	22.9	27.9
CENTRALLY PLANNED ECONOMIES	1250.7	1458.3	1352.1	1616.0
U.S.S.R.	581.8	672.0	557.2	597.8
Germany (Dem. Rep.)	56.6	66.8	45.1	56.9
Poland	202.9	240.1	242.8	266.6
Czechoslovakia	101.7	116.4	117.8	129.2
Hungary	95.5	107.0	127.3	164.2
Romania	97.3	116.1	113.4	151.1
Bulgaria	25.0	30.9	51.7	57.1
China (Mainland)	82.8	101.0	75.7	158.3
Other countries	7.2	8.0	21.0	34.8
OTHER COUNTRY	349.4	402.2	267.6	341.8
South Africa	349.4	402.2	267.6	341.8
UNSPECIFIED	32.3	46.4	205.3	210.6

* Data is in millions of U.S. Dollars, Monthly Averages.
Source: O.E.C.D., *Statistics of Foreign Trade*, Monthly Bulletin (March 1980), pp. 42–43.

Notes

[1] The Treaty was signed on 27 March 1957.

[2] Commission of the European Communities, *The Regions of Europe* (Brussels: January 1981), p. 19.

[3] The increase in France came mainly in the Île de France area, the regions bordering Italy, and in Corsica. The Lazio region around Rome experienced significant increases in density throughout the period. Other parts of central Italy had declines in the 1960s while there was increased density in the north. In the 1970s, Sardegna and the southeast experienced the greatest increase in density. Germany had increases in population density in the northeast and southeast as well as in the Düsseldorf and Arnsberg regions. The central-southern regions of the Netherlands and the Drenthe region had experienced the greatest increases in density while the coastal regions of Freisland, Zuid-Holland, and Zeeland had experienced decreases. Similarly, the coastal region of Belgium experienced a decline whereas the greatest increases were in the central regions. The picture in the United Kingdom is rather interesting as the areas that experienced the greatest increases in the 1960s, the South West and the East Midlands, had declines in the 1970s.

[4] Commission of the European Communities, *op. cit.*, p. 19.

[5] *Ibid.*

[6] For a particularly good review of this period, see Hugh Clout, ed., *Regional Development in Western Europe* (London: John Wiley, 1975).

[7] For a good overview of the post-1973 era, see Commission of the European Communities, *European Economy — Special Issue* (Brussels: 1979).

[8] In presenting this overview, the meaningfulness of many of these broad measurements is glossed over. The difficulties inherent in many of these concepts are particularly well discussed by Simon Kuznets in his writings: E.S. Simon Kuznets, *Six Lectures on Economic Growth* (New York: Free Press, 1961), pp. 13–28.

[9] Commission of the European Communities, *The Regions of Europe*, p. 104.

[10] *Ibid.*, p. 109.

[11] When a farmer has neither employment outside agriculture nor works a minimum of 2200 hours per year on his farm, he is considered underemployed.

[12] Commission of the European Communities, *The Regions of Europe*, p. 69.

[13] For further details on this section, refer to the Commission of the European Communities, *The Regions of Europe*, pp. 67–69 and pp. 80–87. It was found that other industrial regions, as well as the peripheral (agriculturally oriented) regions, tend to have relatively little public-sector employment.

[14] For a current assessment, see Commission of the European Communities, *European Economy*, No. 9 (Brussels: July 1981), pp. 21–44.

[15] Eurostat, *Regional Statistics: Community's Financial Participation in Investments 1978* (Luxembourg: 1980), p. 9.

[16] For additional information, see Wellem Molle with Bas van Holst and Hans Smit, *Regional Disparity and Economic Development in the European Community* (Farnborough: Saxon House, 1980), p. 158.

[17] Commission of the European Communities, *Europeans and Their Regions* (Brussels: December 1980), p. 52.

[18] For a useful, country-by-country discussion of the problems, see Geoffrey Parker, *The Countries of Community Europe* (London: Macmillan, 1979).

[19] Eurostat, *op cit.*, p. 9.

[20] Office for Official Publications of the European Communities, *The European Community — Member States, Regions, Administrative Units* (Map) (Luxembourg: 1981).

[21] Calculated from EEC trade data, in European Documentation, *The Customs Union* (Luxembourg: 1977), p. 16.

[22] For further details, see Commission of the European Communities, *European Economy — Special Issue*, pp. 62–78.

[23] *Ibid.*, p. 62.

National Policies and Instruments for Regional Development: A Synthesis

2

I. Introduction

This section provides an overview of national policies and instruments for regional development among the European Economic Community member states. A substantial literature exists on the subject, detailing particular country programmes and cataloguing the various incentives on a comparative basis.[1] This chapter draws on a cross-section of such material and also on interviews and a number of on-site examinations. The chapter is divided into a discussion of the overall frameworks and philosophies behind regional policies between 1945 and 1981, followed by a synthesis of the main regional policy instruments, with some comments on their perceived value. A number of issues, of comparative relevance to the Canadian situation, are then suggested.

At the outset, one main observation should be noted. This is that the 'explicit' instruments are often of less real importance to regional development than broader fiscal, monetary, and sectoral policies and activities — for example, the national tax structure; external trade protection arrangements; the investment decisions of state corporations; major policy approaches for energy, transportation, agriculture, and urban development; and so on. This aspect has been under-emphasized in many reviews on regional policy instruments in the EEC, the attention tending to focus on 'explicit regional instruments' and their mechanics. Many reasons might be given for such an underemphasis, including the difficulties of relating broader policies and activities to their regional implications, the greater degree of manageability of a review, for example, of regional incentives for industrial development, and the fact that regional specific aids (such as roads or industrial estates) are more visibly 'regional development' activities.

II. Frameworks and Philosophies: 1945–1981

There appears to be some consensus, in the literature on West European regional policies, that the post-war period can be broken into three eras: the era of national reconstruction, the era of national economic growth and regional experimentation, and the post-1973 era. The European Economic Community began its life at the start of the second era.

The Era of National Reconstruction

Supported by the Marshall Aid plan, the decade following the Second World War saw an emphasis on rebuilding the West European economies. National economic growth (largely perceived along sectoral lines) was of paramount concern, requiring the reconstruction of damaged industrial plants, transport systems, and war-ravaged farms and agricultural land. In some countries (most notably West Germany), 'emergency areas' were designated each year — on the basis of unemployment indicators.[2] The inflow of refugees from Eastern Europe accentuated the problems.

Critics of most member-country regional policies, of this era, tend to view the regional policy approaches as somewhat *ad hoc* during this period. In short, there was little alternative given the urgency of getting economies back on the move, and, therefore, actions (not unnaturally) tended to precede 'comprehensive' plans. The 'obviously necessary' was tackled first, often making use of the most up-to-date technology as in the case of the Port of Hamburg. At the city level, however, as distinct from the national levels of regional policy, there was much more evidence of more comprehensive planning approaches, for example, the cases of Rotterdam, Hamburg, West Berlin, Caens, and Plymouth, to name but a few.

The Era of National Economic Expansion and Regional Experimentation

National economic 'miracles' were quite widely talked about during this period, stretching from the late 1950s to 1973. A greater degree of self-confidence and affluence became apparent, based on the immediate post-war economic developments and the accomplishment of the Treaty of Rome. Conservative groups felt that a more balanced approach to regional development 'could now be afforded'. Such views were reinforced by those who argued that greater regional balance 'could not be delayed any longer', both because of inflationary demand pressures from the rapidly growing national economies and from obvious supply bottle-necks. In addition, some regional groups were becoming politically threatening.

Substantial areas of Europe, especially of Italy, showed many of the characteristics of a 'dual economy': the benefits and opportunities of the industrialized and urban sectors were bypassing the more rural, less 'dynamic' regions. For example, Gravier spoke of 'the French desert', pointing out that the population of Paris had increased

threefold over the preceding hundred years, while the French population, *as a whole*, had only increased one sixth.[3] The drift from
agriculture and rural activities to the towns placed strains on urban
infrastructure. At the same time, large pockets of declining industry
and social infrastructure scarred such areas as Genova and Newcastle,
aggravating their disadvantages in the face of competition from
countries such as Japan and Korea (e.g., in shipbuilding). A growing
number of studies were documenting the harshness of regional
inequalities within member countries.[4]

During this era, every member country developed a number of
incentive programmes to encourage industrial development in problem regions, and, in general, the scale and coverage of aids mush-
roomed. In part this reflected competition between countries; however,
competition between richer and poorer regions within the same
country also fuelled the growth of incentive programmes. Concur-
rently, a variety of physical infrastructure programmes, manpower
training programmes, worker mobility programmes, government
corporations with a mandate to invest in poorer regions or to allocate a
percentage of their investments in such regions, and marketing
support and employment subsidy programmes were embarked upon, or
enriched. 'Work to the workers' was increasingly recognized as a
legitimate objective, as well as being politically more attractive than
endorsing measures to reduce the population of poorer regions.

In some countries (for example, the Netherlands), regional policies
and land-use planning went hand in hand; in others (for example,
France), considerable effort was placed on linking regional planning
with the formal, national planning process. In other countries, a more
decentralized approach occurred (for example, the West German
Länder played an extensive — and far from co-ordinated — role with
the federal government). Some countries (notably France and the
United Kingdom) established systems of control (through regulated
permits and congested city tax penalties), primarily to reduce the
congestion of Paris and London, partly to siphon developments to
poorer regions.

During this time, marked by experimentation and quite frequent
changes to regional policies, a variety of 'philosophies' or 'development
theories' were called upon to provide frameworks for regional development activities. (It should be noted that political pressures and
considerations were probably the most pervasive influence, even when
theories might be used as 'pegs' for policy logic.)

Some such theories were evolved in the context of regional studies
(for example, 'growth centres' and the broader idea of 'pôles de
croissance');[5] other theories were borrowed from the concepts particularly associated, during the same era, with the development planning
activities of developing (Third World) and newly independent coun-

tries (for example, balanced and unbalanced growth).[6] However, the quantitative progress, which had been made with the national accounts and had helped anchor Keynesian concepts for macro-economic policy, lagged substantially at the regional level; not merely did the problems of disaggregation and greater specificity loom larger, but also the conventional national indicators became less obviously useful performance indicators, particularly in the more peripheral regions of the Community, where regional disparities were often extreme and a rural or 'quasi-rural' structure was of considerable importance.[7] Thus, for example, measures of average per capita income fail to capture many subsistence-linked activities, or the contributions of many women working outside the wage sectors, while measures such as unemployment rates have been more oriented to industrial and urban market economies.

Looking back at this era, one can say that each member country harnessed a variety of regional policy instruments, called upon a mishmash of development theories and agencies to justify and help bring coherence to such activities, and a great deal was learned (at least with the benefit of hindsight) about how to (and how not to) analyse and seek to influence regional development. Over the period, an awareness of the advantages of approaching regional problems from the vantage point of a number of disciplines became more apparent. The importance of harmonizing regional and sectoral frameworks and of viewing regional goals and strategies in the context of broader, national social, political, and economic policies also became more widely emphasized. The desirability of linking land-use planning with environmental and regional planning was another 'lesson of the era', as well as the need to link economic insights and frameworks of logic at *both* micro and macro levels of analysis. The concept of growth centres became quite widely viewed as a useful planning framework. At the same time, a cynicism emerged about expecting physical infrastructure investments to pay off, regardless of location, existing demand, and allied incentive programmes. Experience has shown, in Europe as in Canada, that infrastructure alone does not guarantee economic development.

In short, the era was one of development and experimentation on broad fronts, coloured with a considerable degree of optimism about the prospects of more balanced (and equitable) regional development. The attitudes were developed in an international context of sustained economic growth. Substantial adjustments are always easier in such circumstances, when employment and investment alternatives are relatively easy to find.

The Post-1973 Era

The post-1973 era has been dominated by the impact of oil price increases and uncertainties, the twin spectres of inflation and higher levels of unemployment and, a further by-product, upward-creeping interest rates.

Regional development policies, at the European national levels, appear to have been somewhat less innovative, on the 'grand scale' of the previous period. This is widely perceived to be a result of the economic problems at the international level. The focus has been particularly on energy exploration, production and, to varying degrees, conservation. An additional reason, but one that can be accorded less weight, was the realization that increased harmonization of effort was badly needed — regardless of available resources — hence, an emphasis on greater consolidation of existing programmes.

One recent review of regional policy instruments concluded:

The post-1973 period saw the main regional incentives remaining very much as they were, although there was undoubtedly above-average growth of what might be called the 'small end' of the incentive market (key-worker mobility schemes, schemes to aid product development, schemes to provide venture capital, etc.) as countries facing increasingly severe expenditure constraints tried both to plug gaps in their incentive programmes and to exploit potential opportunities not covered by their main incentive schemes.[8]

The same review, drawing on work sponsored by the European Commission and federal German agencies, identified a number of shifts in regional programming in the post-1973 era. In summary they were as follows:

1. A few countries (including France and the United Kingdom) have encouraged service-industry mobility without (it is suggested) much success to date.

2. Controls have fallen into relative disuse. The reasons given are the lack of an expansionary climate for manufacturing industry anyway, and the political difficulties of implementing controls in times of high national unemployment.

3. Plans to disperse major blocks of government offices have tended to be put in abeyance. The reasons cited are both the general economic conditions and the particular problems facing the major towns. What was not suggested, but is probably significant, is that most member-country governments (regardless of political creed) have tended to become more conservative in the post-1973 period: the emphasis has been on contracting government activities, not expanding them. Dispersement of government offices has not generally been noted as a method for cutting down staff.

4. Rather than massive dispersements of whole departments of 'senior' levels of government, there has been a tendency in a number of countries (France, the United Kingdom, Italy, and Ireland are cited as main examples) to devolve the administration of policy, at least for details. A number of reasons are suggested for this: increased administrative efficiency (e.g., project vetting and monitoring is often best done on-site), local knowledge can make for improved programming, and an "attempt to meet (if not defuse) some of the political aspirations of the problem regions."[9]

The review also expressed concern that "changes in the *national* incentive sphere . . . namely the very rapid growth in national and sectoral aids" will have a negative impact on regional policy effectiveness. Schemes in the Netherlands and the United Kingdom were cited by way of examples.[10]

If the 1973–1981 period can be viewed as a time of consolidation for EEC member governments regarding regional policy, it is difficult to determine quite what is in store for the next decade. The energy impact has caused national/regional policies to play a generally subservient role to energy and broader development and employment policies. Moreover, the countries with the more extreme regional problems (notably Italy, the United Kingdom, and now Greece) also face some of the tougher macro-economic and societal problems. It is apparent that one cannot view any one of these three main problems in isolation from the other two.

It is also apparent that while new regional development directions are being sought by the member governments, past efforts to rationalize regional development have encountered, in many countries, flood barriers of habits and 'systems of approach' that are very solidly entrenched in the programmes of the particular government departments.

Finally, the quality of national development planning, for regional development, differs quite radically from country to country. West Germany, the Netherlands, France, and Denmark have incorporated some of the more consistent philosophies and approaches to regional development, in each case viewing — it should be emphasized — regional development as requiring help from policy instruments on a very broad level of fronts.

III. Instruments for Regional Development Policy: A Smorgasbord of National Techniques

Overview

Estimates of the numbers of national instruments that are specifically designed to implement regional development policies concur on one point — the number is large. At least fifty such instruments are

currently in use, as a conservative guestimate. Essentially they fall
into the following categories:

- Assistance to new (and expanding) industry and service-sector
  activities (such as tourism). Such aid focuses on designated regions
  (but many are so designated) and consists largely of grants, interest
  subsidies, and a plethora of tax concessions.

- Infrastructure aid to designated regions.

- Regional allocation of public purchases.

- Regional allocation of public investment and other forms of
  leadership by public corporations that are not established primarily
  for regional development purposes.

- Development corporations that are established for regional development or planning purposes.

- Control and disincentive mechanisms.

- Labour mobility and training instruments.

Table 2.1 itemizes financial incentives applied in the framework of
regional economic policy, by eight of the member countries, over the
period 1973–1980. According to that table, it can be noted that five
types of incentives are most common. All member countries provide
capital grants for both buildings and equipment as well as soft loan
schemes. Most members provide aid to labour in the form of training
and mobility incentives. Incentives available in the case of Luxembourg are not specifically for designated areas (so are not included in
Table 2.1), while Greece just joined in 1981.

Appendix 2.1 is a synthesis, by the Commission of the European
Communities, of direct aids to industry.

In Table 2.2, a distinction is drawn between the degrees of
administrative discretion allowed in determining regional incentives.
As can be seen, Italy appears at the end of the spectrum where rates
are relatively fixed, with less administrative discretion. Belgium and
Denmark, in contrast, allow considerable administrative judgement to
play a role. The case for administrative discretion basically emphasizes the risks of giving away public funds 'unnecessarily' or
without a 'fine enough tuning' of regional objectives. The case against
such discretion rests heavily on problems faced by industry of knowing
precisely what it might be eligible for, as it calculates whether or not
to expand or locate in a region. There is the further difficulty of
developing an adequate administrative capability to form reasonable
judgements, expeditiously, on such matters. The European experience
cannot be said to produce any clear preference, but, on balance, the
case for automaticity appears the more convincing and relevant for
Canadian consideration.

Table 2.1
FINANCIAL INCENTIVES APPLIED IN THE FRAMEWORK OF REGIONAL ECONOMIC POLICY IN THE COUNTRIES OF THE EEC

Category	B	DK	G	F	IRL	I	NL	UK
1. Capital grants (investment grants & investment allowances)								
—buildings	A	A	A	A	A	A	A	A
—equipment	A	A	A	A	A	A	A	A
—working capital	—	B	—	—	B	—	—	—
—rationalization & reorganization	—	—	B	—	B	B	—	—
2. Ready built factories	—	B	—	—	B	—	—	B
3. Ready built factories & industrial sites at reduced prices (including factory rent concessions)	B	A	—	A	B	B	B	B
4. Soft loan schemes (interest rebates and/or concessionary loans)	A	A	A	B	B	A	B	A
5. Credit facilities								
— medium and long-term credit banks	—	—	—	..	—	B	—	—
— loans with state guarantee	B	B	B	—	B	—	B	—
6. Labour grants (employment premium)	B	—	—	B	B	—	—	A*
7. Tax exemption								
— accelerated depreciation allowance — or special depreciation allowance	B	—	A	A	A	B	A	B
— from profits	—	—	B	B	B	A	—	—
— from income	—	—	B	—	—	—	—	—
— export profit tax relief	—	—	—	—	A	—	—	—
— from consumption of energy (oil, natural gas)	—	—	—	B	—	B	—	—
— other tax exemptions (business tax exemptions, local registration fees, turnover tax, property income)	B	—	—	A	B	B	—	—
8. Training (very often applied nation-wide)	—	B	B	B	B	—	B	B
9. Transfer premiums								
— decentralization indemnity & decentralization allowances	—	B	—	B	—	—	—	B
— decentralization grant for artisanal subcontractors	—	—	—	B	—	—	—	—
10. Incentives to incite labour to leave problem regions	—	—	—	—	—	—	—	B
11. Incentives to incite labour to move to problem regions	—	B	B	B	—	B	B	B
12. Capital removal grants or allowances for the relocation of firms	—	B	B	—	B	—	B	B
13. Equity participation	—	—	—	B	B	B	—	B
14. Reduction of public utility tariffs								
— transport	—	—	—	B	—	B	—	B
— electricity	—	—	—	—	—	—	—	—
15. Preferential regime for public tender	—	—	B	—	—	B	—	B
16. Regional allocation of public orders (government expenditure)	—	—	B	—	—	B	—	B
17. Regional allocation of public investment	—	—	—	—	—	B	—	—
18. Social security concessions	—	—	—	—	—	A	—	—
19. Marketing assistance to firms	—	—	—	—	—	B	—	—

20. Location controls (disincentives included)							
— location tax (levies)	—	—	—	A	—	B	B	—
— building licence	—	—	—	A	—	—	—	A
— notifications in respect of new industrial buildings, installations and offices	—	—	—	—	—	B	B	—
21. Deconcentration of administration, consultancy & data processing activities (research activities grant included)	—	—	—	B	—	—	B	B
22. Redistribution of fiscal receipts	—	—	B	—	—	—	—	—
23. Artisanal schemes	—	—	—	B	—	—	—	—

Legend: A — a major instrument of a country's regional policy.
 B — an instrument available for some very specific regional purposes.
 * — The regional employment premium was abandoned in January 1977; however a labour premium is applied in Northern Ireland.
Source: N. Vanhove and L.H. Klaassen, *Regional Policy — A European Approach* (Farnborough: Saxon House, 1980), pp. 310–12 (drawing on a series of OECD and EEC publications).

Before commenting on these main instruments, some cautionary comments are in order.

First, staff of the Commission of the European Communities have recently attempted to aggregate the amounts spent by national governments on regional aid,[11] but, as with other attempts, the numbers are seriously deficient. For example, they do not include estimates of the value of tax concessions, social security subsidies with a regional character, and infrastructure supports. They also fail to capture all the direct assistance to companies subsidized. No numbers are therefore cited here; it is not felt that adequate data currently exist to support estimates of the relative quantities of aid, government by government, for regional development purposes.

Secondly, the differences of economic, physical, and constitutional structures of the respective countries inevitably cause different approaches to regional development. The mere cataloguing of instruments does not reflect this. For example, centralized countries (France being a good example) tend to treat regional programmes rather as a geographical breakdown of the national plan. In contrast, planning in federal nations (for example, the Federal Republic of Germany) tends rather to be built up from the regional base, with the national government playing more of a co-ordinating and catalytic role.

Main Instruments

Comments will now be made on the main instruments that, traditionally, have been associated with regional development policy among the member countries.

Table 2.2
MAIN REGIONAL-INCENTIVE DISCRETION[a] BY COUNTRY AND TYPE

Country	Incentive Name	CG	IRS	TC	DA	LS
Belgium	Interest subsidy		D			
	Capital grant		D			
	Accelerated depreciation				D	
Denmark	Company soft loan		D			
	Municipality soft loan		D			
	Investment grant	D				
France	Regional-development grant	A/D				
	Local-business tax concession			A		
Germany	Investment allowance	A				
	Investment grant	D				
	ERP soft loan		A			
	Special depreciation				A	
Ireland	Capital grant — new	D				
	Capital grant — re-equipment	D				
	Export-profit tax relief			A		
Italy	Capital grant	A				
	National soft loan		A			
	Social-security concession					A
	Tax concesssions			A		
Luxembourg	Capital grant	D				
	Tax concession			D		
Netherlands	Investment premium	A/D				
United Kingdom	Regional-development grant	A				
	Soft loan		D			
	Interest-relief grant		D			

Source: Douglas Yuill, Kevin Allan, and Chris Hull, *Regional Policy in the European Community* (London: Croom Helm, 1980), p. 232.

Notes: [a] Abbreviations of discretion categories: D, administrative discretion in award, rates *up to* a maximum: A, little or no administrative discretion in award, rates *fixed*; A/D, basically automatic, but with an element of discretion for large projects.

[b] Abbreviations of incentive types: CG, capital grant; IRS, interest-related subsidy; TC, tax concession; DA, depreciation allowance; LS, labour subsidy.

1. Direct Assistance to Industry

Capital grants have been widely used in all member countries, except Belgium and Denmark. Capital grants enjoy advantages of flexibility (they can be readily made available to projects in particular sectors, in special areas, of certain project sizes, etc.), of promotional visibility (for political advertising), of straightforward measurability by both the company (in assessing their commercial value) and by the government (in determining their scale in the context of broader economic costs and benefits). They can be linked to various conditions (e.g., new rather than old machinery, and so on).

As with any incentive, they can also be viewed, in some cases, as 'windfall gains' and can be vulnerable to political whims (especially when a fair degree of discretion is accorded to the project grant officers). There is some apprehension that investment grants can make companies adopt more capital-intensive production methods than otherwise. There is also some concern that the companies may pull out after using up the grant.

Not only are capital grants the most common form of direct incentive, they were found to be the most valuable incentive on offer, "ranging from 2.7 per cent of value added . . . [discounted to present value] . . . in Luxembourg to 8.9 per cent in Italy. Soft loans or interest rebates are ranging from 0.9 to 3.2 per cent of value added, and accelerated depreciation allowances from 0.6 to 2.0 per cent of value added."[12] The advertised rates of grant were found, in a recent review,[13] to range from a "maximum of 15 per cent of eligible investment in Luxembourg to maxima of 50 per cent or more in Ireland, Italy and Northern Ireland. In all other Community countries the . . . rates . . . lie . . . around 25 per cent . . . except in Belgium where . . . there is no *direct* capital grant." (See also Appendix 2.1 for further details.)

According to the Commission's review (Appendix 2.1), *interest subsidies* of between 5 and 8 per cent, as well as deferred payment privileges, are available in Belgium and Denmark. Interest subsidies play a less central role in Germany, Italy, and the United Kingdom (albeit the Italian subsidy can be particularly generous — up to 70 per cent of the market rate of interest).

Whereas capital grants have a relatively 'clean-cut' character, interest subsidies can have a number of relative disadvantages, particularly when the lending agency's guide-lines are unclear and its own performance assessment is uncertain. For example, the temptation to lend to the commercially more viable projects (that really need no interest subsidies at all) could well be strong if a development bank's guide-lines are unclear about 'preferred customers' and the degree of 'acceptable' risk. On the other hand, interest subsidy programmes — linked to special areas and associated with agencies such as the European Investment Bank — can save a great deal of administrative problems to the member country that might be funding the subsidy programme. In the current era of high and escalating rates, a discount linked to prime rates (e.g., a 3 or 5 per cent rate subsidy) is obviously a less precarious form of governmental aid than, say, an 8 per cent flat rate guarantee — the government committing itself to paying the difference as prime rates escalate.

Fiscal concessions have been quite widely used and are often claimed to have the political convenience of being 'unpublicized revenue forgone', in contrast to more identifiable government subsidies. They are generally less readily fine tuned to relate to specific company circumstances.

Ireland and Italy offer the highest nominal tax incentives (e.g., Irish export-profits tax relief is a full concession for fifteen years, with partial extensions thereafter).

In some countries, the capital grants and interest subsidies are viewed as taxable income, in others not so (e.g., the French concession at the other extreme is for a maximum of five years in the case of local business tax, with no national profits concession at all).

Explicit employment subsidies have been most widely used in Italy, though a number of governments do relate grants to job creation and maintenance (see Appendix 2.1).

There is a good deal of hypocricy evident in the manner employment subsidies are treated, given the attitudes of unions and the public to feather-bedding. While it is true that explicit wage subsidies are not widespread, the structure of programmes such as unemployment insurance (in the manner they enable workers to integrate it with seasonal activities), mobility, and even housing grants are often only a short step away from a straightforward wage subsidy.

The general attitude in the European Commission to regional employment subsidies is probably fairly expressed by the former regional commissioner, C. Thomson:

> The feeling in the Commission so far has been that the difficulty about operational assistance is that it tends to turn into long term, permanent subsidy and then, within Community terms, leads to a permanent distortion of competition; whereas the advantage of aid given in the form of direct help to investment — if it is given wisely — is that it has the best chance of promoting long self-sustaining growth.[14]

2. Infrastructure

Aid for both economic and social infrastructure, in designated regions, is given by all member governments. Industrial estates have been accorded particular priority over the past two decades, to such a degree that officials of the European Commission have noted that "there seems at present to be a surplus of industrial estates in the Community, . . . largely due to the economic crisis."[15]

It is useful to distinguish, at the start of these comments, between physical infrastructure and current account (non-capital) expenditure infrastructure. Both play a major role, and while they should not be viewed in isolation, it may be helpful to identify some of their different characteristics at the beginning.

Capital. Physical or capital infrastructure might be broken into three divisions.

1. *Capital infrastructure aid for individual firms* includes industrial estates, advance/ready-built factories, direct pipeline, electric power, rail and road links to main systems, and so on. All problem regions have access to programmes offering such facilities — some at more generous rates (to the firms) than others. Often the factories (which can either be advanced, that is, of some standing design, or custom built) are rented at subsidized rates, or sold at less than commercial prices. Most appear to be rented. From the private-sector vantage point, industrial estate systems can reduce significantly the pre-operational phase, assuming many services are routinely available on the site, as distinct from the problems of establishing in greenfield sites or areas without such facilities. Industrial estates have proven, when well designed as in the case of Ireland (especially at Shannon), the Netherlands, and many in West Germany, to be an excellent form of linking regional policies to land-use, housing, and environmental planning.

2. *Capital infrastructure at the local/community level* covers a very wide range of physical facilities — from housing to hospitals, from sewage plants to training institutions. The quality and appropriateness of such facilities varies radically between member countries and within regions of member countries. On the one hand, the Netherlands and much of West Germany have achieved almost uniformly high standards; on the other hand, Italy and the United Kingdom give the impression of a good deal of patchiness and bureaucratic rigidities.

The matching of local infrastructure to regional development goals necessitates a far clearer idea of where local areas are really trying to go (over the longer run) than is frequently to be found. It places emphasis on local participation in the development process, as well as the careful use of experienced and multi-disciplined planning staff. On the one hand, one can point to the successful achievements of the Brugge area in Belgium, in conserving a magnificent old town and still developing new industry; on the other hand, one can point to the far from impressive performance of communities, such as Blankenberge and Ostende, that are close neighbours in the very same country and where tourism, industrial, urban and seaport development clash harshly with the environment and with each other. Even in Italy, so patchy in its co-ordination of efforts compared to West Germany, France, and the Netherlands, one can point to effective local infrastructure developments, for example, on parts of the Italian Riviera. But this is in juxtaposition to the chaos of Genova and the open sewers and slums of smaller towns such as Coreira.

One conclusion clearly is that the quality of local political and public-service competence is of fundamental importance. This argues strongly for greater efforts to foster appropriate training and educational programmes, as well as for improved regulatory procedures, especially for land-use planning, on a nation-wide basis.

3. *Capital infrastructure of broader, regional dimensions* includes energy systems, transport and communications networks, and medical, government and educational buildings.

Historically, many member countries saw the major infrastructure networks dominated by the considerations of the capital city and a few other major hubs. Thus the English and French transport systems were very much feeder networks for London and Paris, and, even today, it is far quicker and easier to travel by train to London and then to re-trace much of one's path, in order to reach towns that may be quite close geographically, than to run the gauntlet of local train, bus, and taxi systems that seem designed to impede local travel.

While many of the existing infrastructure systems were seriously damaged during the Second World War, much plant still remained. Essential for more balanced development within member countries of the EEC, and for the Community as a whole, has been a more evenly distributed (and less national capital dominated) system of physical infrastructure. Whether in the name of regional development or not, massive expenditures have been made by each member country on such systems. Thus excellent motorways now connect Milano with Napoli and Taranto, Lyons with Marseilles and Paris, London with Glasgow. At the same time, international links are now often superb — thus from Amsterdam to Düsseldorf or from Roma to Marseilles run first-class motorways.

The logic for much post-war infrastructure has been sectorally dominated. Not all has been 'balanced'. Massive overbuilding of roads, at the expense of other regional priorities, could readily be argued in the case of Northern Italy; incredible expense has been lavished on main highway lights in Belgium, again showing a very odd sense of priorities. Hospital complexes and secondary schools have often been built like military barracks, on a grand scale, when broader, alternative approaches to medical and educational systems might have been in better order, for example, in the United Kingdom, and so on.

While it is clear that much of the infrastructure development (by member countries) over the past twenty-five years has not been aimed *primarily* at balanced regional development, nevertheless such considerations have had influence. Thus, the current (VIIth) National Plan of France contains twenty-five priority action programmes, embodying the principal actions the state intends to take or support.[16] Many reflect regional concerns. For example, Programme Number 5 has the goals of opening up the west of France, the southwest, and the Massif Central. "This aims to improve communications in these regions by modernizing the major transverse routes and by linking the regional centres more effectively with the national road and rail networks by developing and improving the road and motorway networks and rail connections." Programme Number 6, of a similar kind, "aims to develop heavier navigation on the Rhône and the Saône by completing improvements in hand during the VIIth Plan and bringing works on the Rhine-Saône Canal into Burgundy."

Programme Number 21 includes "the completion of new towns: Cergy-Pontoise, Evry, Marne-la-Vallée, Melun-Sénart et Saint Quentin-en-Yvelines in the Paris region, L'Isle d'Abeau, Lille-Est, the banks of the Lake of Berre and Vaudreuil in the provinces. This action aims to strike a satisfactory balance between employment and habitat and to provide the collective equipment that these places need to become living towns of reasonable size, with a sure future."

It became apparent, from field visits, that some administrators have been far more thoughtful in the manner in which main regional systems have been integrated with more local regional development goals. Thus, for example, the West German *autobahns* have frequent, well-marked, access links to the local road networks — without any apparent disruption of the traffic flow. Moreover, there is open access (in terms of no tolls to pay). On the other hand, French and Italian motorways are often inadequately linked into the regions they cross, while the toll barriers result in very questionable economics; for example, the local road from Grenoble to Lyons is a crowded, truck-ridden, and very dangerous road, whereas the (high-toll price) superb Grenoble to Lyons motorway is grossly underutilized and poorly linked into the local road system. For another example, the superbly engineered Parma–La Spezia highway bores through mountains and majestically crosses huge valleys, linking mountains like beads on a necklace, but poorly serves many of the villages perched on the hills because of inadequate links to the motorway (again with much excess capacity). Such examples can be multiplied many times over. They illustrate that there is great scope, at little cost, for more effective regional development through more careful infrastructure planning.

The integration of soundly conceived capital projects into dynamic regional development has rarely proven straightforward. Parts of Western Europe, just as parts of North America, have substantial infrastructure — in such forms as industrial parks, power plants, and roads — that have not related efficiently to their surroundings. Sometimes this is due to a lack of appreciation of the environmental and social dimensions and implications, sometimes it results from an inaccurate assessment of future demand patterns, and quite often it appears to be the result of inadequate attention to the scale of, and responsibility for, future operating costs.

Non-Capital Assistance. Grants to local levels of government for capital facilities often do not take into account the operating cost implications. Lack of adequate maintenance is a serious difficulty in many of the problem regions of Italy and the United Kingdom, albeit cultural attitudes to public property also must play a substantial part. A comparison of the standards of cleanliness and general upkeep, for example, between the London and Brussels metro systems, or between the Italian and West German post offices, suggests this.

Some important infrastructure aid is not so directly linked with capital maintenance, but rather with broader regional systems. Thus the manner in which university and other research programmes (not necessarily buildings) are planned and supported can be important. For example, the Faculty of Science of the University of Grenoble had a positive impact on the development of the electronics industry in that region.[17] The sponsoring of research units and similar programmes in universities and colleges, as part of a regional development programme, can prove a constructive step. Unfortunately, however, universities and research institutes, both in Europe and North America, have frequently prided themselves on the distance their research has taken them away from local problems. Longer-term research grants, tied to specific areas of applied focus, can play a useful role. The foundation of the Limburg State University at Maastricht and the Limburg Institute for Development and Finance incorporate such ideas, as does the deliberate policy of preferential treatment of regional universities by the French government in its efforts to reduce the dependency on Paris.

Some non-capital, 'regional infrastructure' aid is of a non-recurrent nature. Examples include the development of town and country planning guide-lines, the compilation of rural development plans, and the designing of urban plans. The French regional programmes include many such provisions.[18] Among their current regional programmes might be cited Programme Number 4, which aims to "improve the telephone system, . . . including . . . to reduce the waiting period for telephone connection and to raise the standard of service." Programme Number 10 "aims to assist those seeking jobs, . . . [expanding the National Employment Bureau] . . . rationally throughout the country in line with local labour market needs." Programme Number 23 aims to "protect beauty spots and countryside better, to organize the development of recreation and tourism. . . ." Programme Number 1 includes "the renovation of the table-wines sector" (restructuring and renovation of the southern vineyards).

Other non-capital, 'regional infrastructure' aid is of a longer-term character, and falls into the category already warned against by Thomson.[19] Regional transport subsidies (e.g., various rate subsidies on railway freight within poorer regions), energy subsidies (e.g., gasoline subsidies for trucks, electrical energy rate subsidies for certain kinds of manufacturing, etc.), and other input subsidies (e.g., fertilizers and pesticides) are quite widely used — although little has apparently been done to assess their respective costs and benefits for regional development. While it is true that such subsidies can create inefficiencies as a consequence of distorting 'real costs' (so-called), it must be said, in their defence, that they themselves are often in response to imperfect market conditions.

3. Control and Discouragement Measures

There have been two basic approaches to controlling and discouraging regional development. The one, which is substantially discussed in the literature and is more tangible, is an explicit approach — consisting of particular regulations and penalties with declared goals. The other is far harder to grapple with — it is implicit and, while representing a policy position, is undeclared or, at least, unpublicized. It generally consists of the non-intervention by government, whether in terms of not building a structure such as a public building or bridge, or not encouraging a company to locate in an area by offering preferred alternatives.

Explicit controls. The most popularized forms of these measures are tied to congested areas, where governments seek to restrict further investments — of at least certain categories.

The United Kingdom was apparently the first to introduce explicit disincentive measures (1948) in the form of the Industrial Development Certificate. Essentially this instrument (since modified) requires manufacturing firms wishing to build, or even expand, floor space in excess of a certain dimension (e.g., 1100 square metres was one limit) to obtain a permit from the central government. In 1965, the system was extended to include office space requirements. The onus is on the firm to make a strong case to justify the permit; long-run efficiency, export earnings, and London's international commercial role appear to be key criteria.[20]

In the case of France, the primary concern has been the congestion of Paris — and a permit system has been imposed somewhat similar to that of London, together with a special tax on industrial and office space construction (not a recurring tax); the rate depends on the part of the Paris region in which the building is located. The French also levy a "transport tax" (about 2 per cent of gross wages) on all firms in Paris employing more than nine people. The negative instruments are attuned to incentives to encourage firms to move from Paris (and Lyon) to the development regions. These include assistance to workers, a decentralization grant, tax incentives, and so on.[21]

Implicit controls. Such controls are less readily documented, but can nevertheless play a significant role.

1. The very location of power systems, highways, hospitals, and so forth, in one place implies a decision against other localities. Industry frequently looks for positive attitudes by government in the form of longer-term public investments; the failure to make such commitments can be construed as a warning away from a particular location. Such controls, on the basis of various interviews, were found to be quite widespread. They were not simply linked to broad regional approaches (such as the London/Paris congestion problem) but to very local views of the *appropriate* style of development (environmental, urban/rural balance, etc.) for developing areas. The rejection of refinery proposals for the port industrial complex at Zeebrugge is an example of this kind of control. Such control decisions are often not publicized — they are simply taken. Sometimes the regional frameworks are quite clear; at other times, they are more *ad hoc* and dependent on the judgement of local politicians and officials.

2. The allocation of public funds into infrastructure for regional development has been discussed. One offshoot of this is the decentralization/regional build-up of government offices. While the United Kingdom, France, Italy, and the Netherlands are probably the best known users of such an approach, to varying degrees it is done in each country. In the 1950–1973 era, governments expanded rapidly in terms of direct employees, thus the establishment of offices in poorer regions did not present as difficult a problem as it would today in providing alternative employment opportunities for those unwilling to move. Subsequently, with governments seeking to 'belt-tighten', office decentralization appears to have been less easy.

The decentralization process should not, however, be viewed solely as a mechanism for providing more direct employment in the 'development areas'. It also has reflected a widespread concern, in the Community, for greater regional participation in government decision making and planning. The application of computer systems has facilitated the possibilities of decentralized offices, as has the improvement of regional transport systems in each member country. The trend would appear to be 'more of the same', albeit the policy is far tougher to implement in times of government austerity.

3. The allocation of public funds, through the activities of state corporations for regional development purposes, has been most clearly done in Italy. Thus "in 1978 over 27 per cent of state-holding-sector employment was located in the Mezzogiorno, compared with 18 per cent in 1965 and 13 per cent in 1958."[22] Italy has some three hundred and fifty state-holding groups (into which many of the firms are organized), the largest being IRI and ENI. From 1957, a designated, minimal percentage of the total state-holding company allocation had to be placed in the Mezzogiorno, but it has not proven easy either to monitor *meaningfully* or to decide upon the system of measurement.

The employment numbers appear rather more significant measures of this programme.

In the case of other European Community members, the allocations of state corporations for regional development play significant roles, but, on balance, it is probably fair to say that the regional dimension plays more a part in decisions not to close, rather than in decisions to expand into new locations (e.g., the case of the state steel industry in the United Kingdom).

4. Government purchases are a further instrument widely used for regional development purposes — and again there is the question of explicit as distinct from implicit activities. Moreover, the monitoring of the real sources of the goods or services is far from straightforward. To purchase goods or services from an agent/firm in region A or B is one thing while to purchase 'home-made regional content' is frequently quite another matter. Officials of the European Commission are finding it a difficult enough task to monitor activities from a competition policy vantage point at the national level. At the regional level the information is most patchy. That said, the Italian government, nevertheless, does seek to assure the South "30 per cent of the value of each government contract for current purchases of industrial goods," as well as a 40 per cent share of the investments programmed by public administrations.[23] The approaches by other governments to explicit regional preferences appear to have been more guarded, albeit they undoubtedly continue to practise some forms of preference. The problems of patronage and 'unfair practices' have always made this aspect, particularly at the regional level, less politically attractive to publicize as an explicit policy.

4. Regional Development Agencies

There is no clear, common pattern among the national governments regarding regional development policy formulation and execution. Essentially they all face the following main tasks:

- *Research* — as the basis for problem analysis and possible solution identification.

- *Policy formulation* — the selection of the broad strategies and particular policies.

- *Co-ordination* — many departments and other national agencies are involved in significant pieces of regional development policy and implementation. A co-ordinating role to mesh policies is important. This has to include an adequate mechanism for public participation, to make sure the proposed 'beneficiaries' really do get heard.

- *Promotion and implementation* — this set of functions calls for both the promotion of programmes in the governmental network, as well as for the promotion of the programmes (and regions) to potential investors. At the same time, the implementation of infrastructure building requires specific units with clear lines of authority and responsibility. The development of regional and area plans, linking land-use planning, economic planning, and so on, also falls into each of the three headings above. The implementers, however, have to be quite sure that these plans really are clear and practical, if they are to be effective 'doers'.

- *Monitoring* — this function is necessary at various stages. For example, there is the role of a typical financial management agency (such as a treasury board) where financial control is the operative consideration. Then there are requirements of programme-implementing agencies, and central policy analysts, of the ongoing monitoring of progress, with emphasis both on physical indicators of progress and also on the attainment of the end goals of the policy. Such a monitoring process requires both post-project evaluation (and follow-up), as well as broader macro-level assessments of the regional impact of such activities.

These are complex functions, and given the different kinds of government structures among Community members, it is inevitable that they will allocate functions in a variety of ways.

In the case of certain countries, for example, Italy, some agencies have very far-reaching powers — such is the case of the Cassa per il Mezzogiorno, created in 1950 as an executive body for the South under the direction of a Committee of Ministers.[24] While the Cassa has considerable powers on paper, it has serious problems in ensuring that measures (and funds) going into the Mezzogiorno are additive rather than simply replacing funding for programme components and projects that would (were it not around) be the routine responsibilities of other ministries.

In the case of France, for another example, the Délégation à l'aménagement du territoire et à l'action régionale (DATAR), created in 1963, was placed under the direct authority of the Prime Minister. As such, it is a national agency with an overall role for French regional policy. Its influence is viewed as being derived from the following:

- The quality of its staff

- The money it can distribute (through the Fonds d'Interventions pour l'Aménagement du Territoire)

- The political influence/importance of its leaders.

The DATAR has no official goal-setting role, that being the task of the Planning Commission, but obviously, in practice, it does play a substantial part. In each urban centre, the DATAR has planning commissions to study the problems and develop master plans.[25]

In the case of other countries, the regional development agencies may be more research, or specific programme development, or advisory, or promotion oriented.

The United Kingdom, for example, has been subdivided into eleven economic planning regions, each with an economic planning council and board. The councils consist of members drawn from industry, the trades unions, the local authorities, and other similar groups, but they have no executive functions. They are very much advisory arms. The economic planning boards, on the other hand, consist of officials from the regional offices of government departments and are supposed to play more of a co-ordinating role with the various implementing departments, as well as to relate (as administrators) to the councils in their work on regional development advisory strategies.[26] Such mechanisms appear somewhat weak; they are very dependent on the clout of a few individuals, particularly at the political level.

In the case of the Netherlands, "the Minister of Economic Affairs co-ordinates and decides on all regional measures directly designed to stimulate economic activity (investment grants, relocation grants, modernizing shopping centres and the contingency fund)."[27] Land-use planning has underpinned development for generations — in large part because of population pressures — and regional planning has been a natural and integral part. In that sense, despite the existence of particular agencies with regional titles, it is probably fair to say that every agency is a regional planning agency in some manner — 'development in the Netherlands is regional development'.

From the cross-section of material on regional development agencies, it became clear that countries with strong, central governments (e.g., France and the United Kingdom) are having some difficulty incorporating local ideas and interests in the final 'regional development programme products'. The regional economic councils are really, it appears, somewhat weak — in contrast to central agencies such as the Treasury. On the other hand, West Germany with its federal system has faced a somewhat different problem — one of harmonizing quite clear ideas about regional development from each state into a nationally consistent fabric. This became particularly clear in the context of industrial incentive programmes.

It is apparent that when agencies are established with clear regional development responsibilities, there is a tendency for other agencies to 'walk away' from their own regional development responsibilities, on the grounds that 'that is a regional development agency problem'. On the other hand, on the basis of the often sweeping style of some of the regional agencies, they in turn face the temptation of 'empire building', focusing on 'their own programmes' at the expense of playing more of a policy formulation, co-ordinating, and effectiveness-monitoring role.

5. Labour Mobility and Training Instruments

Two points should be made, by way of preface. First, since 1968, based on the objectives of Articles 48 and 49 of the Treaty of Rome, workers (of the member countries) may move freely between these countries. Greece is currently being phased in.[28] Secondly, two 'schools of thought' polarize extreme positions for regional policy, among member countries. They are (1) work to the workers; and (2) workers to the work. On balance, the emphasis of the labour mobility and training programmes is probably weighted in favour of the (politically less difficult) 'work to the workers' school.

Migrant Workers. As of 1980, the Community contained some six million migrant workers, or about twelve million migrants (when families are included). About 70 per cent of these migrant workers came from outside the Community. Non-EEC nationals are mostly citizens of the British Commonwealth and the Mediterranean-rim countries of Turkey, Portugal, Yugoslavia, Spain, Algeria, Greece, Morocco, and Tunisia. The remaining 30 per cent are EEC member-country nationals working in other member countries. Thus, for example, about 650,000 Italians and 450,000 Irish are working in other member countries.

Although Germany is host to the largest number of migrant workers — approximately two million — the proportion of foreign workers (as a percentage of the employed labour force) is highest in Luxembourg (36%), followed by France (11.1%), Germany (9.5%), Belgium (8.3%), and the United Kingdom (7.4%). At the lowest end of the spectrum are the net-exporters of migrant workers, Italy and Ireland (with only about 0.4%).[29]

Nationals of member countries who work elsewhere in the Community are now afforded the same basic rights as native-born workers. They may move freely between member countries, without the need for work permits. Their residence permits (five years at least) are automatically renewed, and access to the social security benefits of the host country is routinely available, just as if they were nationals of that country. Thus, for example, the family of a migrant worker will benefit, in cases of illness, from the social protection of their country of residence (as distinct from origin) and a retired Italian can draw his German pension (i.e., earned for work in Germany) whether he returns to Italy or continues to reside in Germany.[30]

The major exception to these rights is in the area of political privileges, although there are a number of other practical problem aspects; for example, migrant workers, of all origins, frequently obtain low-rental, subsidized housing only after considerable delays because of the general shortage of such housing.[31]

Whereas Germany migrant workers enjoy almost all the rights accorded to the nationals, those from outside the Community are dependent on bilateral arrangements between the host country and their country of origin. Work permits are required, and migrant workers from outside the Community are subject to severe entry restrictions as the Community seeks to tackle its growing, internal unemployment difficulties.

Regional Policies Regarding Mobility. At least six of the member states (Denmark, Germany, France, Italy, the Netherlands, and the United Kingdom) have financial incentives to facilitate the movement of labour to 'problem areas'.

For example, in the United Kingdom, the 'Key Workers Scheme' provides assistance to all firms, moving to an assisted area, that wish to transfer a limited number of key workers.[32] Denmark has a similar programme under which a maximum of 4,000 DKR may be granted, per employee, for transfer costs.[33] The Netherlands instituted a Relocation Costs Scheme in 1977, the aim of which is to increase the mobility of the unemployed and to subsidize the relocation of business.[34] Similar programmes are present in the other countries.

Efforts to move people out of regions of higher unemployment would appear to have been far less advertised or explicit. There are a number of good reasons behind this. For example, the Community has experienced a very substantial shift of people from rural to urban areas — and this, in turn, raised difficult urban infrastructure problems, and, in some cases such as Paris, London and the Dutch 'Rimcity', efforts to reduce urban congestion became a mainspring of regional policy. Secondly, there is substantial evidence (albeit not conclusive in any 'purist' sense, as times and circumstances change) that those who most readily leave 'problem' regions tend to be the younger, more versatile, and relevantly trained members of the labour force, who would be the potential entrepreneurs and skilled workers who could contribute most to the region's development.[35] Thirdly, there is the broader dynamic of the multiplier effect working negatively as workers leave, causing a further contraction in the level of demand for regionally produced goods and services.

Nevertheless, national employment service offices often do make considerable effort to inform people of employment opportunities in other parts of the country (and Community). This seems widespread throughout the Community, although the degree of efficiency varies considerably between countries and regions. Private firms also have their own recruiting systems.

A number of additional activities in such fields as training, broader education, and transportation and communications clearly play an important role — both in upgrading the quality of the labour force in the 'problem regions', and thereby making it more attractive for firms to expand or move into the region, as well as, conversely, to give the trainees skills that enable them more readily to find employment outside the region. All countries in the Community provide widespread educational and vocational training opportunities, and these have been seen as a critical element in both national and regional development. Most poorer regions now boast quite elaborate training facilities.

Training. The distinction between basic education and specific training should not be overstretched in the context of regional development. Both play their role and the cut-off point between them is very arbitrary. It is often the broader educational system, at school and university levels, that helps or hinders development — depending on its quality, philosophical orientation, and social relevance. The literature on regional development in Europe tends to focus exclusively on specific vocational training as an instrument of regional policy, treating the broader educational system cavalierly. However, throughout Western Europe, it is apparent that the educational system, as a whole, has broadened its range, depth, and local coverage very substantially in the post-war decades. While many poorer regions have been included in this process, it is clear that the quality has been extremely variable.

In the case of training programmes, as distinct from the broader educational system, three main approaches can be identified among the member countries — a focus on vocational training, or apprenticeship programmes, or a combination of both.[36]

In Germany and Denmark, the apprenticeship system predominates; in France, Belgium and Italy, full-time vocational education predominates; in Luxembourg, the United Kingdom, the Netherlands, and Ireland, a mixture of the two training approaches is employed.

Since the formation of the EEC, strides have been made to reduce the complications caused by the different qualification systems of the member countries, acting (as they often have done) as barriers to inter-country mobility. Throughout the Community there appears to be a growing awareness of the value *both* of practical experience and on-the-job training *and* of vocational education in schools and other institutions. This is likely to foster a greater degree of conformity among the member countries' training systems.

While the European Social Fund is covered in a later chapter, the manner in which it has given priority to enriching training programmes of the member governments, in the poorer regions, should be noted. This emphasis, together with the programming approach pursued by the European Regional Development Fund, could result in a greater degree of rationalization of the mobility and training instruments, in the Community, as an explicit part of regional development policy.

On balance, mobility and training instruments appear — somewhat uneasily and certainly not explicitly — to be in general support of 'bringing work to the workers', yet, at the same time, serving as a safety valve — so that would-be migrants are not trapped in areas that, however diligent the efforts may be to develop them, nevertheless have a somewhat dubious future.

IV. National Policies for Regional Development: Some Points for Canadian Review

Without repeating the details and many points raised in the earlier part of this chapter, several conclusions from the European experience (at the member-government level of regional policy) will be isolated as meriting consideration in any reappraisal of Canadian regional policy.

1. The quality of regional development planning and the capacity to rationalize and execute regional policies have varied *very substantially*, at the national levels of government in the European Community. The same has been true in the case of the provincial governments in Canada. Quite often it would appear that the regions with the most severe problems have governments that are least capable of tackling them. This is only, in part, it would appear, a function of financial capacity; quite frequently it seems, in Europe, to be a reflection of administrative capacity and of political and broader social will. Inequalities and unbalanced development appear, in many cases, to be reinforced, rather than ameliorated, by the actions of some EEC governments.

2. Regional development theories and philosophies have played some role in providing frameworks to EEC national-level regional policies, although it is not clear whether they have been 'engines behind the policies' or 'crutches to give them respectability'. Two particular underpinning theories might be highlighted:

- That of 'balanced' as distinct from 'unbalanced' growth. This does appear to have had some influence behind European approaches: the issue (which can never be fully resolved) is one of defining an 'acceptable level' of 'balance', and of justifying its rationale.

- That of 'growth centres', and a slightly broader concept of 'pôles de croissance'. This has played a very important role in many European countries — France, the Netherlands, and Italy being in the vanguard.

In the Canadian situation, there appears to have been less effort to link regional development programmes to broader frameworks of theoretical logic or experience, albeit the jargon has periodically been referred to by way of justification after the event.

3. National governments in the EEC have developed a variety of regional instruments, many of which have their counterparts in Canada. Several countries have made a point of emphasizing the need for close integration of national regional policies with national development priorities as a whole (for example, the Netherlands and France in particular). Other national governments appear to have been less well integrated (for example, the United Kingdom, Belgium and, in many ways in practice, Italy).

4. A few EEC member governments have very successfully and deliberately integrated regional planning with physical (both urban and rural) and environmental planning. In such cases, geographers (land-use planning specialists in particular) have worked closely with sociologists, architects, economists, engineers, and representatives of other disciplines. The Netherlands and the Federal Republic of Germany are particularly to be noted in this case.

Unfortunately, in Canada, such an integration has generally not occurred. The economics and commerce graduates have tended to work in isolation from the engineers/physical planners, and vice versa. This becomes very noticeable when regional programmes and projects are assessed, on site. Not merely does the problem seem to stem from work approaches in the field, but also from the relatively narrow professional training that is still quite widespread in some Canadian universities.

5. Industrial parks, linked to towns of various sizes, have been a main framework for the galaxy of incentives offered by most national (EEC) governments. Overall this appears to have been a useful approach to economic development and to urban and rural land-use planning. The quality of industrial parks in the Federal Republic of Germany and southern France is particularly impressive. In the Italian case, as a main cautionary example, the social infrastructure and planning (including environmental) regulations have not kept pace — while a combination of lack of political stability and the actual form of tax aids may have resulted in somewhat lower standards of industrial plant on many sites.

Industrial parks have also played a role in regional development programming in Canada; the standards vary quite considerably across the country. With some exceptions (for example, on the outskirts of Toronto in the Don Mills area), Canadian industrial parks do not appear as carefully planned as most in West Germany and southern France. In the latter two countries, the relationship of the sites with main transport arteries, housing and, of great importance, the broad social and ecological environment is very noticeable.

6. The containment of urban growth is a problem that has faced regional policy makers in much of Europe. The massive reduction of rural employment (especially in agriculture) and the expansion of urban services has resulted in large urban agglomerations. Many of the largest European towns appear to be balanced precariously. France and the United Kingdom stand out for their efforts to control the expansion of (particularly) Paris and London. The use of 'green belts' to ensure rural areas around the cities is particularly impressive in the London region; the control of ribbon development is quite effectively handled in much of West Germany, the Netherlands, and southwestern France.

Canada faces similar urban growth problems especially in southern Ontario, Calgary, Edmonton, and the lower British Columbia mainland. There are few Canadian urban areas, however, that could not benefit from a very careful assessment of the more successful urban planning (and industrial estate management and design) experiences of the EEC countries.

7. Training cannot reasonably be viewed outside the broader systems of education. All member governments appreciate the importance of education to regional and national development. Some place more weight on an apprenticeship approach to the vocational training aspects (e.g., West Germany and Denmark); others place more emphasis on full-time vocational education (e.g., France, Belgium, and Italy). Luxembourg, the United Kingdom, the Netherlands, and Ireland employ a mix of the two approaches.

Substantial strides have been made to reduce the complications caused by different qualification systems between the countries, facilitating greater job mobility. However, one overriding point should be made — namely that while the mobility and training instruments, on balance, appear to be in general support of 'bringing work to the workers', they are viewed also as 'safety valves'. If work does not materialize, in sufficient quantity, in the poorer regions, then would-be migrants should not be trapped there because of inadequate training and mobility aids.

8. Particularly in France and Italy, state corporations have provided considerable leadership in the development of some poorer regions (e.g., the Mezzogiorno). There is scope for a review of the potential role of Crown corporations, as instruments for Canadian regional development. Any such review should not merely include an assessment of specific regional Crown corporations (such as the Cape Breton Development Corporation), but of even greater importance is the potential regional role of nation-wide corporations such as the Canadian National Railways.

9. The members of the European Community have agreed to impose ceilings on the amount of direct aid that can be given, as regional

incentives, to industry locating in various parts of the country. This is differentiated depending on the particular government's perceptions of where the main problem areas lie. The intent, on paper, is to design a more co-ordinated European system of regional development incentives to industry and tourism. As yet, there is little effective effort to monitor the process, and one might be sceptical that it will work in the foreseeable future. But the idea is interesting.

At the present juncture of federal-provincial relations, it is unlikely that the establishment of such ceilings would be acceptable for the Canadian setting. It does, however, have great logical appeal.

10. Finally, regional development instruments — without reasonably clear regional policy frameworks — can be shown to be 'busy', in terms of real or alleged impact on such indicators as direct employment or income generation. But the recital of changes in such data can often serve to obscure rather than to focus on the reasons for regional problems. Symptoms may get treated, but the root causes of problems can be neglected. That is a conclusion that can be gleaned from the experiences of most member countries, at one stage or other in the post-1945 era. In no country is it more clearly to be noted than the United Kingdom or Italy.

A review of speeches by many Canadian federal and provincial ministers will show that this country has not been immune to such 'window dressing.'

V. Conclusion

The oil embargo in 1973 was a watershed for the world as a whole. Canada and the European Community were integrally involved. The decade prior to 1973 was essentially one of rapid economic growth; the EEC national governments (nine) had all attempted a variety of quite imaginative approaches to more balanced regional development. The Canadian federal government had done the same. Since 1973, the nine member countries and the Canadian federal government have moved into something of a 'waiting pattern', so far as regional policies are concerned. Relatively minor programme adjustments have been the norm rather than the exception. In the case of the nine, two main points might be highlighted.

First, the national governments have passed on world energy prices more rapidly to consumers than has Canada, and they have tended to view energy strategies and programmes as essential elements of regional development policies. At the European Community level, such approaches have been encouraged by the influence and financial support of both the European Investment Bank and the European Regional Development Fund.

Secondly, the European Community, particularly through the European Regional Development Fund's activities, has played a growing role as a catalyst, harmonizing influence, and 'collective conscience' on regional disparities in its relationship with the nine member governments. An increased degree of coherence, and comparative assessment of their respective regional policies and problems, has been marked in the case of the nine member governments. However, this should not be read to suggest complete harmony of approach or priorities. A glaring gap is still the lack of any consistent framework for transfer payments between the members of the Community at large. This is further discussed in the section on the Community budget.

In the case of Canada, on the other hand, the initiative for regional policy appears to have slipped from the federal government to the provinces. Alberta, in particular, boosted by oil revenues, has developed aggressive industrial strategies, while the eastern provinces, particularly (including Ontario and Quebec), appear to have generally promoted 'more of the same' — somewhat mesmerized by their past experiences. Adjustments to world energy prices have been generally less complete in Canada, where a complicated maze of subsidies has been erected, and energy programmes (at the federal level) have lacked the degree of regional development strategy that is quite marked in the European Community.[37]

Whereas quite a broad tendency towards greater harmonization is to be found in the European Community approaches to regional integration (for example, freer labour mobility, the removal of trade obstacles between members, and the co-ordination and initiatives taken by the European Regional Development Fund), the Canadian federal government has become immersed in constitutional reform details and has failed to play a harmonizing role regarding post-1973 regional policy. A degree of balkanization has set in with the provincial governments struggling to maximize their separate returns from energy resources, when such are within their 'territory'. Barriers to greater regional integration have been erected rather than reduced, and there now appears to be a greater need, than for many decades, for a more determined and coherent Canada-wide regional development policy framework. While the European Community has certainly faced similar pressures, the *overall* direction of the member governments' regional policies has been one of greater harmony.

APPENDIX 2.1

Measures for Development

The following list of measures for regional development is cited from a recent report by the Commission of the European Communities. While by no means fully comprehensive, it does give a flavour of the kinds of national incentives available.[38]

Direct Aid to Regional Development

—*Belgium*: five-year interest rate subsidy of 5% (or up to 8% in some cases) for loans to finance investment in industry or services; or equivalent capital subsidies or employment premiums. (The last measure has not yet been used.)

—*Denmark*: loans at reduced interest rates (7.5%) with deferred repayment (5 years) for investment in the industrial and service sectors; capital subsidies (cumulative) amounting to a maximum of 25%.

—*Federal Republic of Germany*: 8.75% net investment premium ('Investitionszulage') raised to 15%, 20% or 25% ('Investitionszuschuss') for the 31 growth points ('Schwerpunkte') distributed over 20 action programmes.

—*France*: regional development premiums of FF 15 000 (FF 12 000), FF 20 000 (FF 17 000) or FF 25 000 (FF 22 000) for the creation (extension) of jobs in the various zones with ceilings of 12%, 17% or 25% of fixed investment; there is a similar system for the services sector (PLAT), a location premium for certain activities, ranging from FF 10 000 to 30 000 per job.

—*Ireland*:

    (i) capital subsidies amounting to a maximum of 60% of fixed investment in the designated areas and 45% of fixed investment in the rest of the country (limited in practice to 40% and 25%);

    (ii) for companies set up before 1 January 1981, tax exemption up to 1990 for profits earned on goods manufactured for export;

    (iii) until 1 January 1981 accelerated depreciation of 120% in the designated areas (100% in non-designated areas).

—*Italy*: the principal regional aids for the Mezzogiorno are the following:

    (i) degressive capital subsidies (of 40%, 30% and 20% by tranche of fixed investment) raised by 20% of the initial rate for certain priority sectors (determined by the CIPE) or by 20% for particularly handicapped areas which have yet to be defined; these two rates can be combined where appropriate;

(ii) interest rate subsidies (with 30% of the reference interest rate to be borne by the investor in respect to a maximum of 40% of the capital borrowed) for investments amounting to less than LIT 30 000 million;

(iii) exemption from INPS social security charges up to 1986 for new jobs created between 1976 and 1980 in a number of industrial sectors (about 27% of labour costs).

— *Luxembourg*:

(i) a capital subsidy amounting to a maximum of 15% and an interest rate subsidy of 3 percentage points over 5 years are granted to industry;

(ii) an interest rate subsidy of 4 percentage points and a capital subsidy amounting to 25% for equipment and to a maximum of 15% for buildings are granted to handicrafts, trade and tourism.

— *Netherlands*:

(i) either, an investment premium amounting to a maximum of 25% of the amount of fixed investment for both the industrial sector and the services sector, for new investment and for extension projects;

(ii) or, a 15% investment premium plus an amount of HFL 12 500 per job created.

— *United Kingdom*:

(i) Regional Development Grants are capital grants of 20% in the Intermediate Areas and Development Areas and of 22% in the Special Development Areas, given on fixed investment in industry (buildings only in the Intermediate Areas);

(ii) Selective Financial Assistance granted in various forms, mainly concessionary loans, may be combined with the Regional Development Grants; it also applies to services; it is linked to the creation and maintenance of jobs;

(iii) renting of industrial buildings at reduced rates (no rent payable for an initial period of 2 to 5 years);

(iv) the same system exists in Northern Ireland but on more favourable terms (development grants of 40% to 50%); in addition, there is a Regional Employment Premium of UKL 2 per employee per week.

Infrastructure Linked to Regional Development

The regional development programmes generally attach major importance to the various types of infrastructure, both economic and social. Special emphasis is, however, placed on industrial estates as instruments of regional development directly linked to industrial investment. Though they have played an important role in the past, there seems at present to be a surplus of industrial estates in the Community, a situation which is largely due to the economic crisis.

Most of the programmes also attach importance to the development of other types of infrastructure designed to improve the economic efficiency of the regions, such as transport infrastracture (roads, waterways, ports and airports), telecommunications, water supply and purification and the development of tourist areas. Thus, Italy attaches some priority to water supply projects mainly for agricultural development, France focuses attention on the revitalization of rural areas and Ireland singles out the improvement of road and telephone systems and sanitary services. Some countries, particularly Ireland and the Netherlands, include other infrastructure investment (schools, hospitals, subsidized housing and vocational training centres). Some programmes rely in this respect on regionalized national planning of infrastructure (Belgium and France).

Measures Under Other Policies

With a few exceptions, little or no analysis is provided of the regional effects of other policies, both national and Community, such as agricultural, industrial, transport, physical planning and environmental policies, although in certain cases the regional impact of these policies is clearly identifiable. However, it would be wrong to regard regional policy as a residual policy intended to offset the negative effects of other policies whether sectoral or general. The aim must rather be to ensure consistency and indeed convergence between regional policy and sectoral policies.

Physical Planning

Except for the Netherlands, which applies integrated planning,[39] and to some extent Denmark, France, Italy and Luxembourg, the regional development programmes make relatively little reference to physical planning, the environment and socio-cultural measures. The environment and the quality of life must, however, be considered as increasingly important influences on the location of new economic activities. Some countries, such as the Netherlands, apply measures to protect the structure of rural areas and to limit the damage caused by tourism, reflecting a concern for ecology in the pursuit of regional development.

Notes

[1] Among the most comprehensive surveys are the following: Niles Hansen, ed., *Public Policy and Regional Economic Development: The Experience of Nine Western Countries* (Cambridge, Mass.: Ballinger, 1974); OECD, *The Regional Factor in Economic Development: Policies in Fifteen Industrialized OECD Countries* (Paris: OECD, 1970); OECD, *Issues of Regional Policies* (Paris: OECD, 1973); EEC, *Regional Policy Series*, Nos. 1, 2, 4, 6, 7, 8, 10, 11, 12, 13, 14, 16, and 17 (these studies are on the programmes of the member countries and were published between 1977 and 1980 by the Commission of the European Communities, Brussels); Douglas Yuill, Kevin Allen, and Chris Hull, eds., *Regional Policy in the European Community* (London: Croom Helm, 1980); Norbert Vanhove and Leo H. Klaassen, *Regional Policy — A European Approach* (Farnborough: Saxon House, 1980); Paul Romus, *L'Europe et les régions* (Brussels: Éditions Labor, 1979).

[2] Ullrich Casper, "Regional Incentives in the Republic of Germany," in Douglas Yuill, Kevin Allen and Chris Hull, eds., *Regional Policy in the European Community* (London: Croom Helm, 1980), p. 83.

[3] J. F. Gravier, *Paris et le désert français* (Paris: Flammarion, 1958).

[4] For examples, see A. Emanuel, *Issues of Regional Policies* (Paris: OECD, 1973); Hansen, *op. cit.*; EEC, *Report on the Regional Problems in the Enlarged Community* (Brussels: 1973).

[5] F. Perroux, *L'économie du XXᵉ siècle* (Paris: Presses Universitaires de France, 1961) Part II, "Les pôles de croissance." For a more recent and comprehensive review, see A.R. Kuklinski, *Growth Poles and Growth Centres in Regional Policies and Planning* (The Hague: Mouton, 1972).

[6] Especially associated, in those days, with the view of A.O. Hirschman, *The Strategy of Economic Development* (New Haven, Conn.: Yale University Press, 1958); and R. Nurkse, *Problems of Capital Formation in Underdeveloped Countries* (Oxford: Blackwell, 1953).

[7] Succinctly discussed by S. Kuznets, *Modern Economic Growth* (New Haven, Conn.: Yale University Press, 1966).

[8] Yuill *et al.*, *op. cit.*, p. 221.

[9] *Ibid.*, p. 222.

[10] *Ibid.*, p. 223.

[11] Commission of the European Communities, *The Regional Development Programmes*, Regional Policy Series No. 17 (Brussels: 1979), pp. 249–50.

[12] Vanhove and Klaassen, *op. cit.*, p. 318, summarizing work by K. Allen.

[13] Yuill *et al.*, *op. cit.*, p. 233.

[14] Cited by Vanhove and Klaassen, *op. cit.*, p. 330.

[15] Commission of the European Communities, *op. cit.*, p. 248.

[16] For further details, see Commission of the European Communities, *Regional Development Programmes — France, 1976–1980*, Regional Policy Series No. 13 (Brussels: 1978), pp. 11–12.

[17] CEE, *Rapports de groupes d'experts sur la politique régionale dans la Communauté économique européenne* (Brussels: 1964), p. 294.

[18] For further details, see note 16.

[19] See note 14.

[20] For further information, see Yuill *et al.*, *op. cit.*, pp. 193–98.

[21] For further information, see Yuill *et al.*, *op. cit.*, pp. 54–56; and Commission of the European Communities, *Regional Development Programmes*, p. 88.

[22] Silvio Ronzani, "Regional Incentives in Italy," in Douglas Yuill, Kevin Allen, and Chris Hull, eds., *Regional Policy in the European Community* (London: Croom Helm, 1980), p. 138.

[23] For further information, see Vanhove and Klaassen, *op cit.*, pp. 324–25; see also Ronzani, *op cit.*

[24] Vanhove and Klaassen, *op cit.*, p. 325.

[25] *Ibid.*, pp. 324–25. Further information on DATAR can be found in *France: An Opportunity for Investment* (Paris: DATAR, 1980); and *Investment Incentives in France* (Paris: DATAR, 1980).

[26] Vanhove and Klaassen, *op cit.*, pp. 271–72.

[27] For further details, see Commission of the European Communities, *Regional Development Programmes for the Netherlands, 1977–1980*, Regional Policy Series No. 8 (Brussels: 1979), p. 120.

[28] The right of free movement will not apply for Greece until 1988. In fact, Greece has been a net immigration country in recent years.

[29] Commission of the European Communities, *The European Community — A Migrant Worker*, European File (Brussels: June 1980), p. 1.

[30] *Ibid.*, p. 4.

[31] *Ibid.*, pp. 4–5.

[32] Commission of the European Communities, *Regional Development Programmes: United Kingdom, 1978–1980*, Regional Policy Series No. 10 (Brussels: 1978), p. 65.

[33] Commission of the European Communities, *The European Community and Vocational Training*, Periodical 6/1980 (Luxembourg: 1980), p. 28.

[34] Commission of the European Communities, *Regional Development Programmes for the Netherlands, 1977–1980*, p. 49.

[35] Vanhove and Klaassen, *op cit.*, pp. 357–81.

[36] Commission of the European Communities, *The European Community and Vocational Training*, p. 12.

[37] In September 1981, the federal government and Alberta finally reached an agreement on energy policy.

[38] From Commission of the European Communities, *The Regional Development Programmes*, Regional Policy Series No. 17 (Brussels: 1979), pp. 246–48.

[39] Comprising the socio-economic aspects of regional development, physical planning, and social aspects.

The Framework of the European Community

3

I. Towards a United Europe

The concept of a united Europe reaches back many centuries, but the European Community is very much a post–World War II phenomenon.[1] Historically, concern for a lasting peace within Europe had been the main motivating force behind periodic ideas and efforts to achieve greater European unity; it took the devastation of two world wars and the fear of a nuclear holocaust to produce the Treaties of Rome and, on 1 January 1958, the eventual formation of the European Economic Community (EEC) and the European Atomic Energy Community (Euratom).

The ECSC as a Stepping Stone to the European Community

Perhaps the single, most critical, institutional stepping stone to the EEC had been the European Coal and Steel Community (ECSC). Founded in 1951 by the same six countries that were to sign the Treaty of Rome (France, West Germany, Italy, Belgium, the Netherlands, and Luxembourg), the ECSC represented a concern to restore the iron, coal, and steel sectors of Western Europe to fuel a peace-time economy and, crucially, to prevent them from becoming engines of another European war. The revival of the West German economy made a coherent resolution essential, as did the growing threat, as then perceived, of the Soviet Union and its satellites.

Built upon the Schuman Plan, largely drafted by Jean Monnet, the key idea behind the ECSC was the creation of a common market (among the members) for iron, coal, and steel that required substantial economic and social investments and readjustments, as well as the dismantling of national trade barriers in the form of custom duties, quotas, and so on. This path was chosen as distinct from some common form of nationalization. As Monnet wrote: "By the pooling of basic production and the establishment of a new High Authority whose decisions will be binding on France, Germany and the countries that join them, this proposal will lay the first concrete foundations of the European Federation which is indispensable to the maintenance of peace."[2]

A number of basic features of the EEC are drawn from the ECSC experiment, the most notable being its dual structure, incorporating one body (the High Authority, now absorbed into the Commission), which has the power of initiative and acts as guardian of the Community interest embodied in the (founding) Treaty, and a second body (the Council), which comprises representatives of the member states. "It is worth noting that the powers of the High Authority at that time were greater than the corresponding powers of the Commission in the EEC context. The High Authority was in fact vested with certain supranational decision-making powers, which the Commission has inherited in the coal and steel context. The idea of including a Parliamentary Assembly in the institutional framework dates from this period too."[3]

The ECSC and Regional Policy

Although the ECSC was not designed as an instrument of regional policy, (essentially being an agent of industrial strategy along strictly sectoral lines), nevertheless it has had substantial regional policy implications. The sector-rationalization process involved difficult locational choices, such as the closure of coal mines and the selection of new steel plant sites.

The radical nature of the industrial adjustment can be gleaned from the following.

1. Between 1952 and 1978, coal production (in the nine member states) fell some 465 million tonnes to some 210 million tonnes.[4] A recent communication from the European Commission to the Council reads:

> Member States which are *coal* producers, plan to continue with their endeavours to maintain, and if possible increase, production [to reduce oil dependency]. This should rise from 210 million [tonnes] . . . in 1978 to 240 million [tonnes] . . . in 1990. It is clear that these efforts will involve heavy financial costs — even after allowance is made for further rises in the price of oil over the same period.[5]

2. Steel, conversely, went through a period of rapid expansion, climbing from some 60 million tonnes in 1952 to a 'peak' of 156 million tonnes in 1974. Subsequent output has been at a lower level (128 million tonnes in 1980);[6] the future prospects can presently be described as 'cloudy', tied as they are to Western economies that are still adjusting to a new world 'energy order'.

ECSC Programming

Although the three executives (EEC, Euratom, and ECSC) merged in 1958 to form a Commission of the European Communities, the treaties establishing each remain in force. Consequently the funds of the ECSC still have a separate existence, contributing to five types of action:

1. Financing mining and steel firms "by granting loans to undertakings or by guaranteeing other loans which they may contract" [Article 54, Treaty of Paris].

2. Financing low interest rate loans (1%) for the construction of housing for coal and steel workers [Article 54, on the basis of paragraph 2, Treaty of Paris].

3. Financing low interest rates loans "either in industries within its jurisdiction or, with the assent of the Council, in any other industry, . . . for such programmes as it may approve for the creation of new and economically sound activities capable of reabsorbing the redundant workers into productive employment" [Article 56, 1b, Treaty of Paris].

4. Financing vocational training — by way of grants covering half of workers tiding-over allowances, resettlement allowances, and vocational retraining costs (the other half being financed by the state concerned).[7]

5. At the request of national governments, the ECSC has financed or participated in studies and research concerning the creation of new activities to re-employ redundant workers.

II. The European Economic Community

Introduction

The Treaty of Rome, establishing the European Economic Community, was signed on 25 March 1957 and came into effect on 1 January 1958. A separate, sister treaty was signed, at the same time, for the European Atomic Energy Community. France, West Germany, Italy, Belgium, the Netherlands, and Luxembourg were signatories to both.

The United Kingdom, Denmark, and Ireland subsequently joined the EEC on 1 January 1973 (having signed the Act of Accession in Brussels on 22 January 1972). Greece became the tenth member on 1 January 1981.

Essentially the EEC was built on the principles of a customs union; that is, tariffs, quotas, and other impediments to trade between the members were to be removed, phased over a period, while the members agreed to a common external tariff (with special arrangements with countries that had historical affiliations with member nations, for example, the French Overseas Departments).

Far freer movement (albeit not 'obstacle free') of factors of production has since occurred in what can only be described as an impressive manner, given the previous traditional patterns. Yet, although the

EEC is still often referred to as 'the Common Market', such a phrase fails to capture at all adequately the full mandate and accomplishments of the European Economic Community.

Article 2 of the Treaty of Rome points towards this broader role for the EEC: "The Community shall have as its task, by establishing a Common Market and progressively approximating the economic policies of Member States, to promote through the Community a harmonious development of economic activities, a continuous and balanced expansion, and increased stability, an accelerated raising of the standard of living and closer relations between the States belonging to it."

In an overview of EEC external relations, Wellenstein emphasizes: "the characteristic which gives the EEC Treaty its pre-eminence is . . . its wide scope, not only product-wise but also policy-wise."[8]

Ever since the Treaties of Rome, the EEC was viewed by external nations as a *general* integrative undertaking of considerable political significance, and not an exclusively economic agreement. Indeed, under the EEC founding Treaty, new policies can be created by the institutions themselves.[9]

Politics and Co-operation

The Commission of the European Communities has recently published the following conclusion regarding the first twenty years of the EEC life.[10] In so far as such judgements can reasonably be made of so complex a process, the comments form a useful attempt at synthesis.

The Community's initial approach can be classed as liberal. It concentrated on removing trade barriers and obstacles to economic expansion. It was less concerned with mapping out completely new policies to push economies in a particular direction, or with changing economic and social structures within Europe. Its goal was the creation of an economic area where individual entrepreneurs and firms could operate on a large scale. This was the essence of the Common Market. But, with the passage of time increasing emphasis has been laid on developing regional, social and public investment policies designed to reduce economic and social disparities within the Community.

There are a number of reasons why the Treaty should have laid stress on the removal of obstacles to expansion. The traumatic foray into protectionism and the upheavals in trade and finance of the thirties together with an urgent need for economic reconstruction, ensured that leaders gave priority to what they saw as the foundations of future progress. This is what in fact happened. The Community's early years were characterized by an unmistakable, if rather artificial, euphoria. The Community experienced no great

difficulty in respecting the time-table for dismantling trade barriers, establishing a customs union, and laying the foundations of
the Common Market. But progress did not stop there. The political
momentum was harnessed to finalize and successfully launch a
common agricultural policy and sow the seeds of an external
economic policy. In the early sixties, the Commission still wielded
considerable influence in the balance of institutional power within
the Community.

This initial euphoria was later dissipated by a nationalist
backlash, then by the difficulties of reconciling economic integration
with political decision-making procedures, and finally by the
problem of agreeing on new positive policies in sensitive areas — a
problem aggravated by the emergence in the seventies of a
structural crisis in Western economies. . . .

Such a conclusion inevitably glosses over many of the cracks in the
Community's edifice. Governments have changed within each member
country, and with such changes came different political and personal
loyalties and, quite often, different attitudes to, and appreciation of,
the background of the European Community. When the six expanded
into the nine, (and now the ten), adjustment problems became even
more complex. The Irish situation is very different to that of Germany,
the Danish regional problem is minute compared to those of Italy and
Greece. In sector policy areas, such as agriculture and transport, to
which the Treaty of Rome makes specific mention, a miscellaneous set
of activities often became 'rationalized' with the title of "Community
Policy," albeit such activities were often far from harmonious in
practice or 'watertight' in concept. They were invariably the product of
political compromise and trade-offs. Thus France became perceived as
the major beneficiary (followed by Ireland on a per capita basis) of
EEC 'agricultural policy', West Germany of 'industrial policy', and,
inasmuch as there was ever a 'regional policy', Italy became popularly
viewed as the main net recipient. The United Kingdom fared
relatively well under the regional and ECSC policies, but very badly
under the agricultural policy. No coherent agreement (and formula)
has been reached to provide an overall framework for coherent fiscal
equalization purposes in the Community, member state by member
state. This has meant that the financial framework, at the Community
level, has been somewhat piecemeal from the vantage point of any
coherent regional strategy. Different Community instruments, such
as the European Regional Development Fund, have their own clear
and consistent financial frameworks (and in that example national
quotas), but there is no consensus on the overall degree of fiscal
equalization that is the umbrella frame for the various parts. The
Community budget, itself, really fails to address this issue in a direct
manner.

Notwithstanding this difficulty, a fabric of organizations has been built up under the EEC umbrella, and the European Community is increasingly a 'reference point' for domestic policy considerations as well as for foreign policy outside the EEC. Thus, ideas and regulations, approaches to problems, and broader regional ways of searching out solutions are spawned and cross-fertilized, communicated and refined, by the array of committees and sub-committees that man the highways and by-ways of the EEC operations.

Often it is easy to conclude, after delving into the mechanics of particular EEC 'policies' and agencies, that were such a 'policy' or agency not in existence, then really the world would be little different; some particular member nations would take up the 'slack', others would not even notice its passing. That, however, appears a shallow judgement; it fails to recognize the integrative effect (indeed often achieved by stormy dialectic and subsequent compromise) of the process as a whole. Pieces of the fabric, as of a house, could be dispensed with — but at some point the edifice crumbles. Unlike in the case of a building, where foundations and key structures are readily identifiable as crucial, different aspects appear to have been of greater or lesser importance in the experience of the EEC to the overall edifice at different phases; some indeed only appear important with the benefits of hindsight. Even after twenty-five years, the 'end product' is far from clear. Preferences among nations, and between political groups and individuals, range widely from wanting the EEC to be a relatively 'loose market arrangement' (an especially common view in the United Kingdom), to a clear federation (quite widely argued for in continental Europe). At this juncture, the European Community stands somewhat uneasily between the two poles. Nor indeed are the eventual boundaries of the EEC clear. At what point, and on what criteria, should a confining line be built around the membership? Will the ten become, as part of a deliberate strategy, fifteen or twenty? If so, over what time frame?

It is not only from within the EEC that the 'Community positions' are widely sought. The members have been increasingly challenged by external forces to adopt common approaches; examples include the North-South dialogue, the energy crisis, the Helsinki (1975) Conference on Security and Co-operation in Europe and, more recently, the Afghanistan crisis, the Moscow Olympics, and the Polish question.

The fact that the Community does not always live up to external expectations, indeed that some members emphasize their independent diplomatic roles, does not reduce the international pressure. Such may be resented and viewed by European politicians as a reflection of a lack of understanding (particularly by the Americans) of the historic tapestry of European realities, but the external expectations for the European Community are unlikely to reduce over time.

Institution Development

1. Summary Outline

Four major institutions have been established within the administrative framework of the EEC: the European Commission, the Council
of Ministers, the European Parliament, and the European Court of
Justice.

In addition to these main institutions, each with many branches and
supporting funds and committees, the Treaties also created a number
of other organs that contribute to the Community purpose. They
include the following:

*   The Economic and Social Committee (ESC) for the EEC and
    Euratom. Its 156 members represent producers, workers, farmers,
    consumers, the self-employed, and so on. This Committee has to be
    consulted by the Council and the Commission on most of the legal
    provisions they propose adopting, though the Committee's opinions
    are not binding.

*   The European Investment Bank.

*   The court of Auditors, which ensures that the rules are complied
    with as regards Community revenue and expenditure.

2. Location of Main Offices and Activities

The Council of Ministers has its secretariat in Brussels, where the
Commission's main office is also located. The ESC is likewise in
Brussels, as are two of the important Commission branches to be
elaborated on later — the European Regional Development Fund and
the European Social Fund.

The Court of Justice, the European Investment Bank's head office,
and the Secretariat of the Parliament are located in Luxembourg. The
Commission has a subsidiary office there also, including the statistical
office.

The European Parliament used to meet regularly in Luxembourg
until it recently doubled its number of members. Now it meets in
Strasbourg, borrowing the Council of Europe chambers. There is
considerable competition emerging for the prestige of housing the
Parliament, with no clear venue in apparent sight.

3. The European Commission

The European Commission, the largest of the institutions with a
staff of some ten thousand has (in 1981) a membership of fourteen
individuals appointed for four years by agreement between the ten
member governments. Once appointed they are solely answerable to
the European Parliament. The Commission's main functions are as
follows:

- To initiate proposals for legislation to develop the Community along the lines prescribed in the Treaty of Rome and subsequently enlarged upon by later meetings of the Council of Ministers. Suggestions for policy development come from a variety of quarters, including member governments, the Council of Ministers itself, trade associations and industry pressure groups, consumer groups, and so on. Not only does the Commission have the sole responsibility for proposing the legislation, it also has the role of steering it through the Council, which can amend proposals only by unanimous vote. It acts, accordingly, as an 'unbiased' broker between governments. In many ways it has served as the 'engine' of community action.

- To advise the Council on specifics and in a general manner, by the development of official communications and guide-lines about a wide range of matters, such as energy developments and environmental policy suggestions.

- To ensure that the Treaties and secondary legislation are properly applied. It can take proceedings against member states that violate such legislation.

- To administer and implement common rules (a task for which it has exclusive power), it has its own decision-making powers in connection with the implementation of numerous Treaty provisions (e.g., the rules of competition), and is the only body on which the Council can confer powers to apply the regulations it adopts.

- To represent the Community as a whole, on international bodies such as the United Nations and the International Labour Office, as well as to negotiate international agreements between the Community and non-member countries, which the Council then concludes.

The present Commission was formed in 1967, as a consequence of the Brussels Treaty (1965), which merged the High Authority of the ECSC, the Commission of the EEC, and the Euratom Commission.

The Commission is divided into some twenty directorates general, plus a number of other services (e.g., Statistical Office, Legal Service, etc.). Directorate General XVI is charged with 'Regional Policy'.

4. The Council

The present Council of Ministers was established under the Brussels (1965) Merger Treaty. Comprising (January 1981) one member for each of the ten governments, each representing his or her state, the Council is charged with two functions:

It shall (Treaty of Rome, Article 145)

- "ensure coordination of the general economic policies of the Member States"

- "have power to take decisions," on the adoption of the legal instruments proposed by the Commission (i.e., regulations, directives, general decisions) for the attainment of the Community's objectives.

Drew comments that "if the Commission is the European conscience of the Community, the Council of Ministers is the guardian of the interests of individual member countries. A Commission proposal can only become law when all . . . [member] governments agree through their representatives at the Council of Ministers."[11]

This requirement for unanimity has led to frequent problems. The Commission's own review is surprisingly frank on the subject:

> . . . the Council's modus operandi has become steadily less satisfactory and the institutional set-up is being distorted in such a way as to jeopardize the whole decision-making process.
>
> Following the institutional crisis of 1965, which led to the 1966 agreement to disagree known euphemistically as 'the Luxembourg compromise', certain Member States refused to accept majority voting on major issues not so much on legal as on practical, political grounds. This disagreement led to the practice of the Council adopting legislation only when unanimous agreement has been reached. It will be readily understood that at the end of the day this systematic search for unanimity — which in fact has the effect of giving each and every Member State the power to determine the course taken by the rest — has greatly reduced the Council's capacity to take decisions.[12]

The controversy of 1965, to which the Commission statement refers, was over majority voting when the French withdrew for six months from the Community. The 'Luxembourg compromise' enables a member nation to declare, in discussions of any issue on which majority voting is permitted under the Treaty, that its vital interests are at stake; unanimous agreement is then required.

Each country takes a six-month turn to chair Council of Ministers meetings, the respective country's external affairs minister serving as President of the Council. Unlike the members of the Commission, the ministers do not reside in Brussels, but spend most of their time working in their home capital. Moreover, the ministers attending Council meetings change with the topics. Thus, if transport is to be discussed, the minister is likely to come from the national ministry of transport; if agriculture, from the ministry of agriculture; if regional policy, from the appropriate national ministry.

The Council of Ministers is served by representatives of each member country, who meet in the Committee of Permanent Representatives (COREPER) to prepare agendas, agree on non-contentious items, and so on. The permanent representative of each country has ambassadorial rank and is served, in turn, by an embassy support staff. Since many issues are of a highly technical nature, they draw extensively on officials from the home civil service.

5. The European Council

Not to be confused with the Council of Ministers, which takes its authority back to the Treaty of Rome, is the European Council. This body consists of the ten heads of government and meets several times annually. It provides a forum for broad policy discussion by the heads of government and has served as an opportunity to give shape to EEC main policy directions. When deadlocks are reached by the Council of Ministers, the European Council is one route for resolution of outstanding problems *in principle*. The 'in principle', however, should be emphasized, since the European Council is outside the framework of the Treaty of Rome, and any agreements by it do not have legal validity. This means that topics still have to be referred back to the Council of Ministers for ratification, via the route of formal proposals from the Commission.[13]

6. The European Parliament

Article 138, of the Treaty of Rome, accorded to the European Parliament the responsibility of drawing up "proposals for elections by direct universal suffrage in accordance with a uniform procedure in all Member States." The initial body, also in accordance with the original Treaties, was composed of delegates designated by "the respective Parliaments from among their members in accordance with the procedure laid down by each Member State." The number of delegates (36 for each of the four larger countries, 14 each for Belgium and the Netherlands, 10 each for Denmark and Ireland, and 6 for Luxembourg) was a somewhat arbitrary number (not accurately reflecting population proportions).

In 1979, electors in each member country directly voted for their European parliamentary candidate, some of whom were also members of their own national governments — but that was not a requirement. There are a number of inter-country anomalies still to be worked out, but the step to direct elections was clearly a very large one with widespread implications for the future development of the Community.

The new Parliament (as of 1981) comprised 434 members (81 each from the four larger countries, 25 from the Netherlands, 24 from

Belgium, 16 from Denmark, 15 from Ireland, and 6 from Luxembourg). The accession of Greece has added a further 24.

The future role of the European Parliament is still at an embryonic stage of development. Article 137 of the Treaty of Rome requires it to "exercise the advisory and supervisory powers which are conferred upon it by this Treaty."

At this juncture, it is apparent that Parliament is "primarily a consultative body."[14] Parliament is generally asked to give an 'opinion' on Commission proposals for Council Regulations before the Council can discuss them, but the Council is not bound to accept such opinions.

The roles, in short, comprise the following:

1. By an appropriate majority of the votes cast, Parliament can pass a motion of censure on the Commission to resign as a body (N.B. the Council has the decision-making powers on legislation, not the Commission).

2. To ask questions and call the Commission to account in committee debates, and so forth.

3. To pass resolutions.

4. To be consulted in accordance with the Treaty requirements (consultation does not imply more than an advisory role).

5. To exercise control over parts of the budget (about 20% in total) and to adopt the budget as a whole.

It is widely felt that, over the coming few years, the European Parliament is going to seek to stake out a larger role. Now that the members are directly elected and have to face 'home constituencies' in a very direct way, it is likely that the Parliament will attempt to strengthen its position. The fact that they delayed approval of the 1980 budget, as a whole, is an indication of their determination to acquire more powers. The relationships between the European Parliament, national member governments, the European Commission and, perhaps above all, the Council of Ministers could well change in the near future.

The Commission itself describes the present situation as "less than satisfactory as regards democratic control. The fact of the matter is that:

• On the one hand, Community Activities escape the control of the national Parliaments, who cannot deliberate the content of rules adopted by the Community's institutions. These are imposed on them, are directly applicable, and prevail over the laws that national parliaments pass, yet national parliaments are denied the opportunity to speak for or against them or even to claim advance notification.

- On the other hand, there is no equivalent parliamentary control at European level."[15]

Given the political will, the European Parliament could well become the most influential Community institution during the course of the 1980s, and, as such, with direct links back to the home electorates, it could acquire a number of powers traditionally associated with federal governments, for example in the fields of taxation and transfer payments. At this juncture, however, it appears destined to play a very modest role in comparison, say, to the federal governments of West Germany, the United States, Australia, or Canada. The political will for greater unity should not be mistaken for a will to surrender national sovereignty. It is in such a setting that the EEC regional policy experiences have to be interpreted.

7. The Court of Justice

The Court of Justice, consisting (in 1981) of ten judges and a number of advocates-general, has the responsibility for ensuring that European law is observed and uniformly interpreted across the Community. It is the ultimate interpreter of the Treaties of Paris and Rome that underpin the Community.

Among its wide-ranging functions is the review of the legality of acts of the Council of Ministers and Commissions, such acts being subject to appeal by individuals as well as member states. Additionally, the Court hears cases regarding the alleged non-compliance of member states to their obligations under Community law, as well as settles disputes by individuals or organizations in such fields as EEC competition policy. Increasingly, preliminary rulings are given to facilitate the interweaving of national and Community law.

While the Court can sit in two chambers, normally it sits as a full court — giving one judgement without dissenting or separate judgements being permitted.

8. The Community Budget

In reviewing the gradual evolution of a philosophy regarding the Community budget, Prest writes:

It seems a fair appraisal to say that, in the first twenty years of its history, fiscal policy has been much more a matter of making the customs union work — at least in respect of manufactured goods — than one of setting up a Community Budget.[16]

Prest goes on to cite the progressive abolition of customs duties, directives aimed at harmonization of value added taxes (VAT), attempts to reduce disparities in the levels and coverage of excise taxes within the Community, attempts to improve the flow of capital (especially the Neumark report), and so forth. He continues to note, as the major attempt to break away from a narrow role for overall Community fiscal policy, the economic and monetary union (EMU) proposals of the Werner report, proposals that are still under review.

Subsequent to Prest's assessment, there has been the crisis over the equity of the United Kingdom's share to the budget, temporarily patched up in the shadow of the need for Community solidarity (regarding the Afghanistan and then the Polish situations in particular), but far from resolved, as a principle, for the long term.

Several main threads will be sketched in this brief overview, with the particular aim of providing broad background to the regional development focus of this review.

First, the European Community budget (since 1967 comprising most of the activities of the Council, European Commission, and Euratom) is relatively small in relation to both the overall GNP of the ten member economies and to the budgets of the larger of their governments. Thus, for 1978, the Community budget amounted to some 0.8 per cent of the Community's GNP, or some 2.5 per cent of the combined national budgets of the nine. While it was some two and a half times the size of the Irish government's budget and one fifth the size of the Belgian, it was only one eighth the size of the French national budget. As measured in European units of account (EUA),[17] the total

Table 3.1
ESTIMATED REVENUE FOR 1981
BESIDE THE 1980 OUTTURN
(million EUA/ECU)

	1980 outturn	1981 estimates
Agricultural levies	1,535.4	1,902.0
Sugar and isoglucose levies	466.9	571.1
Customs duties	5,905.7	6,274.0
Financial contributions (GNP)	—	168.8
VAT own resources	7,256.4	10,251.1
Surplus from previous financial year	458.6	token entry
Balance of VAT own resources from previous financial year and adjustments to financial contributions	261.0	token entry
Miscellaneous revenue	153.0	160.6
Total	16,037.0	19,327.6

Source: Commission of the European Communities, *Fourteenth General Report on the Activities of the European Communities in 1980* (Brussels-Luxembourg: 1981), p. 58.

Community budget was some 12,362 million EUA for 1978. Table 3.1 shows the budget for 1980 and estimates for 1981.

Secondly, before examining tables of revenue and expenditure sources and allocations, it is necessary to emphasize that the budget represents only a segment of the European Community's activities. The abolition of customs duties between members, for example, is essentially not an activity that shows up in the Community budget. Similarly, the influencing of national industrial or regional development policies, by the powers of suasion through improved information systems and by the exertion of pressures in a variety of ways, does not show up in the Community budget, except in a relatively small manner; for example, via the cost of the Commission's information services and research, through the cost of some of the project activities of the European Regional Development Fund and the European Social Fund that might have proved influential in changing national programmes and priorities, and so forth. Even the major financial institution of the Community, the European Investment Bank, does not have its activities encompassed within the Community budget, since it borrows most of its funds on the capital markets and does not substantially draw upon taxation sources.

Thirdly, the question of which countries are 'subsidizing' which is frequently raised. For example, the extent to which West Germany is 'bankrolling' Italian or Irish 'inefficiency', and quite where France and the United Kingdom sit in the scheme of things, are very frequent issues (see Table 3.2). But they are not ones that can be answered intelligently from the budget numbers, because so much of the European Community function (e.g., in the dismantling of tariffs and customs duties between member countries) is not adequately reflected in the budget.

Fourthly, the scale of the budget appears to be severely constrained under present arrangements. According to the MacDougall study group,[18] a growth of Community budget expenditures to about 1 per cent of Community GNP is in progress. This approximate figure seems to be what the current sources of revenue can be expected to support, that is, Common External Tariff (CET) and Common Agricultural Policy (CAP) levies, plus the ceiling of 1 per cent of value added tax (VAT) contributions.

Fifthly, the lion's share of expenditures (generally over three quarters) has been spent within the framework of the agricultural policy (largely on price support schemes). Although the Social Fund and, more recently, the Regional Development Fund, have begun to eat more into the total, they are still small in comparison (see Table 3.3).

Sixthly, the question of a reappraisal of spending priorities (which was raised by the United Kingdom crisis over the budget contribu-

Table 3.2

ESTIMATED OWN RESOURCES TO BE PAID BY EACH MEMBER STATE FOR 1980[a]

(EUA/ECU)

Member State	Sugar and isoglucose levies	Agricultural levies	Common Customs Tariff duties	Own resources accruing from VAT	Total
Belgium	33,000,000	198,300,000	366,000,000	324,718,858	922,018,858
Denmark	20,100,000	14,600,000	135,000,000	187,615,340	357,315,340
Germany	140,900,000	289,500,000	1,713,000,000	2,345,191,752	4,488,591,752
France	170,600,000	116,500,000	825,800,000	1,764,305,795	2,877,205,795
Ireland	5,400,000	4,500,000	63,000,000	61,335,784	134,235,784
Italy	60,700,000	407,000,000	552,000,000	779,325,259	1,799,025,259
Luxembourg	—	100,000	4,000,000	14,431,949	18,531,949
Netherlands	43,000,000	283,300,000	536,000,000	432,958,478	1,295,258,478
United Kingdom	30,800,000	405,400,000	1,473,000,000	1,241,147,635	3,150,347,635
Total	504,500,000	1,719,200,000	5,667,800,000	7,151,030,850	15,042,530,850

Source: *Official Journal of the European Communities* (OJL 241) (15 September 1980), Table 3, p. 45.
Note: [a] The actual revenues for 1980 were 16,037 million, shown in Table 3.1. Table 3.2 comprises estimates, running to 15,042 million when made. However, it does serve to show the order of approximate magnitude of revenues from the nine member countries.

Table 3.3
BUDGETARY EXPENDITURES, 1980
(as Percentages of the Total)

	Appropriations for Commitment	Appropriations for Payment
Agriculture		
EAGGF — Guarantee Section	65.66	70.97
EAGGF — Guidance Section	2.56	1.96
Other	0.36	0.47
Social		
Social Fund	5.20	4.33
Other	0.36	0.42
Regional		
Regional Fund	6.66	2.49
Interest Subsidies	1.14	1.24
Other	0.68	0.74
Research, Energy, Industry, Transport	2.54	2.35
(Third World) Development Co-operation	4.60	3.96
Miscellaneous (incl. special payments to Greece and U.K.)	4.88	5.27
Administration and Other Institutions	5.36	5.80
TOTAL	100% 17,491,895,261 EUA	100% 16,182,497,261 EUA

Source: Commission of the European Communities, *Fourteenth General Report on the Activities of the European Communities in 1980* (Brussels-Luxembourg: 1981), condensed and calculated from p. 51.

tions, but far from resolved) obviously can be tackled in two main ways. On the one hand, the total contributions to agricultural policy (well entrenched as it is under the Treaty of Rome) could be modestly increased *if* the total budget were expanded (say towards a figure of 2.5 per cent of Community GNP), and still the bulk of the increased revenue could be allocated to other activities (such as the Regional Development Fund). On the other hand, the total budget could be held within the present framework and limited to some 1.0 per cent of the Community GNP, in which case the Community would face (particularly in light of the slower economic growth envisaged for the first half of the 1980s for many of the economies) an increasingly difficult trade-off between agricultural aid and other activities. At this point it is too early to be confident of the outcome, although the formation of the European Parliament might well augur an expansion of the Community budget and some reordering of priorities.

Seventhly, if the Community budget is to grow proportionately to GNP and the national budgets of the ten, 'at whose expense' will be a crucial question. The MacDougall report was certainly not advocating growth at the expense of the private sector; it was rather through taking over some of the activities of the national governments that growth was contemplated.[19] The potential importance of the European Parliament again comes to the fore, as a mechanism for shaping the extent to which the European Community might move further into the role (at this juncture, very embryonic indeed) of a federal government. If such indeed is to happen, the process is unlikely to be rapid.

Eighthly, and it is here that the regional development issues come centre stage, the issue is increasingly emerging as to how far transfers between richer and poorer national governments (of the members) are to be expected. The matter is already of concern to the ten; it will become even more a consideration when the Community expands to include countries such as Spain and Portugal.

Much of the debate over the United Kingdom budget contribution crisis centred on concern over not giving more than was being received in return. In the United Kingdom situation, while certainly a degree of inequity appeared to have crept in (partly one might deduce as a fair consequence of its failing to accept the initial risks and be one of the founding members of the EEC in 1957), the question nevertheless continues to recur as to how far wealthier members might be expected to subsidize poorer members, for how long, and with what goals in mind.

One of the serious question marks is the degree to which inefficiency or 'different' historical attitudes about their social and economic internal disparities are to be 'rewarded' by transfer payments from the 'richer' to the 'more inefficient' members. For example, both Italy and the United Kingdom indeed display problematic productivity measures and also quite extreme social and economic disparities and poverty. But both countries also display much evidence of large segments of affluence, evidence of a very questionable sense of priorities (from the vantage point of balanced development), and evidence of much mediocre planning. Should West Germany, France, or the Netherlands 'reward' them for this? These, of course, are very loaded questions. The same kind of questions can be asked of some of the poorer provinces within the Canadian federation. The expansion of the nine to the ten and thence to the twelve is bound to raise such issues even more.

Officials of the Commission (e.g., in the Regional and Social Funds) indicated much interest in the fiscal transfer programmes (especially equalization payments) of the Canadian federal system. While there may be merit in developing such a system within the European Community, it should be noted that poorer Canadian provinces tend to have a far more limited mix of resources than is the case of the 'poorer' European countries. Italy, for example, while having many extreme problems, also has a vast wealth of technical skills and natural and financial resources, albeit there appear to be grave inequities in its allocation and serious problems to be overcome before reallocation will be politically acceptable. The United Kingdom, while not so extreme in contrasts, nevertheless displays many of the same characteristics, as does Ireland. However, as poorer countries are given membership in the European Community, so a more coherent approach to transfer payments will inevitably be sought.

III. EEC Instruments for Regional Development

Four EEC policy instruments are reviewed in this volume because of their importance for regional development in the Community. Two are described in quite considerable detail, since it is believed they contain a number of useful ideas for future Canadian regional policy formulation. They are the European Investment Bank (established in 1958) and the more recent European Regional Development Fund (1975 origin). The other two instruments reviewed, the European Social Fund and the Common Agricultural Policy, are surveyed somewhat more broadly. Each instrument, in its way, serves to highlight a number of comparative points.

Table 3.3 illustrates, for 1980, the relative size of three of these activities in terms of budget appropriations for commitment and for actual payments. The dominant costs of the agricultural subsidy programmes stand out. It can be noted that both the Social Fund and the Regional Fund had authorization to commit rather more than was actually paid in 1980; as will be described later, this was because these two funds make payments to the governments after they, in turn, have actually spent the money on agreed projects.

The European Investment Bank's activities are not reflected in the budget, since it raises its funds on the capital markets rather than from Community taxation. In 1980, the EIB loaned 2,950.8 million ECU,[20] which was two and a half times the amount appropriated for commitment by the European Regional Development Fund, or some four times the amount actually appropriated for payment by the Fund in 1980.

Inasmuch as one of the main thrusts of the EEC has been internal trade liberalization, through the dismantling of internal trade barriers, it should be noted that the budget numbers do not capture this important aspect of the EEC record. Nor is this aspect examined in this review on instruments of regional development policy. That huge subject is beyond the scope of the study.

Notes

[1] For an interesting historical review, see Dennis Swann, *The Economics of the Common Market*, 4th ed. (Harmondsworth: Penguin Books, 1978), Chapter 1 and pp. 74–160.

[2] In the Schuman Declaration.

[3] Commission of the European Communities, *The Community Today* (Brussels-Luxembourg: 1979), p. 13.

[4] *Ibid.*, p. 109; see also note 5 below.

[5] Commission of the European Communities, *Energy Objectives of the Community for 1990 and Convergence of Policies of Member States*, a Communication from the Commission to Council, COM (79) 316 final, Brussels, p. 7. For a further, useful overview on energy and the European Community, see N.J.D. Lucas, *Energy and the European Community* (London: Europa Publications, 1977), pp. 159–65.

[6] Commission of the European Communities, *The Community Today*, p. 109 and Eurostat, *Quarterly Iron and Steel Bulletin* (Brussels: 1980–1981).

[7] Commission of the European Communities, *The Community Today*, p. 110.

[8] Edmund Wellenstein, *25 Years of European Community External Relations* (Luxembourg: European Documentation, 1979), p. 13.

[9] *Ibid.*

[10] Commission of the European Communities, *The Community Today*, p. 15.

[11] John Drew, *Doing Business in the European Community* (London: Butterworths, 1979), p. 13.

[12] Commission of the European Communities, *The Community Today*, p. 23.

[13] Rosemary Fennell, *The Common Agricultural Policy of the European Community* (London: Granada, 1979), p. 25.

[14] Commission of the European Communities, *The Community Today*, p. 27.

[15] *Ibid.*, pp. 27–28.

[16] Alan R. Prest, "Fiscal Policy," in *Economic Policies of the Common Market*, edited by Peter Coffey (London: Macmillan, 1979), p. 76. The article is a particularly useful one.

[17] In 1978, one EUA equalled approximately US $1.3. See the Glossary for a further explanation of the Community currency.

[18] *Report of the Study Group on the Role of Public Finance on European Integration*, chairman D. MacDougall, Vols. I and II (Brussels: Commission of the European Communities, 1977).

[19] *Ibid.*

[20] At the suggestion of the EIB, all economic and financial data concerning the Bank have been given in ECU, although the EIB converted to ECU only on 1 January 1981.

The European Investment Bank: An Instrument for Regional Development

4

I. Introduction

The European Investment Bank (EIB), established in 1958 under Article 129 of the Treaty of Rome, is the Community's major investment finance body. Over its twenty-two year existence, the EIB has loaned 17,263.6 million ECU[1] (to 31 December 1980). Of this amount, 14,882.3 million ECU have been loaned for projects inside the EEC; 41.4 per cent went to investment in Italy, followed by the United Kingdom (23 per cent), France (15.5 per cent), Ireland (7.2 per cent), and the Federal Republic of Germany (6.1 per cent) (see Table 4.1).

About 70 per cent of EIB loans, within the Community, have been for projects in regions that are economically less developed or are confronted with industrial conversion problems.[2] This has been in response to Article 130a of the Treaty of Rome, which gives the Bank's first task as to finance "projects for developing less developed regions," and the directive agreed upon by its Board of Governors, in December 1958, that the Bank would "devote a large part of its resources to the financing of projects likely to contribute to the development of less developed regions."[3] (See Appendix 4.1 for the Treaty establishing the Bank).

The Bank has to be viewed in the context of a family of sources of finance serving the Community. The other chief sources are the European Regional Development Fund (not established until 1975), the European Social Fund, the European Agricultural Guidance and Guarantee Fund, the European Coal and Steel Community, the European Atomic Energy Community, and the New Community Instrument for Borrowing and Lending. The EIB is also responsible for the loan management of these last two agencies and for their project assessment, tempered by their particular guide-lines.

II. EIB Profile

Administration of the EIB

The EIB has a Board of Governors, consisting of ten ministers, one drawn from each of the member states. A Board of Directors reports to the Board of Governors and comprises nineteen seats (18 nominated by member states, 1 by the Commission; under the Bank's statute, which forms part of the Treaty of Rome, directors are to be "chosen from persons whose independence and competence are beyond doubt; they shall be responsible only to the Bank"). Below that is a Management Committee, responsible for the day-to-day operations of the Bank, and an Audit Committee.

The EIB statute requires that outstanding loans and guarantees may not exceed the equivalent of 250 per cent of subscribed capital. To enable the recent growth in Bank activity, the subscribed capital was doubled by decision of the Board of Governors, on 19 June 1978, to bring it to 7,087.5 million ECU.[4] Only a small fraction of the subscribed capital has actually been paid up; the balance constitutes the Bank's guarantee for its borrowings on the capital markets of member and non-member states and on international markets. Since the Bank raises its capital on the open market, its own rates of interest have to be adequate to finance the loans and to cover administrative costs of the operation.[5]

AAA Rating

The scale of the EIB operation, its successful track record and, an essential ingredient, the member-state guarantees provide the EIB with an AAA rating; these first-class terms are reflected in its lending rates (for a sample, see Table 4.2). Smaller projects are not charged higher interest rates than larger projects, nor are 'riskier' projects thus penalized. Interest rates are not directly subsidized by the EIB. However, complementary programmes of the Commission, and of member states, are linked and provide subsidies in selected cases[6] (see Table 4.1).

Loans for Specific Projects

The Bank's loans are for financing specific projects and are intended to cover only a part of the cost of a project, supplementing the borrower's own funds and credits from other sources. The EIB does not itself loan more than a proportion of a project's fixed asset costs (currently limited to 50 per cent), although complementary financing from other Community sources could push total contributions above this level (e.g., from the New Community Instrument (NCI)[7] or the ERDF. See Appendix 4.2).

The Bank's Activities: 1980

A profile of the EIB's main activities, focusing on 1980, will provide a current picture of its role.

1. During 1980, the EIB loaned 2,950.8 million ECU for industrial and agricultural projects, energy and other infrastructure develop-

ments in EEC member states, or projects outside EEC territory but of very direct interest to the Community (for projects in Austria and Tunisia that will supply electricity or gas to EEC member countries). This was some 15.0 per cent more than in 1979 (2,558.2 million ECU), representing a consolidation, in real terms, after a period of rapid growth. Half of the Bank's lending, since it began in 1958, has taken place in the last three years alone — against, in the Bank's words, "a difficult climate for investment throughout the Community, coupled with tensions on the Capital markets."[8] Over 80.0 per cent of the EIB

Table 4.1
EIB FINANCING PROVIDED 1958–1980

	1980		1973–80		1958–80	
	Amount (million u.a./ECU)	%	Amount (million u.a./ECU)	%	Amount (million u.a./ECU)	%
COMMUNITY						
Belgium	153.2	5.2	318.6	2.6	385.8	2.6
Denmark	99.3	3.4	307.1	2.5	307.1	2.1
Germany	14.2	0.5	547.4	4.4	901.0	6.1
France	279.0	9.5	1739.8	14.0	2310.2	15.5
Ireland	376.0	12.7	1076.9	8.7	1076.9	7.2
Italy	1290.3	43.7	4752.7	38.2	6165.0	41.4
Luxembourg	—	—	—	—	9.0	0.1
Netherlands	—	—	62.3	0.5	105.2	0.7
United Kingdom	688.0	23.3	3421.3	27.5	3421.3	23.0
Non-Member Countries[a]	50.8	1.7	200.8	1.6	200.8	1.3
Sub-total[b]	2950.8	100.0	12426.9	100.0	14882.3	100.0
OUTSIDE THE COMMUNITY						
From the Bank's own resources	371.4	67.8	1381.5	69.3	1537.2	64.6
From budgetary resources	176.3	32.2	613.2	30.7	844.1	35.4
Sub-total	547.7	100.0	1994.7	100.0	2381.3[c]	100.0
TOTAL	3498.5	—	14421.6	—	17263.6	—

Source: European Investment Bank (Luxembourg: January 1981), unpaged.
Notes: [a] Loans granted for energy projects in Austria, Norway, and Tunisia but of direct importance to the Community.
   [b] Including loans from the resources of the New Community Instrument for borrowing and lending (1979:277 million u.a., of which 105.3 million in the United Kingdom, 86.7 million in Ireland, and 85 million in Italy; 197.6 million u.a., of which 137.8 million in Italy, 41.7 million in Ireland, and 18.2 million in Denmark).
   [c] Of which 351.4 million u.a. in Greece prior to its accession to the Community (341.4 million u.a. own resources; 10 million u.a. budgetary resources).

Table 4.2
EIB LENDING RATES
SAMPLE ILLUSTRATION

INTEREST RATES ON THE BANK'S LOANS
AT 12.12.1980

Loans disbursed in several currencies

Sample combinations:

Term	DM	FF	£	FB	hfl	US $	Sfrs.	Yen	interest rate
8 years	30%	—	—	20%	15%	35%	—	—	12.45
"	30%	—	20%	—	15%	35%	—	—	12.70
"	30%	—	—	—	15%	35%	—	20%	11.55
"	30%	—	—	—	15%	35%	20%	—	11.00
10 years	30%	—	—	20%	15%	35%	—	—	12.45
"	30%	—	20%	—	15%	35%	—	—	12.70
"	30%	—	—	—	15%	35%	—	20%	11.55
"	30%	—	—	—	15%	35%	20%	—	11.05
12 years	30%	—	—	20%	15%	35%	—	—	12.50
"	30%	—	20%	—	15%	35%	—	—	12.75
"	30%	—	—	—	15%	35%	—	20%	11.60
"	30%	—	—	—	15%	35%	20%	—	11.05
15 years	30%	20%	—	—	15%	35%	—	—	12.80
"	30%	—	20%	—	15%	35%	—	—	12.85
"	30%	—	—	—	15%	35%	—	20%	11.60
"	30%	—	—	—	15%	35%	20%	—	11.10

The proportion of each currency in these combinations or "cocktails" may be modified according to the wishes of the borrower or as dictated by the currencies the Bank has at its disposal at the material time: in either event, the rates applied are modified accordingly.

Single currency loans

Term/years	5	6	7	8	9	10	11
US $	14.60	14.60	14.60	14.60	14.60	14.60	14.60
Swiss francs	6.50	6.55	6.60	6.60	6.65	6.70	6.70
Japanese yen	9.25	9.25	9.25	9.25	9.25	9.25	9.25

Term/years	12	13	14	15	16	18	20
US $	14.60	14.60	14.60	14.60	14.70	14.80	14.90
Swiss francs	6.65	6.65	6.60	6.60	6.65	6.70	6.70
Japanese yen	9.25	9.25	9.25	9.30	9.35	9.35	9.35

Source: EIB Information Services.

loans, in 1980, have been in areas of relatively high unemployment (in excess of 7.5 per cent unemployment rates).

2. Some 44 per cent of the EIB loans, in 1980, went to investment in Italy, 23 per cent in the United Kingdom, 13 per cent in Ireland, and 9 per cent in France (Table 4.1).

3. Over the Bank's life, and particularly since 1973, an increasing proportion of EIB loans has gone to projects in the energy sector. Thus, in 1980, some 40 per cent of all EIB lending in the Community was to energy projects. Water supply projects, irrigation, drainage and sewage works (many in the Mezzogiorno region, in Ireland, and parts of the United Kingdom), as well as communication projects have continued to receive a large proportion of EIB funds for infrastructure (Tables 4.3, 4.4, and 4.5).

Loans to industry, despite the economic uncertainties of 1980, increased in aggregate in 1980 over 1979, including loans advanced by the EIB through its 'global loan' system. Global loans are basically lines of credit opened to regional or national financial institutions that, in turn, make sub-loans to small- and medium-sized industrial ventures, chosen in agreement with the EIB.[9] However, loans to industry, over recent years, have decreased as a proportion of total financing (albeit the actual amount has increased substantially), the weighting being more on infrastructure loans.[10] This is not a reflection of changing EIB priorities, but rather of the generally low level of industrial investment in Europe, coupled with increasing calls on EIB finance for energy projects, as major investment programmes have been bunched to reduce dependence on oil imports.

4. In addition to internal loans, the EIB advanced, during 1980, a further 547.7 million ECU in thirty countries outside the Community that have signed agreements of co-operation with the EEC. Of this amount, the bulk (402 million ECU) was loaned to Mediterranean-region countries and most of the rest to African and Caribbean countries that signed the first Lomé Convention. Two thirds (271.4 million ECU) were in the form of loans from the Bank's own resources (usually with interest subsidies paid either from the Community's budget or by the member states), with the remainder (176.3 million ECU) as finance on special conditions, from budgetary funds that the Bank manages on the Community's behalf.

To finance these expanded activities, in 1980, the EIB borrowed 2,455.8 million ECU on the capital markets. Of this total, 1,509 million ECU were raised in public bond issues, 874.5 million ECU in private placings, and 83.3 million ECU from the sale to third parties of participation in EIB loans, guaranteed by the Bank. Main currencies borrowed were Deutsche Marks (34%), US dollars (27.8%), Swiss francs (11.5%), Dutch Guilders (9.2%), Japanese Yen (6.8%), and French francs (5.5%).[11]

Table 4.3
EIB FINANCING PROVIDED WITHIN THE COMMUNITY, 1958–1979: BREAKDOWN BY ECONOMIC POLICY OBJECTIVE

1958–79[a]

Amount (million u.a./ECU)		%	Objective
			From EIB own resources
8551.1		**100.0**	**Regional development**
	83.8	1.0	Belgium
	134.9	1.6	Denmark
	372.6	4.3	Germany
	1287.6	15.1	France
	606.7	7.1	Ireland
	3951.1	46.2	Italy
	4.0	—	Luxembourg
	70.5	0.8	Netherlands
	2039.9	23.9	United Kingdom
243.3		**100.0**	**Modernization and conversion of undertakings**
4457.8		**100.0**	**Common European Interest**
3165.8		**70.9**	**Energy**
	2524.1	56.5	Development of Community resources
	213.0	*4.8*	*Hydroelectric and geothermal*
	1420.8	*31.9*	*Nuclear*
	666.8	*14.9*	*Oil and natural gas deposits*
	220.9	*4.9*	*Solid fuels*
	2.6	—	*Alternative sources*
	74.0	1.7	Energy saving
	567.7	12.7	Import diversification[b]
	472.9	*10.6*	*Natural gas*
	94.8	*2.1*	*Electricity*
850.8		**19.1**	**Communications**
	760.6	17.1	Transport
	103.9	*2.3*	*Railways*
	550.6	*12.4*	*Roads, bridges and tunnels*
	47.9	*1.1*	*Shipping*
	58.2	*1.3*	*Airlines*
	90.2	2.0	Telecommunications
21.2		**0.5**	**Other infrastructure**
25.6		**0.6**	**Protection of the environment**
364.4		**8.2**	**Industrial co-operation**
30.0		**0.7**	**New technology — Research**
−1597.7		—	*— Deduct to allow for duplication in the case of financing justified on the basis of several objectives*
11654.5			**Total**

Source: European Investment Bank, *Annual Report 1979* (Luxembourg: 1980), p. 25.
Note: [a] Amounts at current prices and exchange rates. A summary of financing provided over such a long period should be interpreted cautiously; data for successive years are affected by price movements and exchange rate variations occurring between 1958 and 1979.
[b] For example, gasline projects, schemes helping to increase electricity imports, fitting out power stations to run on imported coal, etc.

Table 4.4
EIB FINANCING PROVIDED WITHIN THE COMMUNITY, 1980: BREAKDOWN BY ECONOMIC POLICY OBJECTIVE

Objective	From EIB own resources Amount (million u.a./ECU)	%	From NCI resources Amount (million u.a./ECU)	Total Amount (million u.a./ECU)	%
Regional development	**1815.7**	**100.0**	145.7	**1961.4**	**100.0**
Belgium	6.2	0.3		6.2	0.3
Denmark	17.5	1.0		17.5	0.9
France	148.4	8.2		148.4	7.5
Ireland	318.7	17.5	41.7	360.4	18.4
Italy	825.4	45.5	104.0	929.4	47.4
United Kingdom	499.5	27.5		499.5	25.5
Modernization and conversion of undertakings	**31.4**	**100.0**		**31.4**	**100.0**
Common European interest	**1213.0**	**100.0**	108.0	**1321.0**	**100.0**
Energy	1094.4	90.2	108.0	1202.4	91.0
Development of Community resources	*673.7*	*55.6*	*31.1*	*704.8*	*53.3*
• Hydroelectric and geothermal	163.6	13.5		163.6	12.4
• Nuclear	432.6	35.7		432.6	32.7
• Oil and natural gas deposits	38.6	3.2	16.7	55.3	4.2
• Solid fuels	38.9	3.2	14.4	53.3	4.0
Energy saving	*125.3*	*10.3*	*35.2*	*160.6*	*12.2*
Import diversification[a]	*295.4*	*24.3*	*41.7*	*337.1*	*25.5*
• Natural gas	137.6	11.3	41.7	179.3	13.6
• Electricity, coal	157.8	13.0		157.8	11.9
Communications	111.7	9.2		111.8	8.5
Transport	*94.7*	*7.8*		*94.7*	*7.2*
• Roads, bridges and tunnels	29.6	2.5		29.6	2.3
• Shipping	16.1	1.3		16.1	1.2
• Airlines	49.0	4.0		49.0	3.7
Telecommunications	*17.1*	*1.4*		*17.1*	*1.3*
Protection of the environment	5.1	0.4		5.1	0.4
Industrial co-operation	1.7	0.2		1.7	0.1
— Deduct to allow for duplication in the case of financing justified on the basis of several objectives	−306.9		−56.1	−363.0	
TOTAL	2753.2		197.6	2950.8	

Source: European Investment Bank, *Information EIB*, No. 24 (Luxembourg: February 1981), p. 5, Table 2.

Note: [a] For example, gasline projects, schemes helping to increase electricity imports, fitting out power stations to run on imported coal, etc.

Table 4.5

EIB FINANCING PROVIDED WITHIN THE COMMUNITY, 1980: SECTORAL BREAKDOWN

Sector	Own resources million u.a./ECU	%	NIC resources million u.a./ECU	%	Combined million u.a./ECU	%
ENERGY, COMMUNICATIONS AND OTHER INFRASTRUCTURE	**2167.8**	**78.7**	**197.6**	**100.0**	**2365.4**	**80.2**
Energy	1078.0	39.1	108.0	54.7	1186.0	40.2
(Production)	(893.2)	(32.4)	(49.3)	(24.9)	(942.4)	(31.9)
Nuclear	432.6	15.7			432.6	14.7
Thermal power stations	116.5	4.2	9.0	4.5	125.5	4.2
Hydroelectric power stations	213.9	7.8			213.8	7.2
District heating plant	29.5	1.1	9.2	4.7	38.7	1.3
Development of oil and natural gas deposits	88.5	3.2	16.7	8.4	105.2	3.6
Solid fuel extraction	12.2	0.4	14.4	7.3	26.6	0.9
(Supply systems)	(184.9)	(6.7)	(58.8)	(29.7)	(243.7)	(8.3)
Power lines	47.3	1.7	17.1	8.6	64.4	2.2
Gaslines and oil pipelines	137.6	5.0	41.7	21.1	179.3	6.1
Communications	532.9	19.4	77.1	39.0	610.0	20.7
(Transport)	(206.3)	(7.5)	(37.3)	(18.9)	(243.6)	(8.3)
Railways	47.2	1.7			47.2	1.6
Roads, bridges and tunnels	58.6	2.1	37.3	18.9	95.9	3.3
Shipping	46.9	1.7			46.9	1.6
Airlines	53.6	1.9			53.6	1.8
(Telecommunications)	(326.6)	(11.9)	(39.8)	(20.1)	(366.4)	(12.4)
Water schemes	416.6	15.1			416.6	14.1
Agricultural development	195.2	7.1			195.2	6.6
Water catchment, treatment and supply	221.4	8.0			221.4	7.5
Other infrastructure	118.7	4.3	12.5	6.3	131.2	4.5
Global loans (unallocated portion)[a]	21.6	0.8			21.6	0.7
INDUSTRY, AGRICULTURE AND SERVICES	**585.4**	**21.3**			**585.4**	**19.8**
Industry	433.8	15.8				
Mining and quarrying	0.7					
Metal production and semi-processing	30.4	1.1				
Construction materials	16.6	0.6				
Woodworking	14.7	0.5				
Class and ceramics	22.1	0.8				
Chemicals	18.4	0.7				
Metalworking and mechanical engineering	67.6	2.4				
Motor vehicles, transport equipment	23.7	0.9				
Electrical engineering, electronics	31.4	1.2				
Foodstuffs	59.2	2.2				
Textiles and leather	15.0	0.6				
Paper and pulp	16.9	0.6				
Rubber and plastics processing	22.6	0.8				
Other	2.6	0.1				
Building — civil engineering	0.1					
Industrial estates and buildings	91.8	3.3				
Agriculture, forestry, fishing	16.7	0.6				
Services	1.0					
Tourism	0.9					
Other	0.1					
Global loans (unallocated portion)[b]	133.9	4.9				
TOTAL	2753.2	100.0	197.6	100.0	2950.8	100.0

Source: European Investment Bank, *Information EIB*, No. 24 (Luxembourg: February 1981), p. 6, Table 3.

Notes: [a] Difference between the sum of global loans granted for infrastructural works in 1980 (59.9m u.a./ECU) and the sum of allocations approved during the year from current global loans (38.3m u.a./ECU).

[b] Difference between the sum of global loans granted for industrial investment in 1980 (265.5m u.a./ECU) and the sum of allocations approved during the year from all current global loans (131.6m u.a./ECU).

III. Operational Principles for the EIB to Aid Regional Development

The Spaak Committee, when drafting the basic Treaty of Rome, had rejected the idea of one, specific regional development fund:[12] rather it preferred to see regional problems tackled by elements of other, more generalized, programmes. Regional problems, indeed, were clearly not viewed as central to the issues facing the emerging EEC: European security, political clout in relationship with the United States and the Soviet Union, economic growth and rationalization of key sectors such as agriculture and heavy industry — these appear to have been the central issues. The liberalization of internal trade and factors of production were largely to be the means of such increased growth and political strength.

As in North America at that time, 'reasonable' regional balance or development seems to have been viewed as an almost inevitable by-product of the national, economic growth process. With the reduction of trade, labour, and capital mobility barriers, it was viewed as 'natural' that some out-migration of labour would occur from poorer regions and, at the same time, that lower wages and other costs would attract some capital to labour-surplus areas, thereby helping the regions climb closer to the EEC (or North American) average. To foster such a process, there was an acknowledged need to strengthen the mosaic of infrastructure links between and within poor and rich regions — from energy networks to financial systems and manpower training programmes.

The EIB was a central product of that viewpoint. It was not to be a grant or soft-loan agency. It was to establish itself as a prudent investor within the Community, helping to strengthen the national financial systems and competing (as an efficiency safeguard) for funds on both member and international capital markets. It would be a bridge for financial institutions and, of great importance, would concentrate attention on viable projects linking member countries more closely together (some 40 per cent of projects aided have fitted this general category — many also being in poorer regions, hence being 'double counted' in the ratios cited), as well as strengthening the poorer regions by lending to 'viable', economic projects.

In determining its approach to regional development, the EIB cited the following as its declared principles:

1. The Bank respects the regional development priorities laid down by the appropriate national authorities, which are being coordinated at Community level.
2. It strives to focus its lending on those regions with the gravest problems. ... [in 1980, two thirds of lending for regional development went to those areas given top priority under

Community regional policy; Ireland, the Italian Mezzogiorno, Northern Ireland, and Greenland.]

3. In selecting projects, it attaches utmost importance to their contribution to the economic development of the regions concerned and their place in regional development programmes, where such exist.

4. It finances both essential infrastructural works offering an indirect or long-term return, but which lay down the base for economic growth and permit industrial development, and productive enterprise itself.

5. In industry, it supports not only major undertakings likely to form the backbone of development centres, but also seeks to help a variety of labour-intensive smaller businesses which assure the growth of a broader economic structure: since 1969, the EIB has aided smaller businesses via a facility known as global loans, whereby a loan is made to an intermediary financing institution which, in agreement with the EIB and subject to the Bank's normal intervention criteria, selects projects from amongst its own clients and parcels out the funds accordingly.[13]

IV. Effectiveness Assessment by the EIB Itself

In 1980, the EIB evaluated its past three years of activities (1976–1979) from three different vantage points.[14] They are quoted extensively to indicate the criteria the EIB uses for its self-assessment:

1. *The impact made on employment by various EIB financed projects.*
   These are estimated as follows:
   "a. The direct creation of around 52,000 permanent jobs, plus the safeguarding of 23,500 more, principally in industry;
   b. The temporary, direct, and indirect, effects on employment during construction periods (often lengthy) and also on employment involved in supply of necessary services and materials — this mainly concerns large-scale energy and infrastructure works; the total effect of projects financed for the first time in 1979 can be estimated at about 500,000 man-years of work, a figure roughly comparable to that for operations in each of the previous two years. This 500,000 corresponds to up to 145,000 jobs for a year in 1979 and 1980, progressively fewer thereafter;"

2. "*The long-term effects of most infrastructure projects* — water supplies and communications for example — which create few permanent jobs directly but which are of fundamental importance for economic growth;"

3. *"The impact in potential oil import savings of the energy projects which it has helped to finance.* (38% of total [EIB] lending within the Community in the [three-year] period concerns energy). Very approximately, and barring unforeseen circumstances, energy investment financed in 1977–1979 should, when completed, provide extra resources or enable economies equivalent in total to over 38 million tonnes of imported oil per year (= ± 8% of the Community's imports in 1979)."

V. Further Comments on the EIB

Effectiveness

As an international development bank, with the EEC as its focal region, the European Investment Bank has an impressive record. It has raised the vast proportion of its capital requirements in the markets, not from government budgets, and has participated in the financing of a wide spectrum of projects through loans and guarantees. Its scale of activities has rapidly expanded and yet much has been directed into the poorer regions. Even with the increased emphasis of the European Community on energy developments and the stimulation of economic growth, the EIB has still managed to maintain its concentration of effort in the poorer regions of the EEC. Viable projects have been found; the necessary capital has been raised under competitive circumstances.

In the EIB's 'self-assessment' of the 1958–1978 record, two points are given some prominence.[15] On the one hand, the Bank is said to epitomize Schuman's declaration: "Europe will not be built in a day, nor to an overall design; it will be built through practical achievements that first establish a sense of common purpose." On the other hand, although estimating "that close to a quarter of a million jobs have been directly created or safeguarded by the investments which the Bank has helped to finance," the EIB report cautions that, even though the Bank has been so vigorous, "it also demonstrates rather soberingly the extent and persistence of some of the economic problems which are still at the heart of the Community."

The EIB and Its Cementing Role

Those two quotations place the Bank's challenge and accomplishments in useful perspective.

On the one hand, the EIB has played a 'cementing' role for the European Economic Community. When substantial disagreements on such issues as agricultural policy or the apportionment of the EEC budget have threatened the shape of the Community, and when internal tariff reductions have created adjustment difficulties, the EIB, as an agency of the EEC, has continued to raise funds on the capital markets and has continued to finance projects of a practical nature, with credentials of economic viability and logic — mostly in the poorer regions — and frequently of an inter-country linkage nature. While there are usually many alternative sources of funds and while, on a project-by-project basis, a thesis could no doubt be developed showing that many projects could have 'gotten off the ground' without EIB involvement, the facts are that they did get EIB assistance, on 'reasonable' terms (given the market conditions within which the EIB operates and its non-profit-making framework and member state guarantees).

In short the EIB has been a flagship of the European Economic Community. It has shown tangible results through involvement in the long list of projects. These projects have helped give the Community an identity that is more directly tangible, in some respects, than the important benefits from mainstream policies such as internal tariff reductions.

The EIB and the Scale of Regional Problems

On the other hand, there is the dimension and complexity of European economic problems — many of which are concentrated in less developed regions and areas with grave problems of social and industrial decline and readjustment. Unemployment and low productivity are among the symptoms. The energy crisis has simply compounded long-standing weaknesses. The European Investment Bank, despite its rapid growth and the huge scale of its endeavours, is only — in this overall scheme of things — one ship on a very large ocean. Moreover, it is apparent that only so much can be done to achieve more balanced and growing regional development activity in Europe, if economic viability (narrowly interpreted at the project level) is a *sine qua non* for Community-level financing. By 'narrow economic viability', it is meant that, whether it is private or public enterprises, public authorities or other financial institutions that are borrowing the funds for particular projects, they do have to finance the full repayment of the principal and interest of the loans (normally over a duration of between seven and twenty years, depending on the activity). There is little 'softness' to an EIB loan.

Rather than broaden the EIB mandate further in expanding the attack on regional disparities, and thereby risk confusion between a lending and a grant-allocating agency, the European Community wisely established additional, subsequent resources — chief of which is the European Regional Development Fund.[16] The New Community Instrument further extends the Community's financial armoury.

Cost-Benefit Appraisals

Even though the EIB is operating essentially along commercial lines, the author was somewhat surprised to learn, in discussion with representatives of the Bank, that broader cost-benefit appraisals of Bank-funded projects, along the lines of those undertaken by the World Bank, do not appear to be either a routine or a periodic procedure. While security of the loan might quite reasonably be a Bank concern in terms of repayment, nevertheless appraisals that take into explicit (rather than rather vague or implicit) account socio-economic and environmental considerations would appear a desirable procedure. As it is, the Bank's assessments of social benefits (as outlined above) are very broad in character.

A further comparison with the World Bank might be added. Whereas the World Bank has instituted an effective and widely used publication system for samples of its project case experiences, normally along sector lines, the EIB has not embarked upon such a venture. Such a procedure, it is suggested, could be of great value to officials in lending agencies receiving EIB support, agencies generating loan requests to the EIB, and a wide range of national and other development banking institutions within the European Community.[17]

To balance these suggestions, particular emphasis should be placed on the excellent standard of the general information publications by the Bank and by the extremely well-informed nature and helpful style of the Bank's information and public relations service.

VI. Ideas From the EIB for Canadian Policy Review

There is no agency in Canada with a mandate comparable to that of the European Investment Bank. The nearest example would be the Federal Business Development Bank (FBDB), a somewhat expanded version of the Industrial Development Bank, its predecessor. But while the officials of the FBDB have much of the necessary experience to operate a Canadian equivalent of the EIB, the FBDB is focused on small- and middle-sized business. The FBDB can provide loans, guarantees and, on occasion, take equity positions in companies. It is intended to be a Bank of Last Resort, by which is meant that loan applicants must show evidence of having been refused a loan request by a commercial lending agency — on 'reasonable' terms. Like the EIB, the FBDB is not intended to be a competitor to the commercial banking system, but rather an energetic 'gap-filler'. Frequently the FBDB, as the EIB, marshals funds in association with commercial lending agencies — again filling perceived 'gaps' and lending some additional security to the project. Similarly, the FBDB also works closely with provincial lending and other forms of development agencies.

Table 4.6
FEDERAL BUSINESS DEVELOPMENT BANK PER CAPITA DISTRIBUTION OF ACCOUNTS BY PROVINCE AS AT 31 MARCH 1980

	Amounts Outstanding[a] ($ 000)	Number of[a] Customers	Population[b] (1976)	Per Capita* ($)
Newfoundland	61,119	1,565	557,725	109.59
Prince Edward Island	10,859	346	118,229	91.85
Nova Scotia	53,608	1,812	828,571	64.70
New Brunswick	65,730	1,600	677,250	97.05
Quebec	456,691	7,179	6,234,445	73.25
Ontario	537,683	11,559	8,264,465	65.06
Manitoba	53,095	1,020	1,021,506	51.98
Saskatchewan	55,042	970	921,323	59.74
Alberta	190,722	3,633	1,838,037	103.76
British Columbia	538,703	9,961	2,466,608	218.40
Yukon	14,344	142	21,836	656.90
Northwest Territories	10,985	160	42,609	257.81
TOTALS:	2,048,581	39,947	22,992,604	

Source: [a] FBDB 1980 Annual Report, p. 15.
        [b] Canada Year Book, 1978–79, Statistics Canada, p. 155.
* Calculated as: Amounts Outstanding ($ 000) = $ per capita Population (1976 census)

However, the comparison between the EIB and the FBDB should not be overstretched. The EIB focuses heavily on the less-developed regions of Western Europe and, within that framework, on areas of relatively high unemployment. (In 1980, some 80 per cent of EIB loans for regional development purposes went into areas where the un-employment levels exceeded 7.5 per cent.) In the case of the FBDB, there is no clear regional development mandate, although periodically the Bank has been urged to 'step up efforts' in regions such as the Maritimes (and has apparently attempted so to do, within its broad operational limits). However, Table 4.6 demonstrates very clearly that the FBDB pattern of lending has been most haphazard if it is to be assessed from the vantage point of national/regional development problems or priorities. This is not to criticize the lending pattern of the FBDB, which does have its historic explanations and presumably, to some degree, reflects upon gaps in provincial government lending agencies and, perhaps more particularly, the areas where investment opportunities are more readily identified. Having said that, the FBDB lending pattern is in sharp contrast to that of the EIB, which serves to highlight the question of whether the FBDB mandate should be changed or whether there is indeed scope for another type of regional development banking agency.

Other main differences can be noted between the EIB and FBDB. The FBDB does not lend to the kind of infrastructure projects that form a large percentage of EIB activity, nor has the FBDB become heavily involved in energy-producing and energy-saving projects on the kind of proportional scale of the EIB. Pieces of EIB kinds of activities, in the Canadian setting, are spread around a number of federal, commercial, and provincial agencies. There is no comparable Canadian federal agency that closely resembles the EIB. Nor is there such a provincial agency, albeit the Alberta Heritage Fund has some superficial similarities.

Two questions follow. First, is there a good case for some Canadian version of the EIB? Secondly, are there some striking conclusions from the EIB for Canadian policy purposes in regional development, albeit there may not necessarily be a case for a 'Canadian' EIB?

1. *Is there a good case for a Canadian version of the EIB?*

The European Investment Bank, while only one of many public and commercial development financing agencies within the European Community at large, is also an important (it has been here argued) and very practical 'flagship' of the European Community. Not only has it provided a vehicle for capital to be directed to less-developed regions of the Community (as well as outside, which raises many issues of another kind not explored at length in this review), it has also promoted and helped finance many projects that are linked to several member countries, for example, in fields such as transportation, communications, industrial and, of most recent importance, energy linkages. When the Treaty of Rome was signed in 1957, there were many border linkage gaps and almost 'no-man's land' zones on the fringes of countries whose governments had frequently concentrated much of the development around the (often centrally located) capitals and key ports and cities. The Treaty of Rome opened up new locational possibilities for development activities; the EIB helped harness these opportunities.

Whereas the European Community 'federation' is relatively new, the Canadian one is long standing. Already the federal government has fostered many interprovincial links through a variety of programmes, starting with the railway-building age and including, more recently, projects such as the trans-Canada highway. However, many gaps do still remain regardless of constitutional questions. For example, one has only to view objectively the breakdown of the proposed Maritime Energy Corporation or the problems associated with the development of the Lower Churchill Falls project in Labrador. Moreover, as has been argued by the author elsewhere,[18] Canadian regional disparities (whatever the yardsticks that are to be used, and that issue is by no means straightforward) have remained persistently extreme, in many cases, and appear to have been tackled, thus far, in a manner that shows no promise of improved results. It is

Table 4.7
RESOURCES OF THE EUROPEAN INVESTMENT BANK

Capital is subscribed by member states; the bulk of resources, however, comes from borrowings — principally public or private bond issues on national capital markets inside and outside the Community and on the international market.

Capital Structure (as at 1 January 1981, in million u.a./ECU[a]				Borrowings 1961–1980	
	Subscribed capital[b]	Total paid in and to be paid in[b]	%		(million u.a./ECU)
Germany	1575.00	202.50	21.875	1961–1972	1973.5
France	1575.00	202.50	21.875	1973	612.3
United Kingdom	1575.00	202.50	21.875	1974	825.5
Italy	1260.00	162.00	17.50	1975	830.7
Belgium	414.75	53.325	5.76	1976	748.7
Netherlands	414.75	53.325	5.76	1977	1161.5
Denmark	210.00	27.00	2.925	1978	1949.7
Greece	112.50	14.46	1.563	1979	2481.2
Ireland	52.50	6.75	0.729	1980	2466.8
Luxembourg	10.50	1.35	0.146		
TOTAL	7200.0	925.71	100.0	TOTAL	13050.1

Source: European Investment Bank (Luxembourg: January 1981), unpaged.
Notes: [a] The Board of Governors is to examine in 1981 proposals concerning the Bank's next capital increase.
   [b] The capital set to be paid in equals approximately 13% of the subscribed capital; all or part of the remainder could be called by decision of the Board of Directors, should ever the Bank's obligations towards lenders require this.

indeed now argued by some that disparities should really not be viewed as problems at all.[19]

At the present juncture in Canadian affairs, the provincial and federal attitudes to the appropriate framework of 'Confederation for the Eighties' (and beyond) are far from harmonious. Such attitudes are by no means unfamiliar to the European Community, in some ways a more embryonic 'federation', but in other ways, at this time, more constructive in overall terms of 'a spirit to make a success of the co-operative venture'.[20]

The possibility of establishing a 'Canadian Development Bank', with very substantial provincial as well as federal government representation and financial responsibility, should not — it is suggested — be ruled out as untimely or causing duplication. Nor should it be seen as a threat to the private sector. It is believed that a focus on less-developed regions and, also of great importance, projects of interest to more than one province, should be the paramount thrust of any such development bank. At a time of constitutional disharmony, a Canadian development bank could, it is suggested, perform a 'flagship' role, in the same way as the EIB did for the Community. It could become a practical mobilizer of capital to help strengthen the federation, by fostering common projects and by attacking regional disparities across the country. Just as the EIB has identified coherent areas of priority, so could a Canadian development bank. The possibility of provincial ministers being conspicuously at the helm, as well as strong federal representation, is a possible further policy option. Were any reshaped FBDB, or new development bank, to be established, such a move could only be viewed as one step in a process of regional development reform in Canada. It could provide for a more dynamic and direct role for provincial governments in articulating and contributing to national/regional policy formulation and execution.

As in the case of the EIB, it is suggested that any such Canadian development bank should be required to raise its resources in the capital markets, with initial subscriptions from government. As has happened with the EIB, it could readily dovetail with other public programmes (such as federal and provincial interest subsidy measures) and (as with the global loan approach) delegate authority to other agencies.[21] The essential case behind formulating such an agency consists of the following:

- The view that far more can be done to ensure more balanced regional development in Canada, on a *viable* economic basis.

- A large-scale effort is feasible and warranted to tackle key regional problems in a frontal manner.

- Flagship, practical agencies can play an important role in the federal fabric.

- Provincial governments should be challenged to accept a more direct role in assisting each other tackle regional disparities in Canada. The federal government, alone and along traditional lines, shows no likelihood of significant success.

2. *Are there some striking conclusions from the EIB for Canadian policy purposes in regional development, albeit there may not necessarily be a strong enough case for a Canadian version of the EIB?*

Inasmuch as the author suggests that there is a good case for appraising very seriously the role of a possible Canadian development bank, along the lines of the EIB (as discussed above), the response to this second question will highlight some key aspects of the EIB experience that could be of interest to regional policy formulation:

- The European Investment Bank has played a 'cementing role' between member states, particularly through the financing of joint projects; such has clearly proven constructive in a practical, as well as a symbolic, manner. The importance of symbols should not be underestimated in achieving harmonious development.

- With a minimum of government financing (subscription), the EIB has raised huge amounts of capital in a competitive setting and has successfully focused the bulk on projects in the less-prosperous regions. The use of global loan facilities has enabled substantial, effective delegation to occur for smaller project financing in particular. The EIB has itself concentrated on larger-scale projects.

- The involvement of ministers from each member country, as well as a representative from the European Commission, has given constructive political inputs at the level of the Board of Governors. The composition of the Board of Directors has 'bureaucratized' this. The Bank staff themselves, responsible for operational inputs, have been careful to work 'at arms length' from the political process. Projects have to pass the test of 'financial viability'.

- The Bank has developed a professionalism that is essential for such an organization; its rules have not been 'chopped and changed'. Its guide-lines have been relatively clear, albeit necessitating often quite tough decisions. It is a non-profit-making institution, which enables it to lend at somewhat lower rates than would otherwise be the case in some undertakings. However, it generally safeguards itself by requiring guarantees, in such instances, from the national government or other appropriate bodies in whose domain the project is being located. This generally accords with World Bank practice and does seem a useful safeguard. The fact that this is such an operationally 'grey area' calls for substantial development banking acumen on the part of the EIB officials dealing with such projects. Their success record speaks for itself.

- The EIB, it is suggested, could usefully follow the World Bank practice of publishing rather broader socio-economic post-project appraisals of projects, to provide a more 'rounded' assessment of projects. This could, it is believed, serve to improve the quality of some project plans and serve to make certain important cost and benefit implications more explicit, particularly to member governments and their participating development agencies. Such suggestions are of very widespread application to Canadian development agencies, which are also frequently remiss in these activities.

- The EIB annual reports (and report on the first twenty years), as well as the most useful *Information* publications, are much more candid and detailed, in style, than is the wont of Canadian development corporation publications. The style is refreshing. The discussion of objectives in EIB reports, moreover, (while still not quite as precise as might be the ideal model), is considerably more focused and thoughtful than one tends to find in most Canadian development agency publications. The EIB approach could usefully be followed more by Canadian agencies. Even the better Canadian reports that are publicly available (such as the FBDB annual reports) lack the EIB quality of self-assessment.

- The EIB lending often meshes with EEC or member-state interest rate subsidy programmes, normally on the basis of a routine formula. Thus the viability assessment of the project is the responsibility of the EIB staff, avoiding unnecessary duplication of effort and enabling the member country to take advantage of the professional standards of the EIB. Such an approach might be particularly helpful in poorer provinces of Canada, where there are problems of adequately staffing local lending agencies and yet where soft loans are viewed as an important element of provincial development strategy.

- The EIB does not loan more than a proportion of a project's fixed asset cost (currently up to 50 per cent).

The Bank has raised its funds on the European and international capital markets and it has loaned at competitive rates, not charging higher interest rates for smaller than for larger projects, nor for 'more risky' projects. It has been able to remain competitive, in poorer regions, for essentially four reasons:

1. Its scale and efficiency of operation has enabled it to retain an AAA rating for borrowing purposes; a necessary ingredient has been guarantees of its member states.

2. It is a non-profit-making body, capital being subscribed by the member states. However, this should not be overstressed, as the bulk of the resources comes from borrowings (see Table 4.7).

3. Loans in poorer regions are often made more attractive by complementary interest subsidies, through member government programmes or, on occasion, via the budget of the Community. The EIB itself does not give interest subsidies.

4. It has broadened the range of financing available to the poorer countries in general (e.g., Italy) and, in the process, has particularly added another financial dimension for projects in the less-developed regions. As a major financial institution, it has developed a professionalism that has earned the confidence of other financial bodies in its assessment of, and commitment to, the viability of projects funded.

VII. Conclusion

After twenty-two years of extensive international banking experience, it is obvious that the EIB contains a rich mine of comparative ideas for Canadian policy and development banking consideration. As constitutional and federal-provincial fiscal arrangements are redesigned to face current realities, an aggressive, regional development banking corporation could provide one component of a substantially revamped approach to Canadian regional development.

The EIB has by no means 'solved' the problems of regional disparities in the less-prosperous regions of Europe. They remain extreme and, in 1975, the Community established a further instrument, the European Regional Development Fund, to increase the Community's efforts, particularly by the mechanism of grant programmes. That agency will be discussed in the next chapter.

APPENDIX 4.1

Treaty Establishing the European Economic Community of 25 March 1957 (Text dated 1 January 1981)[22]

Article 2

The Community shall have as its task, by establishing a common market and progressively approximating the economic policies of Member States, to promote throughout the Community a harmonious development of economic activities, a continuous and balanced expansion, an increase in stability, an accelerated raising of the standard of living and closer relations between the States belonging to it.

Article 3

For the purposes set out in Article 2, the activities of the Community shall include, as provided in this Treaty and in accordance with the timetable set out therein:

. . . . . .

(j) the establishment of a European Investment Bank to facilitate the economic expansion of the Community by opening up fresh resources.

. . . . . .

Article 92

(1) Save as otherwise provided in this Treaty, any aid granted by a Member State or through State resources in any form whatsoever which distorts or threatens to distort competition by favouring certain undertakings or the production of certain goods shall, in so far as it affects trade between Member States, be incompatible with the common market.

(2) The following shall be compatible with the common market:

(a) aid having a social character, granted to individual consumers, provided that such aid is granted without discrimination related to the origin of the products concerned;

(b) aid to make good the damage caused by natural disasters or other exceptional occurrences;

(c) aid granted to the economy of certain areas of the Federal Republic of Germany affected by the division of Germany, in so far as such aid is required in order to compensate for the economic disadvantages caused by that division.

(3) The following may be considered to be compatible with the common market:

(a) aid to promote the economic development of areas where the standard of living is abnormally low or where there is serious underemployment;

(b) aid to promote the execution of an important project of common European interest or to remedy a serious disturbance in the economy of a Member State;

(c) aid to facilitate the development of certain economic activities or of certain economic areas, where such aid does not adversely affect trading conditions to an extent contrary to the common interest. However, the aids granted to ship-building as of 1 January 1957 shall, in so far as they serve only to compensate for the absence of customs protection, be progressively reduced under the same conditions as apply to the elimination of customs duties, subject to the provisions of this Treaty concernig common commercial policy towards third countries;

(d) such other categories of aid as may be specified by decision of the Council acting by a qualified majority on a proposal from the Commission.

Article 129

A European Investment Bank is hereby established; it shall have legal personality.

The members of the European Investment Bank shall be the Member States.

The Statute of the European Investment Bank is laid down in a Protocol annexed to this Treaty.

Article 130

The task of the European Investment Bank shall be to contribute, by having recourse to the capital market and utilising its own resources, to the balanced and steady development of the common market in the interest of the Community. For this purpose the Bank shall, operating on a non-profit-making basis, grant loans and give guarantees which facilitate the financing of the following projects in all sectors of the economy:

(a) projects for developing less developed regions;

(b) projects for modernising or converting undertakings or for developing fresh activities called for by the progressive establishment of the common market, where these projects are of such a size or nature that they cannot be entirely financed by the various means available in the individual Member States;

(c) projects of common interest to several Member States which are of such a size or nature that they cannot be entirely financed by the various means available in the individual Member States.

Article 148

(1) Save as otherwise provided in this Treaty, the Council shall act by a majority of its members.

(2) Where the Council is required to act by a qualified majority, the votes of its members shall be weighted as follows:

Belgium:	5
Denmark:	3
Germany:	10
Greece:	5
France:	10
Ireland:	3
Italy:	10
Luxembourg:	2
Netherlands:	5
United Kingdom:	10

For their adoption, acts of the Council shall require at least:

— 45 votes in favour where this Treaty requires them to be adopted on a proposal from the Commission,

— 45 votes in favour, cast by at least six members, in other cases.

(3) Abstentions by members present in person or represented shall not prevent the adoption by the Council of acts which required unanimity.

Article 169

If the Commission considers that a Member State has failed to fulfil an obligation under this Treaty, it shall deliver a reasoned opinion on the matter after giving the State concerned the opportunity to submit its observations.

If the State concerned does not comply with the opinion within the period laid down by the Commission, the latter may bring the matter before the Court of Justice.

Article 173

The Court of Justice shall review the legality of acts of the Council and the Commission other than recommendations or opinions. It shall for this purpose have jurisdiction in actions brought by a Member State, the Council or the Commission on grounds of lack of competence, infringement of an essential procedural requirement, infringement of this Treaty or of any rule of law relating to its application, or misuse of powers.

Any natural or legal person may, under the same conditions, institute proceedings against a decision addressed to that person or against a decision which, although in the form of a regulation or a decision addressed to another person, is of direct and individual concern to the former.

The proceedings provided for in this Article shall be instituted within two months of the publication of the measure, or of its notification to the plaintiff, or, in the absence thereof, of the day on which it came to the knowledge of the latter, as the case may be.

Article 180

The Court of Justice shall, within the limits hereinafter laid down, have jurisdiction in disputes concerning:

(a) the fulfilment by Member States of obligations under the Statute of the European Investment Bank. In this connection, the Board of Directors of the Bank shall enjoy the powers conferred upon the Commission by Article 169;

(b) measures adopted by the Board of Governors of the Bank. In this connection, any Member State, the Commission or the Board of Directors of the Bank may institute proceedings under the conditions laid down in Article 173;

(c) measures adopted by the Board of Directors of the Bank. Proceedings against such measures may be instituted only by Member States or by the Commission, under the conditions laid down in Article 173, and solely on the grounds of non-compliance with the procedure provided for in Article 21 (2), (5), (6) and (7) of the Statute of the Bank.

Article 239

The Protocols annexed to this Treaty by common accord of the Member States shall form an integral part thereof.

Protocol on Italy

The High Contracting Parties,

Desiring to settle certain particular problems relating to Italy,

Have agreed upon the following provisions, which shall be annexed to this Treaty:

The Member States of the Community

Take note of the fact that the Italian Government is carrying out a ten-year programme of economic expansion designed to rectify the disequilibria in the structure of the Italian economy, in particular by providing an infrastructure for the less developed areas in Southern Italy and in the Italian islands and by creating new jobs in order to eliminate unemployment;

. . . . . .

Agree, in order to facilitate the accomplishment of this task by the Italian Government, to recommend to the institutions of the Community that they should employ all the methods and procedures provided in this Treaty and, in particular, make appropriate use of the resources of the European Investment Bank and the European Social Fund.

. . . . . .

Treaty Establishing a Single Council and a Single Commission of the European Communities of 8 April 1965

Article 28

The European Communities shall enjoy in the territories of the Member States such privileges and immunities as are necessary for the performance of their tasks, under the conditions laid down in the Protocol annexed to this Treaty. The same shall apply to the European Investment Bank.

. . . . . .

Protocol on the Privileges and Immunities of the European Communities

Article 1

The premises and buildings of the Communities shall be inviolable. They shall be exempt from search, requisition, confiscation or expropriation. The property and assets of the Communities shall not be the subject of any administrative or legal measure of constraint without the authorisation of the Court of Justice.

Article 2

The archives of the Communities shall be inviolable.

Article 3

The Communities, their assets, revenues and other property shall be exempt from all direct taxes.

The Governments of the Member States shall, wherever possible, take the appropriate measures to remit or refund the amount of indirect taxes or sales taxes included in the price of movable or immovable property, where the Communities make, for their official use, substantial purchases the price of which includes taxes of this kind. These provisions shall not be applied, however, so as to have the effect of distorting competition within the Communities.

No exemption shall be granted in respect of taxes and dues which amount merely to charges for public utility services.

Article 4

The Communities shall be exempt from all customs duties, prohibitions and restrictions on imports and exports in respect of articles intended for their official use; articles so imported shall not be disposed of, whether or not in return for payment, in the territory of the country into which they have been imported, except under conditions approved by the Government of that country.

The Communities shall also be exempt from any customs duties and any prohibitions and restrictions on imports and exports in respect of their publications.

Article 22

This Protocol shall also apply to the European Investment Bank, to the members of its organs, to its staff and to the representatives of the Member States taking part in its activities, without prejudice to the provisions of the Protocol on the Statute of the Bank.

The European Investment Bank shall in addition be exempt from any form of taxation or imposition of a like nature on the occasion of any increase in its capital and from the various formalities which may be connected therewith in the State where the Bank has its seat. Similarly, its dissolution or liquidation shall not give rise to any imposition. Finally, the activities of the Bank and of its organs carried on in accordance with its Statute shall not be subject to any turnover tax.

General Directives for the Credit Policy of the European Investment Bank laid down on 4 December 1958

I

The Board of Governors of the European Investment Bank,

Having regard to Article 9 (2) of the Statute of the Bank, under which it falls to the Board of Governors to lay down general directives for the credit policy of the Bank,

Having regard to Articles 2 and 130 of the Treaty of Rome which state the task of the Community and establish general terms of reference for the Bank,

at its meeting on 4 December 1958 laid down the following general directives for the Bank in matters of credit policy.

II

The Bank shall devote a large part of its resources to the financing of projects likely to contribute to the development of less developed regions, which is already one of the major objectives of the European Economic Community: such projects may be in any of the various economic sectors.

The Bank shall finance projects of common interest to several Member Countries, and shall in particular give support to projects likely to further the integration of Member Countries' markets and economies.

The Bank shall participate in financing projects aimed at the modernisation or conversion of enterprises or the creation of new activities furthering the progressive establishment of the Common Market, as soon as the repercussions of the development of this Market on the situation of the enterprises in question can be foreseen with sufficient accuracy.

III

Projects financed by the Bank must fulfil the conditions laid down in the Statute and in particular must meet the provisions of Article 20 with regard to eonomic productivity and profitability.

Furthermore, the Bank shall observe the following principles:

(a) During its first phase of activity, it shall grant loans rather than provide its guarantee for borrowing operations.

(b) It shall confine itself to financing specific projects.

(c) It shall seek to avoid dissipating its resources by employing them in general to finance projects of a certain size.

(d) The granting of loans shall be conditional upon the mobilisation of other sources of finance, whether provided by the borrower or by third parties.

(e) Particular consideration shall be given to projects which involve the pooling of capital from a number of Community countries.

(f) In mounting such operations, the Bank shall pursue the general objective of fostering the progressive unification of Member Countries' capital markets.

IV

These directives may be amended as needs dictate, in line with progress towards the establishment of the Common Market.

The Board of Directors and the Management Committee shall be responsible for ensuring that the Bank is administered in accordance with these directives.

APPENDIX 4.2

The New Community Instrument

The New Community Instrument (NCI), consisting of funds directly borrowed by the European Commission on the capital markets, is a new mechanism for broadening the EIB mandate in conformity with certain priority objectives of the Community, namely unemployment, sluggish investment, and insufficient convergence in national economic performance. The Commission has been empowered by the Council and the European Communities to raise funds (up to specified amounts decided by the Council) on the capital markets in the name of the EEC. These funds are deposited with the EIB for making loans for investment projects. The first 1000 million ECU have been reserved by the Council mainly for infrastructure assisting regional development and energy investment. While the Commission rules on the eligibility of any project for which an NCI loan is sought, in other respects the procedures for obtaining such loans, the interest rates charged, and other terms are comparable to those applying to loans directly from the EIB's own resources. In 1980, the NCI allocations only amounted to 197 million ECU; the bulk went to Italy and Ireland (the first year, 1979, saw loans of 277 million ECU).

Notes

[1] At the suggestion of the EIB, all economic and financial data concerning the Bank have been given in ECU, although the Bank converted to ECU only on 1 January 1981.

[2] Tables 4.3 and 4.4; see also annual reports of the EIB for more details.

[3] European Investment Bank, *Twenty Years: 1958–1978* (Luxembourg: 1978), p. 13.

[4] All these numbers are as of 1 January 1981, including Greece's membership.

[5] For further details, up to 1976, see Dennis Swann, *The Economics of the Common Market*, 4th ed. (Harmondsworth: Penguin Books, 1978). Also the regular *Information* publications of the EIB are of excellent quality.

[6] EIB interest rates follow closely movements on the capital markets where it raises the bulk of its funds. Interest subsidies may, however, be granted by member states or other agencies. Subsidies may also be paid from the Community budget as follows:
  European Monetary System (E.M.S.): to help strengthen the economies of the less prosperous member countries fully participating in the E.M.S. (Ireland and Italy have been so designated), 3% interest subsidies may be applied to selected loans from the EIB's own resources and from those of the NCI. These subsidized loans may total up to 1 billion EUA/ECU per year for the five years 1979–1983.
  European Regional Development Fund: while this is essentially for making grants, there is provision (hardly used to date) to pay 3% subsidies on certain EIB loans.
  Development Outside the Community: an interest subsidy of 2% or 3% is normally paid from the Community budget directly or from other Community special instrument funds, such as the European Development Fund, which the Bank manages on the Community's behalf.

[7] The NCI was a mechanism for further opening up this constraint, in clear response to direct Council of Europe priority guide-lines. See Appendix 4.2 for further details.

[8] EIB, Press Release, Luxembourg, 12 February 1981, p. 2.

⁹ Sources of details: EIB annual reports and information bulletins, especially (for 1979) No. 20, February 1980.

¹⁰ EIB, Press Release, 12 February 1981.

¹¹ This information is drawn from EIB, Press Release, 12 February 1981; and EIB, *Information*, No. 20, February 1980, Luxembourg.

¹² Norbert Vanhove and Leo H. Klaassen, *Regional Policy — A European Approach* (Farnborough: Saxon House, 1980), p. 385.

¹³ European Investment Bank, *Twenty Years: 1958–1978*, p. 13.

¹⁴ This section quotes with minor omissions, from EIB, *Information*, No. 20, February 1980, p. 3.

¹⁵ European Investment Bank, *Twenty Years: 1958–1978*, pp. 7, 9, and 10.

¹⁶ Established in March 1975, the ERDF is reviewed in Chapter Five.

¹⁷ The EIB does make reports after project completion and start-up, reviewing the main characteristics of the project and noting differences compared with the project appraisal. These are internal documents for reasons of confidentiality with the clients. The EIB does not, however, systematically make *ex post* evaluations of projects, with detailed performance comparisons against original objectives, in the same way as the World Bank.

¹⁸ R.I. McAllister, "How to Re-make DREE," *Policy Options* 1 (March 1980): 39–43.

¹⁹ Thomas Courchene, "Regional Economic Disparities: Myth and Reality," notes for a panel discussion at the Canadian Economics Association conference, Halifax, 27 May 1981.

²⁰ The United Kingdom excepted.

²¹ It should be noted that EIB global loans are made to public-sector agencies (e.g., various Italian state-owned organizations financing develoment in the Mezzogiorno) and also, on occasion, to private agencies (e.g., the Midland Bank in the United Kingdom.

²² From European Investment Bank, *Statute and Other Provisions* (Luxembourg: (January 1981), pp. 25–33.

The European Regional Development Fund

5

I. Profile of the Fund

Purpose

Article 1 of the Council Regulation, establishing a European Regional Development Fund, defines the Fund's role as ". . . to correct the principal regional imbalances within the Community resulting in particular from agricultural preponderance, industrial change and structural under-employment" (see Appendix 5.1).

Historical Background

Although not established until 1975, the European Regional Development Fund (ERDF) was no new idea. The Spaak Committee, when drafting the Treaty of Rome, had discussed a regional fund as it considered the potential role of the European Community in achieving more balanced regional development.[1] They opted, instead, for the establishment of the European Investment Bank. However, despite the growth of the EIB and the regional impact of other Community instruments (such as the Social Fund) and despite a proliferation of national programmes with regional development objectives, it became widely recognized that extreme disparities were persisting within the Community, and, in some cases, regional problems were proving somewhat intractable (e.g., the southern Italian situation).[2] As a result, the ERDF was designed to focus exclusively on regional development problems within the Community, largely through the mechanism of grants to national governments to share the cost of regional aids for specific projects.

To give some flavour of the debate on regional imbalances that led up to the formulation of the ERDF, three (of potentially very many) references are cited. Each point was to find itself embedded in subsequent ERDF philosophy.

1. In its first report on regional policy in the EEC (May 1965), the Commission stressed the necessity of co-ordinated action by the regional authorities, both on the national and the European levels, recommending the compilation of regional development programmes.[3]

2. In 1968, the President of the Commission (Jean Roy) stated, in the European Parliament: "Regional policy in the Community should be as the heart is in the human body . . . and should aim to reanimate human life in the regions which have been denied it."[4]

3. In March 1971, the Council made the following resolution:

In order to undertake, without delay, measures in the regional or structural field which are necessary to the ultimate achievement of economic and monetary union, the Council agrees in principle that:

- from 1972 onwards the European Agricultural Guidance and Guarantee Fund may be used for measures to foster regional development;

- a Regional Development Fund be set up, or any other system that will provide the requisite Community resources for regional development.[5]

Administration of the ERDF

The European Commission is responsible for administering the ERDF. Its main offices are in Brussels. Two committees, on which national officials sit, assist the Commission. They are the Regional Policy Committee and the Fund Committee.

The Regional Policy Committee, established in 1975 at the same time as the Fund, is responsible for studying the development of the regions of the Community, for examining the "aims, means, methods and experience of Member States in the field of regional policy, taking account of the Community's other policies,"[6] and for generally contributing towards improved co-ordination of regional development policies by the member states. The Committee is charged with giving advice upon all major infrastructure projects for which ERDF assistance is sought. Thus, in 1979, the Committee gave opinions on 91 such projects as well as on a draft definition of the infrastructure categories that may be financed from the Fund.[7]

The Fund Committee is primarily responsible for formulating opinions on the Commission's draft decisions to grant aid from the Fund.[8]

ERDF: The Core Regional Grant Agency

Over its six years of life, the European Regional Development Fund has rapidly become the central grant financing agency for Community regional policy. However, far from relieving other Community instruments of their regional responsibilities, the ERDF has contributed to reinforcing their regional development roles, as well as to fostering a clearer understanding of the regional problems.

In the field of grant aid to poorer regions, the ERDF has joined the

European Social Fund, the European Agricultural Guidance and Guarantee Fund, and the European Coal and Steel Community.

The European Investment Bank has continued to dominate the lending activities of EEC instruments for purposes of regional development.

Major Features of the ERDF

1. Quota System

The allocation for the ERDF was fixed, in the general budget of the Community, at 1,165 million EUA for 1980; of this all but 58 million EUA were allocated according to a quota system. Some 40 per cent of the quota was to go to Italy, 27 per cent to the United Kingdom, 17 per cent to France, and 6 per cent each to Ireland and West Germany. On a per capita basis, Ireland received most assistance (some 27 EUA per capita), followed by Italy (some 9 EUA per capita). As of 16 December 1980, the Regional Fund Regulation established a quota of 13 per cent for Greece and adjusted those of the other nine members.[9]

2. Projects Aided Largely Infrastructure

Some 12,700 individual projects were approved for aid, under the quota section of the ERDF, between 1975 and the end of 1980. (Table 5.1 summarizes Fund activity in 1980 and over the 1975–1980 period.) Some 30 per cent of the aid went to projects in the industrial and service sectors, while about 70 per cent went to infrastructure projects.

3. New Non-Quota Regulations

In October 1980, the Council adopted five new Regulations providing for additional Fund assistance, to the amount of 220 million EUA, divided over a five-year period as follows: 120 million EUA for certain regions affected by the Community's enlargement (Mezzogiorno, Aquitaine, Midi-Pyrénées, Languedoc-Roussillon); 43 million EUA for areas in the United Kingdom, Italy, and Belgium beset by steel industry problems; 17 million EUA for United Kingdom ship-building areas; 16 million EUA to diversify energy sources in the mountainous areas of the Mezzogiorno; 24 million EUA for the further development of the boarder areas of Ireland and Northern Ireland.

This represents a modest departure from the quota framework that is central to the ERDF financial system. The 220 million EUA are allocated according to a programme principle, rather than tied to specific project approvals (which is the case under the quota framework). At this juncture it appears unlikely, however, that the quota system will be substantially replaced. Nor, indeed, will it be argued in this review that such a change of policy is desirable.

Table 5.1
REGIONAL FUND GRANTS
(by Member State)^a

	1980			1975-80			1980
	Number of investment projects	Investment involved (million EUA)	Assistance approved (million EUA)^b	Number of investment projects	Investment involved (million EUA)	Assistance approved (million EUA)	Payments made (million EUA)^b
Belgium	76	112.26	11.88	232	411.68	51.08	6.585
Denmark	94	57.57	12.16	342	291.37	47.31	9.438
FR of Germany	232	904.17	71.06	1318	4556.17	280.21	50.449
France	271	1397.08	198.76	1756	5470.94	626.93	90.662
Ireland	35	1630.70	78.56	558	3003.50	230.75	69.552
Italy	1522	3579.30	495.80	4506	11222.57	1418.76	249.080
Luxembourg	1	2.14	0.50	6	24.03	3.41	0.992
Netherlands	7	107.79	22.54	34	479.44	70.50	7,698
United Kingdom	324	2291.35	242.72	2993	8448.33	896.25	233.242
Community	2562	10082.36	1133.98	11745	33908.03	3625.20	726.698

Source: Commission of the European Communities, *Fourteenth General Report of the Activities of the European Communities in 1980* (Brussels: 1981), p. 148.

^a The amounts in EUA are indicative only.
^b Including studies (Article 12 of the Fund Regulation).

4. Grants Paid to Reimburse National Governments for Funds Expended

In 1980, actual ERDF payments, under the quota system, were 727 million EUA (out of an approval of assistance to projects amounting to 1,134 million EUA). These payments brought the total expenditures by the Fund to 2,058 million EUA over the Fund's six years of operation (1975−1980); this represented some 55 per cent of total commitments. The distinction between payments and approved commitments is because expenditures are only released from the Fund after payments have been demonstrated to have been made by the national aid programmes, on the basis of which Fund contributions are calculated. The national aids are normally paid out as work on projects progresses.

5. Two Key Principles

Two general principles have been fundamental to ERDF procedures and entrenched in the quota system.

1. ERDF funding is to be viewed as supplemental to the regional development assistance given by national member governments. Hence it is tied to actual aid expenditures by these governments, reimbursing them for a portion. The concept is that this will enable them to finance more ambitious regional development programmes than would otherwise be the case.

2. As a corollary, regions and areas eligible for Fund assistance shall be *limited* to those areas aided by member states, under their own systems of regional aid.

6. Most Aid to Poorest Areas for Infrastructure

Table 5.2 shows the distribution of Fund assistance, by geographical emphasis, for each member country for 1979. Map 5.1 shows the breakdown of ERDF aid between 1975 and 1979, indicating the industry and infrastructure mix. It can be seen that many of the 'poorest' and more rural areas are using Fund aid largely for infrastructure projects. A very different pattern prevails in the more industrialized regions eligible for Fund support. In such cases, grants to industry usually dominate the ERDF aid.

7. The Fund, 1975−79: Sectoral Activities

Tables 5.3 and 5.4 provide more detail on the types of investments financed by the European Regional Fund between 1975 and 1979. They are divided under the two main categories: Industry and Services, and Infrastructure.

Table 5.2
GEOGRAPHICAL CONCENTRATION OF AID

The Fund Regulation states that regions and areas eligible for Fund assistance shall be limited to those areas aided by Member States under their own systems of regional aid. To give maximum impact to Fund assistance, however, priority must be given to investments located in national priority areas, taking account of the principles of Community-level, coordination of regional aids. In 1979, the situation was as follows in the various Member States:

— *Belgium*, 53.1% of the quota available for 1979 has been given to Wallonie to the areas covered by the Commission Decision of 26 April 1972 (1) on aids granted under the Belgian law on economic expansion of 30 December 1980.

— *Denmark*, 83.6% of Fund assistance went to Greenland.

— *Germany*, 58.5% of Fund assistance went to Berlin, to the Zonenrandgebiet and to first priority development poles qualifying for 20% aid.

— *France*, 91.9% of Fund assistance went to the priority regions of Nord-Pas-de-Calais, to the west and South-west, to Corsica and the Overseas Departments.

— *Ireland*, 54.4% of the projects were situated in the designated areas, mainly in the west of the country.

— *Italy*, 96% of Fund assistance went to the Mezzogiorno, the remainder to areas of Friuli-Venezia Giulia struck by the 1976 earthquake (this is the second Fund contribution on behalf of these regions).

— *Netherlands*, 100% of Fund assistance went to the only two priority areas in the north and south of the country.

— *United Kingdom*, some 86.8% of assistance went to projects in priority areas, namely Northern Ireland, the Special Development Areas and the Development Areas.

Source: European Regional Development Fund, *Fifth Annual Report* (1979) (Brussels: 1980), p. 29.

Map 5.1
REGIONAL FUND AID 1975–1979

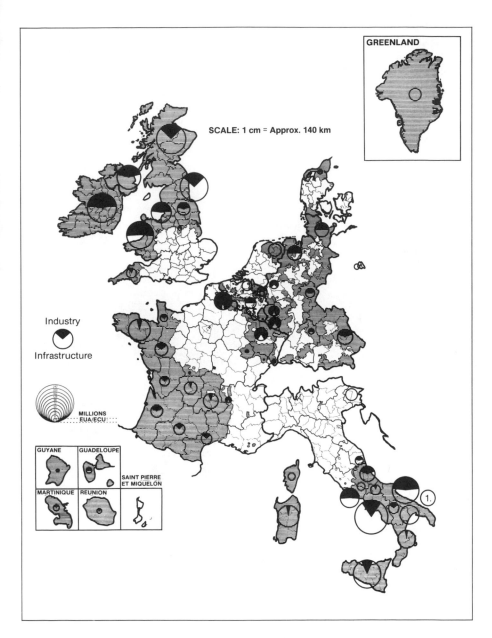

Source: European Regional Development Fund, *Fifth Annual Report* (1979) (Brussels: 1980), p. 30.
Note: [a] Multiregional projects concerning several regions of the Mezzogiorno.

Table 5.3
TYPES OF INVESTMENT FINANCED BY THE REGIONAL FUND:
INDUSTRY AND SERVICES 1975–1979

Type as defined in the Fund Regulation		Total investment (million EUA)	National aid involved (million EUA)	Number of projects and main sectors of activity concerned	
Industry and services	projects of 10 million EUA or more	6,513.69	1,028.89	156 of which	1 Nuclear fuel 1 Mining and processing of metallic ores 9 Metal production and first stage processing 12 Non-metallic minerals 35 Chemicals 2 Artificial and synthetic fibres 4 Metal goods 13 Mechanical engineering 14 Electrical and electronic engineering 27 Motor manufacture and spare parts 2 Other transport equipment 1 Precision, optical and similar instruments 15 Food, drinks and tobacco 1 Textiles 2 Footwear and clothing 3 Timber and furniture 4 Paper, printing and publishing 9 Rubber and plastics 1 Financial institutions
	projects of less than 10 million EUA	4,455.34	866.27	2636 of which	69 Production and first stage processing of metals 214 Non-metallic minerals 137 Chemicals 1 Artificial and synthetic fibres 366 Metal goods 239 Mechanical engineering 248 Electrical and electronic engineering 100 Motor manufacture and spare parts 48 Other transport equipment 55 Precision, optical and similar instruments 236 Food, drinks and tobacco 74 Textiles 79 Footwear and clothing 221 Timber and furniture 135 Paper, printing and publishing 198 Rubber and plastics 71 Catering and hotels 145 Miscellaneous industries and services
	TOTALS	10,968.93	1,895.16	2792 projects	

Source: European Regional Development Fund, *Fifth Annual Report (1979)* (Brussels: 1980), p. 75.

Table 5.4

TYPES OF INVESTMENT FINANCED BY THE REGIONAL FUND: INFRASTRUCTURE 1975–1979

Type as defined in the Fund Regulation	Total investment (million EUA)	National aid involved (million EUA)	Number of projects and main types of infrastructure concerned
Infrastructure projects of more than 10 million EUA	9,186.14	3,939.91	177 of which: 1 Purchase of sites for industry 89 General services to industrial estates (roads, railways, water supply and purification, drainage, etc.) 14 Port development 3 Energy supply 1 Tourist infrastructure 16 General services 31 Road works 7 Airport development 15 Miscellaneous infrastructure (energy production, telecommunications, etc.)
projects of less than 10 million EUA	3,377.90	2,849.91	4892 of which: 31 Purchase of sites for industry 151 Site preparation for industrial estates 1801 General services for industrial estates (roads, water supply, drainage, etc.) 505 Advance factories 1 Other infrastructure of social character 158 Tourist infrastructure 733 Road works 210 Port development 58 Airport 1244 Miscellaneous infrastructure (energy production, telecommunications, etc.)
projects in hill farming areas	292.70	274.17	1321 of which: 1321 General services (roads, water supply, etc.)
TOTALS	12,856.74	7,063.99	6390 projects

Source: European Regional Development Fund, *Fifth Annual Report (1979)* (Brussels: 1980), p. 77.

8. Industry and Services

Between 1975 and 1979, the average amount invested for projects of more than 10 million EUA was 42 million EUA; for projects of less than 10 million EUA, the average amount invested was 1.7 million EUA. The scale of projects for 1979 was considerably above this average, being 72 million EUA for the larger projects and 9.5 million EUA for the projects of less than 10 million EUA.

For 1979, Fund grants were found to equal some 45 per cent of national aid and some 7 per cent of the total investments, in the case of the projects of more than 10 million EUA. In the case of smaller projects, Fund grants were found to equal some 47 per cent of national aid and some 11 per cent of the total investments.

Over the 1975–1979 period, 22 per cent of the larger projects were in the chemical industry sector, followed by the motor vehicle industry (17 per cent). Assistance to smaller projects was far less concentrated than in the case of the larger projects. Metal goods, electrical and electronic engineering, mechanical engineering, timber and furniture, rubber and plastics, food, drink and tobacco, non-metallic minerals, paper, printing and publishing each fall in the range of 7 to 10 per cent of the number of projects assisted. (For further details see Tables 5.3 and 5.4.)

9. Infrastructure

Over the period 1975–1979, some 50 per cent of the large infrastructure projects aided (defined as more than 10 million EUA investments) comprised general services to industrial estates (e.g., roads, railways, water supply, drainage, etc.). Some 40 per cent of the smaller infrastructure projects (defined as less than 10 million EUA investments) were also linked to industrial estates (including site preparation, advance factories, roads, water supply, etc.).

During 1979, the level of Fund assistance averaged some 30 per cent of eligible public expenditure for projects of less than 10 million EUA, and 21 per cent for larger projects. In the case of some large projects, the Commission altered the rate of grant, between the limits of 10 and 30 per cent, to take account of the importance of the project for regional development purposes. Such changes were made after consulting the Regional Policy Committee and the Fund Committee.[10] More precise guide-lines are being developed.

10. Geographical Coverage by the Fund

The Fund Regulation states that regions and areas eligible for Fund assistance shall be limited to those areas aided by member states under their own systems of regional aid. The Fund, within that framework, gives priority to investments located in 'national priority areas'.[11]

In practice, over the period 1975–1979, the regions assisted by the ERDF contain almost 100 million inhabitants (i.e., 38 per cent of the Community's population) and cover 55 per cent of the Community's territory.[12] The relative size of the assisted region varies widely as between member states. They account for 15 per cent of the population in Denmark and in the Netherlands, 33 per cent in Belgium, from 35 to 40 per cent in the Federal Republic of Germany, in France, and in Italy, and 43 per cent in the United Kingdom. Both Ireland and Luxembourg, as a whole, are considered eligible for ERDF assistance. These ERDF areas correspond to the areas covered by national regional policies, except in Belgium, Denmark, and particularly the Netherlands and Italy, where only part of the territory covered by the regional aid of these member states is assisted by the ERDF.[13]

The selection process raises difficult questions. The demarcation of the assisted regions in the member states are based on a number of criteria that are not always clearly defined in national legislation. The criteria most frequently applied by the member states are per capita income and unemployment, both of which are measured against the national average.[14] Other criteria include population density, migration, population employed in agriculture or in declining industries, low economic growth, past or predictable employment trends, and infrastructure levels.[15]

II. Towards a Programming Approach for Regional Development

Initial Guide-lines

The improved co-ordinatiion of national regional policies is "an essential factor in Community regional policy." As a mechanism to improve such co-ordination, and to enable the ERDF to have a reasonably coherent framework for its activities with each and all of the national governments, some basic principles for programming regional development activities were advocated by the Regional Policy Committee. The initial guide-lines are of comparative interest.[16]

For example, specifying that the outline was 'indicative' and 'should be interpreted in a flexible manner', the Committee said that "Regional development programmes should have five chapters: (1) economic and social analysis; (2) development objectives; (3) measures for development; (4) financial resources; (5) implementation."

The Committee continued to enlarge upon the kind of details required under each of the above headings. They then established a proposed timetable for such work, to be completed by the member states. Thus, for example, they stated: "The Italian programmes are expected to cover the period 1976 to 1980, and to be notified during 1977."[17]

Documentation: Guide-lines and Results

The programme documentation that has so far resulted has been somewhat patchy. Among the more tightly organized programmes were those of the Netherlands and the Federal Republic of Germany. It is apparent that different countries have taken the exercise with varying degrees of seriousness.

In a preamble to the collection of all the programmes submitted, the Commission writes:

> From the Community's point of view, the regional development programmes are both a reference tool for assessing projects submitted for ERDF assistance, which must fall within the framework of these programmes, and the most appropriate framework for coordinating national regional policies and the Community regional policy. They need to be updated regularly.[18]

The Commission continued:

> . . . they must in a market economy remain indicative, i.e., outline the main lines of development (types of infrastructure investment and their priorities, main locational advantages for various types of activity), and state the costs of such projects and the financial commitments of the various public authorities, particularly central government.

> The ERDF Regulation stipulates that, in order to benefit from the Fund's assistance, investments must 'fall within the framework of a regional development programme'. This means that the programme should justify the projects, though these do not necessarily have to be listed explicitly.[19]

As a result of the initial programme documents, with different countries designing the work to phase in to the new ERDF requirements and their own national planning periods, the Commission is now calling for a uniform planning period, for all member country programmes, to run from 1981 to 1985.

But the Commission is not just urging harmony in the programme timing; it has also made thirteen recommendations (dated 23 May 1979) to be followed in future programme development. These appear, because of their potential relevance to Canadian policy design, in full (in Appendix 5.2). Three particular recommendations are highlighted.

The Commission recommends that the member states:

1. Communicate to the Commission, in addition to the regional development programmes for regions in which the ERDF is to provide assistance, and in so far as regional policy measures are applied in other regions, the principal measures whose aim is a better regional balance over the whole of the country, including

the so-called disincentives, either in the form of programmes or in another form.

2. Take fuller account, in the analysis of the economic and social situation in each region, on the one hand of the implications of national policies of measures in areas such as the restructuring of certain sectors, transport, energy, agriculture, fishing, the environment, physical planning, certain social measures and vocational training and, on the other of the most significant effects of Community policies and measures, particularly in the fields of agriculture, external trade relations and the restructuring of certain sectors.

3. Provide, where the setting of development objectives for jobs is concerned, at least quantified forecasts of job deficits in each region for the years 1981 to 1985 and to take further account in this connection of the tertiary sector, including tourism, and of the agricultural sector.[20]

III. Complementary Character of Fund Activities: Issues in Practice

The Fund: Passive or Active?

In the Fourth Annual Report (1978) on the ERDF, cited by way of illustration of the general philosophy, the Commission writes:

> During the course of 1978 the Commission services responsible for the Fund intensified their cooperation with the administrations of the Member States at national, regional and local levels, in particular in Italy and the United Kingdom. Indeed, the Commission does not see the role of the Fund as simply waiting for Member States to submit grant applications. It considers that the Fund must be a stimulant to new initiatives and the speeding up of investments already under way.[21]

These comments reflect the experience of the initial years of Fund activities. At first, grants were given to countries for 'shopping lists' of projects (that the member states had already spent funds on), many of which were not really integrated into any very clear 'programming framework', however ambiguously one might choose to define such. As time progressed, and as the programme documents began to be developed according to the very general guide-lines of the Regional Policy Committee (in co-operation with ERDF staff), it became clear that there was room for tightening up (including efforts to use more quantitative yardsticks). At the heart of the problem appear to be two factors.

1. The member states have negotiated a quota arrangement regarding their share of the ERDF funds. From a national government vantage point, this is the really serious part of the exercise — the aggregate size of the quota available. A straight transfer of the quota, without any project details at all, in many ways would best serve their 'interests'. As to how the funding is then allocated would be entirely according to their perceived priorities. The entire process of identifying projects that fit certain categories, or that are 'wrapped up' within broad (ERDF inspired) regional development programme 'frameworks', could be viewed as an exercise in somewhat unnecessary game-playing. Hitherto, the Fund staff may not have carried much real clout in the project assessment process. If one project is viewed (by ERDF staff) as not relating to an appropriate programme guide-line, then there are always others that can be dug out of the system. It is simply a matter of negotiation — and of using the appropriate jargon of the day.

2. From the vantage point of the Fund, their own role is a *complementary* one to the national regional development efforts, but not, in any way, a *substitute* for any parts. The Fund concept is 'additionality', by which is meant that the Fund resources are intended to augment the amounts member states spend to wrestle with regional disparities, not to substitute for them.

But how, one might ask, can one be sure that substitution is not taking place — particularly given the complexities and scale of the range of endeavours involved? The answer clearly is that one cannot be sure — it is simply up to the political process, with appropriate information flows, to keep the general public as well informed as possible on such matters.

Programmes as a Way to Clarify Regional Priorities

In the above situation, the Fund officials appear to believe that they can play a 'shaping' role in the sharpening of national regional development priorities and strategies, through the mechanism of programme guide-lines.

This is probably true when member states are genuinely attempting to work with the ERDF and really do support the basic philosophy of more 'coherent' programming, along the lines of such an approach as recommended in Appendix 5.1. However, in situations where member states (at the political and/or official levels) do not support such an approach (at heart), and view it as either 'simplistic' or 'interference' from the Commission, in those cases the whole exercise is likely to be little more than 'shadow-boxing'. In such situations, the ERDF has a tough 'selling job' ahead of it — and, quite frankly, it is hard to be optimistic about the outcome so long as the quota system is the overall allocative mechanism. This is not, it should be noted, to be critical of the quota system in any overall manner, but just to point out this particular experience. As is indicated in a number of places in this review, the author believes that the quota system is a good way to allocate, and advocates a similar system for Canada. But the ERDF experience shows that, for all its apparent merits, the quota approach is no panacea.

IV. Effectiveness Assessment by the ERDF Itself

New Organization

Inasmuch as the ERDF is a relatively new organization, there is no documentation available that compares with the EIB's *Twenty Years: 1958–1978*. The conclusions, at the end of the Fourth and Fifth Annual Reports of the ERDF are of an 'operational nature', useful from that vantage point and already covered, for the most part, in the previous sections of this review. They do not provide a broad-ranging assessment of past experiences.

Controls

Under the section on "Controls," the Fourth Annual Report summarizes the number of on-the-spot checks (a target of 10 per cent of assisted projects are inspected) and outlines some of the results to date.[22] Given the framework within which the ERDF operates, and the nature of some of those findings (e.g., "In France, Commission officials have not so far been allowed to visit industrial projects"), the very role of the 'controls' must surely be open to serious question. This same point recurs, in a most candid manner, in the Fifth Annual Report.[23]

Co-ordination

Finally, under the section on "Coordination and Programmes," again in the Fourth Annual Report,[24] the whole thrust of the discussion is on the future — with great emphasis being placed on the Resolution of 6 February 1979 (see Appendix 5.1) whereby the Council agreed to take account of the regional consequences of Community policies in its own decisions.

The ERDF consistently emphasizes that "the impact of the Fund cannot be judged in isolation. It is only one instrument of regional policy and must contribute to the achievement of a whole range of objectives defined at Community level and which seek both to remedy the traditional imbalances between regions by improving the situation of the less favoured, and to prevent new imbalances from appearing."[25]

In both the most recent annual reports, the ERDF emphasizes the benefits to be gained from 'regional development integrated operations', and in the Fourth Annual Report (1978) the hope is expressed that the regional programming (being advocated almost as an article of faith) will not merely help the ERDF be more effective in its work with individual regions, but of great importance will (1) foster improved co-operation within member-state agencies responsible for regional project and programme analysis and performance; and (2) generate a greater degree of cohesion in the work of the other EEC instruments when they relate to regional development issues.[26]

Simplistic Employment Indicators

The ERDF has traditionally, and wisely, been cautious about claiming large numbers of new jobs as an outcome of Fund assistance. In the case of its aid to infrastructure projects, the ERDF Annual Report for 1979 states:

> One of the main aims of the Fund is the creation and maintenance of jobs in regions that are heavily dependent on or suffer from industrial change or structural underemployment. In this connection, the fact that most Fund assisted projects in 1979 were for infrastructure, for which precise statistical details on jobs created were not available, makes it difficult to assess Fund assistance in this field. . . .
>
> . . . the Commission does not underestimate the basic role of infrastructure in developing the less favoured regions. Indeed, regional policy must, of its very nature, concentrate principally on medium and long term structural measures such as the improvement of infrastructure since these are essential to the creation and maintenance of permanent jobs in the future.

The report continues to note that "According to information in the applications, projects in receipt of Fund assistance in 1979 in the industrial and services sectors should create and/or maintain nearly 80,000 jobs." The report suggests job creation was higher in member states receiving proportionately more aid for industry (i.e., France and the United Kingdom) and that smaller projects (less than 10 million EUA) were more labour intensive.[27]

V. Some Further Comments

The scale of the ERDF, in the context of the regional problems of the Community, is small. One official likened its budget to the allocation of a packet of cigarettes to each person in the designated regions. He argued that, given its size, one could hardly expect to measure its economic impact in terms of changes in GNP.

Having said that, officials appear (to varying degrees) to be hopeful that qualitative improvements to both EEC and national governmental efforts to tackle regional problems could be an outcome of the

ERDF work. The degree of confidence to be placed in the programming approach now followed ranged from (perhaps over-abundant) optimism to cynicism (given the perceived attitudes of some national governments to the whole approach).

The problem of 'additionality' loomed large in conversations with Fund officials, but once again the cautionary comment was made that it was not merely an adding of resources to existing national projects and programmes that was at issue, it was also a question of improved information flows, analysis of goals and problems, and co-ordination of policies and programmes — all of which could lead to qualitative gains.

The Fund's appraisal of specific projects has, thus far, been somewhat confined (for example, by World Bank standards). The onus has so very heavily been on the shoulders of the national governments. The emphasis has been, and will apparently continue to be, much more on broad policy and broad programme appraisals (by the Fund). Concern, in that context, was frequently expressed about meaningful, objective criteria. Two particular yardsticks were viewed as most helpful: job creation and unemployment. There is a growing interest in more specificity as to goals and targets (numerical so far as practicable).

In assessing the Fund, it is suggested that one can reach one of two main conclusions.

1. The Fund is too trivial to take seriously, given the scale of the problems and also given its tiny size in relation to the resources available to the member states to tackle regional development, if they so choose. The main issue is not to increase the Fund's budget, but, particularly in the case of countries such as Italy and the United Kingdom, for national governments to treat regional development and equity more seriously than appears presently to be the case.

2. The Fund, while admittedly modest (and perhaps it should be much larger), is of great political importance to the Community. In the context of the EEC, it serves to add an additional range to the overall Community fabric of instruments and roles. The Fund projects can be seen as representing 'a sense of direction', albeit modest. The Fund, in many ways like many of the other Commission instruments, represents some more cement to help fill in cracks and bind more closely together the member states. They are, in turn, only as strong as the sum of their regions: the ERDF can play a modest but constructive role.

The writer prefers this latter conclusion, although it is noted that one should not go overboard and conclude that the ERDF is either large enough, or has the degree of political support by the governments of the member states, to become a 'trail-blazer' in the solution of the regional problems of the Community. Substantial eradication of regional disparities will require greater commitment by the member states with the more serious problems; the ERDF can encourage such commitment and can help to bring comparative insights, improved information systems, and objective analysis to the issues. With the support of member states, the ERDF can even be a transfer mechanism to siphon resources from the richer to the poorer countries. But it is unlikely that massive transfers will be supported by the wealthier governments; hence it seems clear that the main responsibility for redressing regional problems is firmly with the national governments of the member states. The further development of the European Parliament, and the greater degree of political direction that might be forthcoming, is unlikely to change this situation very markedly.

VI. Points for Canadian Policy Review

Comparison Between ERDF and DREE

There is no agency in Canada with a mandate comparable to that of the European Regional Development Fund. The organization that most closely resembled the Fund was the recently dismantled (January 1982) federal Department of Regional Economic Expansion (DREE). However, DREE had much wider powers than the ERDF; it had a budget that was, on a per capita basis, much larger than that of the ERDF (albeit quite small in the context of the overall Canadian federal budget); and, at least until its last two years of operation when it worked under the cloud of the constitutional negotiations, it enjoyed a great deal more flexibility in its relationship with the provinces than has the ERDF with the member states. Moreover, DREE did not have to operate within the confines of any formal quota system — which is not to say that some 'rough and ready' balance has not been sought between provinces. But any such quota has been extremely *ad hoc*, in practice.

Observations

Given such differences, it might be asked if there are any points from the ERDF experience that could have Canadian application. The conclusion is in the affirmative, although the suggested lessons are certainly neither dramatic nor comprising any 'panacea' qualities. Five ideas are highlighted.

   1. *The Commission has constantly emphasized that the ERDF can only be expected to play something of a catalytic role in contributing to regional development* — both in terms of influencing other Community instruments (such as Community Agricultural Policy), and the policies of national governments.

   The emphasis has been on the qualitative role of the ERDF, always in co-operation with other agencies and policies. In the case of DREE, historically, the tendency was to concentrate on its own spending programmes, rather than to seek to influence other federal programmes and provincial policies. This became less true in the period 1980–1981 (largely because of the views of its minister), but it was clear that the federal system, as a whole, was not at all sure about the federal government's regional development role. Regional problems tended to be viewed as DREE's problems rather than those of the federal government apparatus as a whole. The establishment of a Ministry of State for Economic and Regional Development (MSERD) in January 1982 has been announced as a step to better co-ordinate and shape federal regional development programming.

2. *ERDF has operated within a formalized quota system.* That framework has been the outcome of negotiation and does not fully reflect regional development differences. If it did, West Germany, for example, would receive no aid, while Italy would receive proportionately more than at present. For the north of Italy not to receive any aid from the ERDF, yet for the Netherlands, Denmark, Belgium, and West Germany to receive some, really does not represent a reasonable distribution according to any criteria of need.

Moreover, the quota system has tended to reduce the clout that the ERDF can carry in screening projects. Not merely does the quota act as a ceiling, it also serves as a norm. Having said that, it is concluded that a quota system, based on carefully worked out and routinely reappraised criteria, would have been an improvement to the manner in which DREE funds were allocated among provinces. A 'post-DREE approach' to federal regional budget allocations is still at a formative stage. The critical conclusions from the ERDF experience, in this regard, are that the negotiation phase is of great importance and requires both competent analysis and open political debate. It can only be concluded, from the manner in which the ERDF quota is drawn, that political judgement preceded objective analysis, and that such analysis as was done was to justify a political balance, not to clarify the disparity problems.

3. *The ERDF is concentrating on improving the quality of member-state regional development programming.* It is doing this primarily by attempting to improve information exchanges, both of problems and policies, as well as to foster (with the aid of the Regional Policy Committee) quality improvements in programme design. Its funds are used as carrots in this regard, although there could be some danger of resentment among member states if this approach is overplayed. The initiatives for project aid, within evolving programme frameworks, have come from the member-state governments. To some degree, the ERDF has served as a transfer agency — drawing funds from the richer member nations and granting them (according to an agreed-upon quota) to the poorer member nations. Similarly, the ERDF has

sought (with some apparent success) to develop regional guide-lines for widespread EEC application among its various instruments.

The major weakness to this process is that the total European Commission budget (of which the ERDF only claims some 7 per cent in 1981) has not reached even 1 per cent of the GNP of the nine. Were DREE to have changed its role to approximate more closely that of the ERDF, it would have had a substantial chance of making greater impact than the ERDF because of the far larger, proportionate size of the Canadian federal budget. The new Canadian MSERD and the reshaped Department of Industry, Trade and Commerce, as of January 1982 known as the Department of Regional Industrial Expansion (DRIE), are similarly placed in a more advantageous position than is the lot of the ERDF.

Attractive aspects of the ERDF experience include the roles played by member states through both the Regional Policy and Fund Committees, the Fund's emphasis on member-state initiatives, the Fund's contribution to the upgrading of regional development pro-gramme quality as a result of the ERDF programme focus and, not to be downplayed in terms of longer-range benefits, the improvements that are likely to be the outcome of improved policy information exchange mechanisms.

It is felt, by the writer, that an ERDF-like agency would really not have been an improvement upon DREE. However, a blend of both ideas does hold some attractions — whereby more onus is placed on provincial government policy inputs (and direction), whereby a quota system approach does become a framework, and whereby some of the regional programme ideas are developed further in Canada, to encourage increased co-ordination (and tailoring) of other federal policies, as well as increased review and harmonization of provincial policies, for the provinces as a whole and not merely for designated areas. Federal government approaches to regional policy in Canada in 1981 appeared to be moving away from, rather than closer to, increased harmonization of federal programming with that of the provincial governments. If this perception is indeed accurate, it should be noted that it is radically different from the emphasis being stressed in the EEC, on the basis of their experiences. The whole emphasis in Canada appeared to be on 'federal' projects and programmes, not on joint federal-provincial programming. With the January 1982 reor-ganization (especially MSERD), the Canadian situation is suddenly more liquid. Some initial concerns are being raised that while improved federal programming may emerge, a federal political concern for visibility and credit for federal programming could be at the expense of close provincial co-operation. It is premature to comment on this.

The fact that both in Europe and Canada such glaring regional disparities exist is not merely a reflection of inadequacies of Community-level or federal regional programming, nor of the 'harsh realities' of some 'unfettered market system'. It is very considerably a reflection of a lack of real concern by, in the case of the European Community, some member-state governments and, in the case of Canada, some provincial governments. It was clear from site visits in Europe that many regional problems are reinforced by government policies, rather than helped by them. The same is clearly also the case in many of the Canadian provinces, for example, on the coast of Labrador and in Cape Breton.

4. *The technical work being fostered by the ERDF, along the lines of Appendix 5.2, does merit review by federal and provincial agencies.* While the quality, at this juncture, is quite variable, there are clearly lessons for Canadian assessment. The emphasis is on developing quantitative goals and performance yardsticks, an emphasis that has not gained great support in the Canadian setting.

At the same time, it is concluded that the ERDF staff, at this point, are probably placing too much hope on the benefits to be gained from qualitative improvements in the form of programme presentations that will serve as bench-marks for project appraisal. More reliance, it is suggested, could usefully be placed (if the ERDF is indeed to screen projects) on the kind of project appraisal process used by the World Bank. Such appraisal, following agreed-upon principles, can still be undertaken at the member-government level and need not be an ERDF responsibility. But the fostering of such an approach could reasonably become an ERDF role within its existing terms of reference. The same is also much needed in the Canadian setting. Project appraisal, in DREE and in many of the poorer provinces, has been a very *ad hoc* and rather chaotic process. It has not generally compared at all favourably with the standards set by the World Bank, which is working in developing countries with far more extreme problems. Moreover, systematic case study reviews, as routinely published by the World Bank, are almost unheard of in Canada.

5. *A continuing review of ERDF activities is, at this formative stage of the ERDF life, likely to be of value to Canadian regional policy* both at the federal and provincial levels of government. At this early juncture in the ERDF's existence, it is premature to suggest how much impact the Fund will have in resolving regional problems in the Community. Of major importance will be the degree of real power and sense of purpose achieved by the European Parliament.

APPENDIX 5.1

Main texts[28]

Updated version of the text of Council Regulation (EEC) No 724/75 of 18 March 1975 establishing a European Regional Development Fund.

Council Regulation (EEC) No 724/75 of 18 March 1975 establishing a European Regional Development Fund (OJ No L 73, 21.3.1975, p. 1) and the amendments arising out of Regulation (EEC) No 214/79 (OJ No L 35, 9.2.1979, p. 1) are hereby coordinated.

This coordination is without legal status. Hence, the preamble has been omitted.

TITLE 1

PRELIMINARY PROVISIONS

Article 1

The European Regional Development Fund, hereinafter referred to as 'the Fund', is intended to correct the principal regional imbalances within the Community resulting in particular from agricultural preponderance, industrial change and structural under-employment.

Article 2

1. As from the financial year 1978, the endowment for the Fund shall be determined annually in the general budget of the European Communities.

2. The annual budget shall indicate for the relevant year under the Fund heading:

(a) commitment appropriations;

(b) payment appropriations.

Save where otherwise provided for in the special provisions laid down in this Regulation, the Financial Regulation applicable to the general budget of the Communities shall apply to the management of the Fund.

3. The following may be financed by the Fund with a view to contributing to the realization of the objectives referred to in Article 1:

(a) Community action in support of regional policy measures taken by the Member States, as provided for in Title II of this Regulation.

   The resources of the Fund intended for financing these activities shall be distributed in accordance with the following table:

Belgium	1.39%
Denmark	1.20%
Germany	6.0 %
France	16.86%
Ireland	6.46%
Italy	39.39%
Luxembourg	0.09%
Netherlands	1.58%
United Kingdom	27.03%

(b) specific Community regional development measures, as provided for in Title III of this Regulation. The sum allotted to such measures shall amount to 5% of the Fund's resources. Resources which cannot be used in time for such measures shall be allocated to the supporting action referred to in (a).

The whole of the Fund's resources for financing these measures shall be used having due regard to the relative severity of regional imbalances in the Community.

Article 3

1. Regions and areas which may benefit from the Fund shall be limited to those aided areas established by Member States in applying their systems of regional aids and in which State aids are granted which qualify for Fund assistance.

When aid from the Fund is granted, priority shall be given to investments in national priority areas, taking account of the principles for the coordination at Community level of regional aids.

2. As part of the specific Community regional development measures referred to in Article 2 (3) (b), the Fund may also, where appropriate, give assistance in regions or areas other than those referred to in paragraph 1, for the solution of problems forming the subject of Community action, if the Member State concerned has also given assistance or does so at the same time.

TITLE II

COMMUNITY ACTION IN SUPPORT OF REGIONAL POLICY MEASURES TAKEN BY THE MEMBER STATES

Chapter 1

Field of Action

Article 4

1. As part of Community action in support of regional policy measures taken by the Member States, the Fund may contribute to the financing

of investments which individually exceed 50 000 European units of account and come under any of the following categories:

(a) investments in industrial, handicraft or service activities which are economically sound and which benefit from State regional aids, provided that at least 10 new jobs are created or that 10 existing jobs are maintained. In the latter case, the investments should fall within the framework of a conversion or restructuring plan to ensure that the undertaking concerned is competitive. Preference shall, however, be given to operations which both maintain existing jobs and create new jobs.

Service activities qualifying for assistance shall be those concerned with tourism and those which have a choice of location. Such activities should have a direct impact on the development of the region and on the level of employment.

For the purposes of this Article, a group of investments which are related geographically and financially, and which together comply with the criteria provided for in this Article, may be considered as a single investment in the field of handicrafts or tourism;

(b) investments financed wholly or in part by public authorities or by any other agency responsible, on a similar basis to a public authority, for the creation of infrastructures, and covering, provided that this is justified by regional development programmes, infrastructures which contribute to the development of the region or area in which they are situated, provided that the total share of the overall assistance granted by the Fund for financing the investments referred to in this point does not exceed 70% of the Fund's assistance.

This percentage must be complied with over a period of three years; however, it may be exceeded by decision of the Council acting on a proposal from the Commission.

In administering the Fund, the Commission shall take account of the particular situation of certain regions on the basis of the programmes referred to above. Member States shall take all steps to enable the provisions of this point to be applied;

(c) investments in infrastructures covered by Article 3 (2) of the Council Directive on mountain and hill farming and farming in certain less-favoured areas, provided that the less-favoured area in question corresponds to or is located within one of the regions or areas covered by Article 3 of this Regulation.

2. The amount of the Fund's contribution shall be:

(a) in respect of investments covered by paragraph 1 (a), 20% of the investment cost without, however, exceeding 50% of the aid accorded to each investment by public authorities under a system of regional aids, such contributions being limited moreover to that part of the investment which does not exceed 100 000 European units of account per job created and 50 000 European units of account per job maintained.

In the case of services and handicrafts, the Fund's contribution may, by way of derogation from the first subparagraph, exceed 20% of the investment cost, provided that the amount does not exceed in such case 10 000 European units of account per job created or maintained, or 50% of the national aid.

The State aid to be taken into consideration shall be grants, interest rebates, or their equivalent where loans at reduced rates of interest are concerned, whether such aid is linked to the investment or to the number of jobs created.

Such aid may include aid granted in respect of an investment in connection with the transfer of plant and workers. The aid equivalent shall be calculated in accordance with an implementing Regulation under the terms of Article 16. Aid granted in the form of rent rebates or exemptions from payments of rent for buildings, including plant, may also be taken into account, provided that the same calculation is possible.

The contribution from the Fund thus defined may, pursuant to a prior decision of the Member State concerned communicated at the same time as the request for this contribution, either supplement aid granted to the relevant investment by public authorities or remain credited to those authorities and considered as a partial repayment of such aid;

(b) in respect of investments covered by paragraphs 1 (b) and (c), 30% of the expenditure incurred by public authorities where the investment is less than 10 million European units of account and from 10 to 30% maximum for investments of 10 million European units of account or more. However, the maximum rate may be 40% for projects which are of particular importance to the development of the region in which they are situated.

The Fund's assistance may consist wholly or in part of a rebate of three percentage points on loans made by the European Investment Bank, pursuant to Article 130 (a) and (b) of the Treaty, in the regions and areas referred to in Article 3 of this Regulation. In that event, the aid from the Fund shall be paid to the Bank in one instalment, the rebate being a capitalized sum expressed as a percentage of the investment.

Chapter 2

Procedural Provisions

Article 5

1. The Fund's assistance shall be decided upon by the Commission according to the relative severity of the economic imbalance of the region where the investment is made and the direct or indirect effect of the investment on employment. The Commission shall examine, in particular, the consistency of the investment with the range of actions undertaken by the relevant Member State in favour of the region concerned, as apparent from information supplied by Member States pursuant to Article 6 and taking special account of:

(a) the investment's contribution to the economic development of the region;

(b) the consistency of the investment with the Community's programmes or objectives;

(c) the situation of the economic sector concerned and the profitability of the investment;

(d) whether the investment falls within a frontier area, that is to say, within regions adjacent to one or more other Member States;

(e) other contributions made by Community institutions or by the European Investment Bank, either to the same investment or to other activities within the same region. Thus contributions from the Fund will be coordinated with other Community contributions, in such a way as to favour a range of converging and coordinated actions within a given region and to guarantee, in particular, consistency between regional policy and structural policy for agriculture.

2. (a) In respect of investments of 10 million European units of account or more, the Fund's assistance shall be the subject of a Commission Decision under the procedure provided for in Article 16.

   In respect of investments in infrastructure costing 10 million or more European units of account, the Commission shall, before obtaining the opinion of the Fund Committee referred to in Article 15, consult the Regional Policy Committee.

   (b) In respect of investments costing less than 10 million European units of account, the Commission shall provide prior information for the Member States in the form of a simplified list of investments for which requests for assistance have been received. The procedure provided for in Article 16 shall apply in the case of:

— draft negative decisions, where the Member State concerned so requests,

— all other draft decisions in respect of which the Commission or a Member State wishes an opinion to be sought from the Fund Committee.

Article 6

1. Investments may benefit from the Fund's assistance only if they fall within the framework of a regional development programme the implementation of which is such as to contribute to correction of the main regional imbalances within the Community which may prejudice the proper functioning of the common market and the convergence of the Member States' economies, with a view, in particular, to the attainment of economic and monetary union.

2. Regional development programmes shall be established according to the joint plan prepared by the Regional Policy Committee.

3. Member States shall notify the Commission of regional development programmes and alterations to programmes already notified.

4. The programmes shall be of an indicative nature and specify the objectives of the development of the region concerned and the means to be employed. They shall be the subject of consultation with the Regional Policy Committee. The Commission shall examine these programmes in the light of the criteria referred to in Article 5 (1) (b) in order to enable it to determine the priorities for assistance from the Fund.

5. Before 31 March each year, Member States shall bring the regional development programmes up to date by providing the Commission with all available information for the current year not contained in the programmes on:

(a) the financial resources allocated to regional development under their programmes;

(b) the priority measures relating to regional development which they intend to implement;

(c) the use they intend to make of Community resources, and in particular of resources from the Fund in implementing these priority measures.

Any other relevant information shall be forwarded to the Commission as soon as available.

6. Before 1 October each year, Member States shall provide the Commission with an overall statistical summary indicating by region for the previous year:

(a) the results achieved in the region in terms of investment and employment;

(b) the financial means employed;

(c) the actual use made of the resources of the Fund.

Article 7

1. Member States shall submit requests for assistance from the Fund to the Commission, and shall indicate any factors which will allow the Commission to assess the value of the investments proposed in the light of Articles 5 and 6.

2. In respect of the investments referred to in Article 4 (1) of less than 10 million European units of account, Member States shall present their global requests at the beginning of each quarter. They shall group these requests by region and shall separate investments referred to in Article 4 (1) (a) from investments in infrastructure.

These requests shall indicate:

(a) in respect of the investments referred to in Article 4 (1) (a), the names of the undertakings concerned, the sector of their activity and the location of each investment, also its character (foundation, extension, conversion or restructuring of the relevant concern), the total amount of investment involved, the predicted overall effect on employment (creation or maintenance), estimates regarding the implementation schedule, total aids granted for which a contribution from the Fund is requested and the schedule laid down for their payment;

(b) in respect of investments in infrastructure, the location of each investment and its character, its contribution to the development of the region, the predicted total costs and the costs borne by public authorities and the schedule laid down for their payment, the name of the responsible authorities, the total contribution requested from the Fund, and estimates regarding the implementation schedule.

3. In respect of investments of 10 million European units of account or more, requests shall be presented separately and shall include the following information:

(a) in respect of the investments referred to in Article 4 (1) (a) the name of the undertaking, the sector of activity, the nature of the investment, its location, the effect on employment, the implementation schedule, the grants, interest rebates or loans at reduced rates of interest and the schedule laid down for the payment of such aids, any other form of aid granted or provided for by public authorities and the financing plan, indicating in particular any other Community aids requested or provided for.

The Member State shall state in its request the total aid which in its opinion should be granted to the undertaking and the contribution it is seeking from the Community;

(b) in respect of investments in infrastructure, the responsible authority, the nature of the investment, its location, its contribution to the development of the region, its cost, its financing plan, its implementation schedule and the schedule laid down for payments.

4. Aid from the Fund shall be determined by the Commission:

(a) in the aggregate for each request covered by paragraph 2;

(b) case by case for requests covered by paragraph 3.

5. Member States shall give priority to the presentation of requests for contributions towards investments of 10 million European units of account or more.

Article 8

1. The amount of the contribution from the Fund defined, where applicable, by calculating the aid equivalent pursuant to the implementing Regulation referred to in Article 4 (2) (a) shall be paid *pari passu* with expenditure upon presentation by the Member State of quarterly statements certifying expenditure and the existence of detailed supporting documents, and containing the following information:

(a) for intermediate payment requests:

— the name of the undertaking concerned, or, for infrastructures, the name of the responsible authority,

— the location of the investment,

— total public expenditure paid after the date referred to in Article 11 and that part of the amount for which payment is requested,

— the amount of the payment requested from the Fund,

— a forecast of future payment requests;

(b) for final payment requests, all the information referred to in (a) except the last indent, together with:

— the sum actually invested and confirmation that the investment made conforms with the initial project,

— the date of completion of the investment,

— the number of jobs created or maintained in being by the investments referred to in Article 4 (1) (a),

— the amounts of public expenditure.

2. In cases where expenditure provided for by the decision referred to in Article 7 consists of aids granted in the form of interest rebates or loans at reduced rates of interest, the contribution of the Fund relating to these aids and which is still due when the investments are completed shall be settled in a single payment on presentation of the certificates covering completion of the investments.

3. Accelerated payments under a decision to grant aid from the Fund may be granted by the Commission to a Member State at the latter's request. They may not exceed 75% of the total amount of the aid from the Fund. Such accelerated payments shall be subject to the condition that at least 30% of the payments constituting the basis for aid from the Fund have been made.

Payments already made pursuant to paragraph 1 (a) under the decision to grant aid shall be deducted from the accelerated payments.

The balance of the aid from the Fund shall be paid in accordance with paragraph 1 as regards payments by the Member States not covered by the accelerated payment.

Grouped applications for accelerated payments shall be submitted on a quarterly basis to the Commission by the Member State concerned.

4. Member States shall designate the authority or the institution authorized to furnish the certification referred to in this Article. The Commission shall make payments to the Member State, to an agency designated by the Member State for this purpose, or if necessary to the European Investment Bank.

Article 9

1. Where an investment which has been the subject of a contribution from the Fund has not been made as planned, or if the conditions of this Regulation are not fulfilled, the contribution from the Fund may be reduced or cancelled, if the Commission so decides after consulting the Fund Committee.

Any sums which have been paid in error shall be repaid to the Community by the Member State concerned or, where applicable, by the European Investment Bank, within 12 months following the date on which the relevant decision has been communicated.

Member States shall repay the Commission the amount of the Fund's assistance wherever national aid used as the basis for calculating the

Fund's assistance has been repaid to the Member State by the investor.

2. Member States shall make available to the Commission all information required for the effective operation of the Fund and shall take all steps to facilitate such supervision as the Commission may consider useful in managing the Fund, including on-the-spot checks. They shall notify the Commission of the cases referred to in the first subparagraph of paragraph 1.

3. Notwithstanding verification carried out by Member States in accordance with national laws, regulations and administrative provisions and without prejudice to the provisions of Article 206 of the Treaty or to any inspection arranged on the basis of Article 209 (c) of the Treaty, at the request of the Commission and with the agreement of the Member State, the competent authorities of that Member State shall carry out on-the-spot checks or enquiries about operations financed by the Fund. Officials of the Commission may take part in these proceedings and the Commission may fix a time limit for carrying them out.

4. The objective of these on-the-spot checks or enquiries about operations financed by the Fund shall be to verify:

(a) the conformity of administrative practices with Community rules;

(b) the existence of supporting documentary evidence and its conformity with the operations financed by the Fund;

(c) the conditions under which the operations financed by the Fund are executed and checked;

(d) the conformity of projects implemented with the operations financed by the Fund.

5. The Commission may suspend payment of aid to a particular operation if an inspection reveals either irregularities or a substantial change in the character or conditions of the project for which the Commission's approval has not been sought.

6. Notwithstanding Article 6 (2) of the Financial Regulation of 21 December 1977 applicable to the general budget of the European Communities,[a] if a project receiving aid from the Fund is not completed or is implemented in such a manner as no longer to justify payment of part of the aid from the Fund granted on behalf of that project, the outstanding part of the Fund's contribution shall be granted to another investment located in one of the eligible regions of the same Member State under the conditions laid down in this Regulation.

Article 10

1. The investors concerned shall be informed by agreement with the Member States in question that part of the aid granted to them has been provided by the Community. For infrastructure projects, the Member States, by agreement with the Commission, shall take all necessary steps to ensure that assistance from the Fund is given suitable publicity.

2. The list of projects which have received contributions from the Fund shall be published every six months in the *Official Journal of the European Communities*.

Article 11

The Commission shall take into consideration for Fund assistance payments made by the Member States as from the 12th month before the date on which it receives the request for assistance, in respect of investments not completed by that date. This period shall be increased to 24 months for payments in respect of investments in Greenland.

Article 12

1. The Fund may contribute to the financing of studies which are closely related to Fund operations and are undertaken at the request of a Member State.

2. Such assistance may not exceed 50% of the cost of the study.

TITLE III

SPECIFIC COMMUNITY REGIONAL DEVELOPMENT MEASURES

Article 13

1. The Fund may participate in financing specific Community regional development measures which differ in whole or in part from the types of measure referred to in Title II. These shall be measures:

— either linked with Community policies and with measures adopted by the Community in order to take better account of their regional dimension or to reduce their regional consequences,

— or, in exceptional cases, intended to meet the structural consequences of particularly serious occurrences in certain regions or areas with a view to replacing jobs lost and creating the necessary infrastructures for this purpose.

These measures shall not have as their object the internal reorganization of declining sectors but may, by establishing new economic activities, promote the creation of alternative employment in regions or areas in a difficult situation.

These measures shall be financed jointly by the Community and the Member State or States concerned.

2. Member States shall provide the Commission with information on regional problems likely to be the subject of specific measures within the meaning of paragraph 1.

3. Without prejudice to the responsibilities of the Commission with regard to State aid under Articles 92, 93 and 94 of the Treaty, the Council, acting unanimously on a proposal from the Commission and after consulting the European Parliament, shall determine for each of these measures to be implemented in the form of a special programme:

(a) the nature of the operations to which the Fund may contribute;

(b) the areas and regions which the Fund may assist;

(c) the national public aid taken into consideration in granting Fund assistance;

(d) the contribution of the Fund;

(e) the categories of beneficiaries of Fund assistance;

(f) the detailed rules for financing.

4. Requests for Fund assistance for these special programmes shall be submitted to the Commission by the Member States. The fifth subparagraph of Article 4 (2) (a) and Article 10 shall apply.

Article 14

1. The Fund may bear all or part of the cost of studies which are closely related to the measures referred to in Article 2 (3) and are undertaken at the request of one or more Member States.

2. The Commission shall decide whether to grant assistance from the Fund in accordance with the procedure laid down in Article 16, after consulting the Regional Policy Committee.

TITLE IV

GENERAL AND FINAL PROVISIONS

Article 15

1. A Fund Committee (hereinafter referred to as 'the Committee') is hereby established. It shall be composed of representatives of the Member States and chaired by a representative of the Commission.

2. Within the Committee the votes of the Member States shall be weighted in accordance with Article 148 (2) of the Treaty. The chairman shall not vote.

Article 16

1. Where the procedure laid down in this Article is to be followed, the chairman shall refer the matter to the Committee either on his own initiative or at the request of the representative of a Member State.

2. The representative of the Commission shall submit drafts of decisions to be taken. The Committee shall deliver its opinion on the drafts within the time limit which the chairman may fix according to the urgency of the questions under consideration. An opinion shall be adopted by a majority of 41 votes.

3. The Commission shall adopt decisions which shall apply immediately. However, if these decisions are not in accordance with the opinion of the Committee, they shall forthwith be communicated by the Commission to the Council. In that event the Commission shall defer application of the decisions which it has adopted for not more than two months from the date of such communications. The Council, acting by a qualified majority, may take a different decision within two months.

Article 17

The Committee may consider any other question concerning the Fund's operations referred to it by its chairman either on his own initiative or at the request of the representative of a Member State.

Article 18

The necessary measures for the implementation of this Regulation shall be adopted in accordance with the procedure laid down in Article 16.

Article 19

1. Member States shall adopt the necessary measures to indicate separately, according to the special characteristics of national budget systems, the sums received from the Fund.

2. At the request of the Commission, Member States shall provide it with information on the allocation of the amounts received from the Fund.

Article 20

Assistance from the Fund shall not change the conditions of competition in a way incompatible with the principles contained in the relevant provisions of the Treaty, as elaborated in the principles for the coordination of the general regional aid schemes. In particular, the provisions of this Regulation shall not prejudice the application of Articles 92, 93 and 94 of the Treaty, particularly as regards establishing and realigning the areas aided for regional purposes referred to in Article 3 and in respect of the amount of the contributions from the Fund.

Article 21

1. Before 1 October each year the Commission shall present a report to the Council, the European Parliament and the Economic and Social Committee on the implementation of this Regulation during the preceding year.

2. This report shall also cover the financial managemment of the Fund and the conclusions drawn by the Commission from the checks made on the Fund's operations.

Article 22

On a proposal from the Commission, the Council shall re-examine this Regulation before 1 January 1981.

Article 23

This Regulation shall enter into force on the day following its publication in the *Official Journal of the European Communities*.

APPENDIX 5.2

COMMISSION RECOMMENDATION[29]
of 23 May 1979
to the Member States on the
regional development programmes
(79/535/EEC)

THE COMMISSION OF THE EUROPEAN COMMUNITIES,

Having regard to the Treaty establishing the European Economic Community, and in particular Article 155 thereof,

Having regard to Council Regulation (EEC) No 724/75 of 18 March 1975 establishing a European Regional Development Fund (ERDF),[a] as amended by Regulation (EEC) No 214/79,[b]

Having regard to the Council resolution of 6 February 1979 concerning the guidelines for Community regional policy,[c]

Having regard to the Commission's opinion of 23 May 1979 on the regional development programmes notified to it by the Member States pursuant to Article 6 of Regulation (EEC) No 724/75,

Whereas regional development programmes are to serve both as a point of reference for projects submitted for ERDF assistance and — in accordance with the aforesaid Council resolution — as the most appropriate framework for the practical implementation of coordination of national regional policies, and of the Community's regional policy;

Whereas, for the purposes of such coordination, the Member States and the Commission must be adequately informed of national policies aimed at achieving a better balance in the territorial distribution of economic activities, including such special measures as are taken with this aim in regions not eligible for ERDF assistance;

Whereas adoption by Member States of a uniform regional programme period would permit a greater measure of comparability between programmes and would make it easier to coordinate them at Community level with the medium-term economic policy programme being drawn up;

Whereas the general economic context and regional implications of the various national or Community sectoral policies are not sufficiently

---

[a] OJ No L73, 21. 3. 1975, p. 1.
[b] OJ No L35, 9. 2. 1979, p. 1.
[c] OJ No C36, 9. 2. 1979, p. 10.

taken into account in the analysis of the regional economic and social situation given in the programmes examined;

Whereas, as regards Community policies in particular, the Commission and the Council made known in the resolution of 6 February 1979 their intention of taking fuller account of the regional impact of such policies; whereas, furthermore, implementation of the specific Community measures referred to in Article 13 of Regulation (EEC) No 724/75 also depends on an accurate assessment of the regional impact of these policies and of the measures taken by the Community;

Whereas a number of special problems arise in certain frontier regions; whereas effective coordination of the regional development measures taken by the Member States concerned may make a significant contribution towards resolving those problems;

Whereas setting quantified development objectives for each of the regions concerned presents various difficulties, notably as regards job creation; whereas, for this reason, the Commission will, as requested by the Regional Policy Committee, accord priority to the study of regionalized labour balance sheets;

Whereas Regulation (EEC) No 724/75 in its amended version has adopted a broader concept of infrastructure than that previously applied (direct link with industrial and service investment) but stipulates, in Article 4 (2) (b), that infrastructure investments may be financed by the ERDF only when the regional development programmes show that they contribute to the development of the region in question;

Whereas, in parallel with regional policy measures proper such as regional aid schemes or infrastructure investments carried out for regional development purposes, Member States take measures, whether of a regional nature or not, under other national or Community policies which have indirect but important effects on regional development: on these the programmes examined in general provide little detail;

Whereas regional policy measures regarded as being of prime importance for regional development are not in all cases described in sufficient detail in the regional development programmes examined; whereas, where ERDF assistance is concerned, Regulation (EEC) No 724/75 provides that the Commission determine the priorities for assistance after having examined these programmes;

Whereas, although the regional development programmes examined generally indicate the State's commitments of finance to regional development, they only rarely mention transfers between different levels of government or finance from regional or subregional sources;

whereas sufficient information on these matters is essential if national regional policies are to be more effectively compared;

Whereas a number of regional development programmes neither provide for multiannual financial programming of infrastructure investment nor give the volume of investments to be made by public enterprises or by major private undertakings under planning agreements;

Whereas effective coordination of national regional policies and of Community regional policy is possible only if information is available on the Member States' intentions as to the future use, at regional level, of Community financial resources from the different financial instruments established for structural purposes;

Whereas the programmes notified generally contain sufficient information on their implementation, although some of them are not specific enough about the timing of the projected investments and the systematic assessment of the impact of the measures taken,

HEREBY RECOMMENDS THAT THE MEMBER STATES:

1. Take the measures necessary to ensure that development programmes communicated to it as reference instruments for projects submitted for assistance from the ERDF reflect all aspects of national regional policies and can thus be used as a framework for policy coordination at Community level.

2. Communicate to the Commission, in addition to the regional development programmes for regions in which the ERDF is to provide assistance, and in so far as regional policy measures are applied in other regions, the principal measures whose aim is a better regional balance over the whole of the country, including the so-called disincentives, either in the form of programmes or in another form.

3. Adopt, for the next regional development programmes to be drawn up, a uniform programme period coinciding with that chosen for the fifth medium-term economic programme (1981 to 1985); for the financial part of this five-year programme two periods could be adopted.

4. Take fuller account, in the analysis of the economic and social situation in each region, on the one hand of the implications of national policies or measures in areas such as the restructuring of certain sectors, transport, energy, agriculture, fishing, the environment, physical planning, certain social measures and vocational training and, on the other of the most significant effects of Community policies and measures, particularly in the fields of

agriculture, external trade relations and the restructuring of certain sectors.

5. Include in the above analysis, where it concerns frontier regions, the specific aspects that stem from their special geographical situation.

6. Provide, where the setting of development objectives for jobs is concerned, at least quantified forecasts of job deficits in each region for the years 1981 to 1985 and take further account in this connection of the tertiary sector, including tourism, and of the agricultural sector.

7. Bring out more clearly, when setting infrastructure objectives, the link that should exist between investments in infrastructure and the conditions that affect the development of a region, thereby making it possible to assess better the need for such investment and the priorities in this field and, more particularly, consider not only regional infrastructure proper but also national infrastructure of real regional importance.

8. Incorporate gradually, among the measures permitting attainment of the development objectives and alongside direct regional policy measures, measures arising from other national or Community policies which vary with the region or which have a clear regional impact. Such measures may concern the policy areas referred to in point 4.

9. Indicate more clearly in regional development programmes the aspects of national regional policy that are regarded as having priority, whether geographical or in terms of the type of measure to be taken.

10. Make the financial programming of regional development more transparent by supplementing the relevant information with details of financial transfers between different levels of government and of finance from regional or subregional sources.

11. Draw up a multiannual financial programme for infrastructure investment, where a programme of this type does not yet exist, and indicate, where such information is available, the volume of investment to be made during the programme period by public enterprises or by major private undertakings as part of planning agreements.

12. Include in future regional development programmes, alongside more detailed information on their intentions for the future use of ERDF resources, information concerning the other Community financial instruments, thereby permitting, at regional level,

greater cohesion between the various financial measures of a structural nature taken by the Community.

13. Give a timetable for implementing the measures planned under regional development programmes and provide a more systematic analysis of the impact of the different regional policy measures, particularly on employment.

This recommendation is addressed to the Member States.

Done at Brussels, 23 May 1979.

For the Commission

Antonio GIOLITTI

Member of the Commission

Notes

[1] Norbert Vanhove and Leo H. Klaassen, *Regional Policy — A European Approach* (Farnborough: Saxon House, 1980), p. 385.

[2] The persistence of the disparities is documented in Commission of the European Communities, *The Regions of Europe: First Periodic Report on the Social and Economic Situation of the Regions of the Community* (Brussels: January 1981).

[3] C.E.C., Première communication de la Commission sur la politique régionale dans la C.E.E. (Brussels: June 1965).

[4] European Parliament, 15 June 1968.

[5] *Official Journal of the European Communities*, No. C38 (18 April 1972). A lengthy list of such examples can be found in Vanhove and Klaassen, *op. cit.*, pp. 385–401.

[6] *Official Journal of the European Communities*, No. L 73 (21 March 1975).

[7] Commission of the European Communities, *Fourteenth General Report on the Activities of the European Communities in 1980* (Luxembourg: 1981), p. 146.

[8] Vanhove and Klaassen, *op. cit.*, p. 423.

[9] "On 16 December the Council amended the Regional Fund Regulation by establishing a quota for Greece and adjusting the quotas of the other Member States as follows: Belgium: 1.11%; Denmark: 1.06%; Federal Republic of Germany: 4.65%; France: 13.64%; Greece: 13.00%; Ireland: 5.94%; Italy: 35.49%; Luxembourg: 0.07%; Netherlands: 1.24%; United Kingdom: 23.80%. These quotas will apply for 1981." *Fourteenth General Report on the Activities of the European Communities in 1980*, p. 147.

[10] Commission of the European Communities, *European Regional Development Fund, Fifth Annual Report* (Brussels: 1980), p. 23. Unless otherwise stated, all 1979 data cited are drawn from this report.

[11] Commission of the European Communities, *European Regional Development Fund, Fourth Annual Report* (Brussels, Luxembourg: 1979), p. 23.

[12] This excludes Greenland and the French Overseas Departments, from the *size* point of view, but they are eligible and do receive ERDF aid.

[13] Cited from Commission of the European Communities. *The Regional Development Programmes*, Regional Policy Series No. 17 (Brussels: May, 1979), p. 240.

[14] *Ibid.*, p. 239.

[15] *Ibid.*, footnote 1, p. 239.

¹⁶ *Official Journal of the European Communities*, No. C69 (24 March 1976), p. 4, cited in full by the Commission of the European Communities, *The Regional Development Programmes*, p. 267.

¹⁷ *Ibid.*, p. 270.

¹⁸ *Ibid.*, p. 7.

¹⁹ *Ibid.*, p. 7.

²⁰ In Appendix 5.2, it can be seen that these points are numbered 2, 4, and 6 respectively.

²¹ ERDF, *Fourth Annual Report* (Brussels: 1979), p. 22.

²² *Ibid.*, pp. 53—55.

²³ ERDF, *Fifth Annual Report* (Brussels: 1980), pp. 57—58.

²⁴ ERDF, *Fourth Annual Report*, pp. 55—58.

²⁵ *Ibid.*, p. 9. Also see ERDF, *Fifth Annual Report*, p. 70.

²⁶ ERDF, *Fourth Annual Report*, p. 9.

²⁷ ERDF, *Fifth Annual Report*, p. 24.

²⁸ Published in *Official Journal of the European Communities*, No. C36 (9 February 1979).

²⁹ *Official Journal of the European Communities*, No. L143/9 (12 June 1979).

The European Social Fund: An Instrument For Regional Adjustment

6

I. Introduction: ECSC Social Programmes

When the European Coal and Steel Community (ECSC) was established in 1951, provision was made for social programmes to facilitate the structural adjustments anticipated for those key sectors.

Retraining of workers for jobs within and outside coal and steel production, mobility and housing assistance (via soft-loan provisions), even help to the member governments to establish alternative employment opportunities — these were all an integral part of the ECSC mandate. Accordingly, over 350 million EUA had been allocated to help some 650,000 workers re-adapt and find jobs inside, and outside, the coal and steel sectors between 1952 and 1980. By 1980, some 150,000 dwellings had also been made available as a result of ECSC financial participation. Essential to the framework of ECSC social adjustment assistance has been the integral co-operation of effort with the governments of the member countries. In recent years, the major beneficiary has been the United Kingdom.

II. The European Social Fund and the Treaty of Rome

The social programmes established by the ECSC were relatively focused; they were linked to adjustment problems of the coal and steel sectors. The social programmes of the European Economic Community have clearly had a far harder time gaining definition because of the scope of the EEC as a whole.

Nevertheless, alongside the ECSC social programmes have evolved those of the EEC, the most important instrument being the European Social Fund. Essentially the rationale has been to "promote the geographical and occupational mobility of workers within the Community, particularly those workers whose jobs were affected by the development of the Common Market."[1] In the process, particular groups have been isolated for special help — including young people, women, the handicapped, and migrant workers.

The rather broad flavour of the Treaty of Rome towards a social mandate is captured in Articles 117 and 118, extracts of which read as follows:

Member States agree upon the need to promote improved working conditions and an improved standard of living for workers, so as to make possible their harmonisation while the improvement is being maintained.

They believe that such a development will ensue not only from the functioning of the common market, which will favour the harmonisation of social systems, but also from the procedures provided for in this Treaty and from the approximation of provisions laid down by law, regulation or administrative action. (cited from Article 117)

and

... the Commission shall have the task of promoting close co-operation between Member States in the social field, particularly in matters relating to:
— Employment
— Labour law and working conditions
— Basic and advanced vocational training
— Social security
— Prevention of occupational accidents and diseases
— Occupational hygiene
— The right of association and collective bargaining between employers and workers.

To this end the Commission shall act in close contact with Member States by making studies, delivering opinions and arranging consultations both on problems arising at national level and on those of concern to international organisations.

Before delivering opinions provided for in this Article, the Commission shall consult the Economic and Social Committee. (cited from Article 118)

Finally, Article 125, of the Treaty of Rome, spells out operational directives:

On application by a Member State ... [the Social Fund is empowered to] meet 50 per cent of the expenditure incurred ... by that State or by a body governed by public law [droit public] for the purposes of:

(a) Ensuring productive re-employment of workers by means of:
    vocational re-training;
    resettlement allowances;

(b) Granting aid for the benefit of workers whose employment is reduced or temporarily suspended, in whole or in part, as a result of the conversion of an undertaking to other production, in order that they may retain the same wage level pending their full re-employment.

The assistance of the Fund is to be granted, in the case of retraining and rehousing, upon the demand of the member state concerned when the recipient worker has been re-employed in his new trade or location for a period of at least six months. In the case of reconversion, the member government is requested to have "previously submitted a plan, drawn up by the concern in question, for its conversion and for the financing thereof." If the Commission approves the project, payment from the Fund will be made to workers once they have completed at least six months' employment with the reconverted enterprise.

III. The European Social Fund

1960–1972

The European Social Fund started very slowly. Indeed between 1960 and 1972, it only allocated some 264 million EUA. This was hardly more than the ECSC social programme (during the same period), albeit the latter was far more concentrated. There appears to have been a dominant view that the Community was to attach secondary importance to social policies, seeing them rather as the preserve of the national governments. "Each country depending on its level of development and the role played by the trade union movement, (had) . . . evolved very complex systems of social security, worker protection and aid for the worst-off social groups."[2]

The European Commission's official documentation for the period gives the following assessment. The Social Fund proved

> little more than a passive 'clearing' house for money spent by Member States on retraining and resettling workers made redundant as a result of economic and industrial readjustments within the Community. The Fund considered vocational retraining and resettlement projects submitted by the Member States and could then reimburse up to half the costs of these projects

> . . . In practice . . . the Fund tended to benefit those Member States whose governments were most adept at claiming reimbursements rather than those with the greatest unemployment and structural underemployment problems. For example, by 1972 Germany had received more than half the total grants made by the Fund even though it consistently had low unemployment. This was because the German Government was more efficient at filing its claims and

because reimbursement of training costs depended upon workers having been re-employed — a relatively easy condition to fulfil in booming Germany. Italy, on the other hand, with high unemployment, fared extremely badly under the old Fund while France appeared to be the main paymaster in the scheme.[3]

1973–1980 — Towards a More Aggressive Social Policy

A number of pressures had been building up for the Social Fund to become more dynamic. On the one hand, the proposed entry of Ireland, Denmark, and the United Kingdom, in 1973, was preceded by a great deal of self-evaluation by the six as they reviewed the appropriate terms and implications of the expansion. On the other hand, a number of reviews had thoughtfully urged a changing attitude to the Social Fund.[4] Moreover, the members, somewhat exhilarated by the economic progress of the 1960s, were viewing the EEC in increasingly wider-ranging terms. There was talk of a common monetary system and, leading to the subsequent Lomé Convention, of a new economic relationship with the Third World countries.

Such additional steps, built on European economic strength in overall terms, could be expected to aggravate the unevenness of the development of the 1960s. Not merely had there been regional problems within the six (e.g., the Mezzogiorno and southwest France were not making appreciable gains in relative terms), but also, within the labour market, underprivileged members of the work-force (e.g., women, the handicapped, migrant workers) were clearly not being adequately catered for.

Therefore, when the nine met for the first time (as a formal group) in Paris, at the end of 1972, they endorsed a 'new deal' for the Community, with four main elements (the social programme being integral, as distinct from the more traditional 'afterthought'). The four main features were the following:

1. Steps to establish an Economic and Monetary Union (initially via the 'snake in the tunnel' mechanism)

2. The establishment of a Regional Development Fund

3. The co-ordination of Community economic and aid policy *vis-à-vis* Third World countries

4. A social action programme — focused on the three broad objectives of full and better employment, the improvement of living and working conditions, and the increased involvement of management and labour in the Community decision process and of workers in their own organizations.

For several reasons, chief of which were the OPEC oil crisis and the departure from central leadership roles of three of the key figures

Table 6.1
APPROPRIATIONS FOR COMMITMENTS
(Authorized for 1980)

(million EUA)

Operations to assist agriculture and the textile industry	29
Operations to assist young people	358
Operations to assist migrant workers	30
Operations to assist women	20
Aid to improve the employment situation in specific regions, industries or groups of firms	395.5
Operations to assist handicapped persons	74
Consequences of industrial conversion	token entry
Pilot schemes and preparatory studies	3
Total	909.5

Source: Commission of the European Communities, *Fourteenth General Report on the Activities of the European Communities in 1980* (Brussels: 1981), p. 133.

Table 6.2
APPLICATIONS APPROVED IN 1980

	Amount (million EUA)	% per state
Belgium	29.1	2.9
Denmark	19.4	1.9
FR of Germany	108.6	10.7
France	195.8	19.3
Ireland	82.9	8.2
Italy	328.5	32.4
Luxembourg	0.9	0.1
Netherlands	18.3	1.8
United Kingdom	229.6	22.7
Community	1013.1*	100.0

Source: Commission of the European Communities, *Fourteenth General Report on the Activities of the European Communites in 1980* (Brussels: 1981), p. 134.

Note: * This total differs from that in Table 6.1 (909.5 million EUA), because Table 6.2 data include unused appropriations for commitments from the previous year, which were available for reallocation.

(Chancellor Brandt, Prime Minister Heath and, through his death, President Pompidou), the shorter-term impact of the summit meeting of 1972 (Paris) was severely weakened. The longer-term effect, however, can be traced. In the particular case of the social action programme, the Social Fund was allocated larger budgets and began to play a more assertive role, essentially (as has been the case with the ERDF) of a catalytic nature.

As one main consequence, the number of interventions has substantially multiplied and, for 1980, the annual commitments had reached 909 million EUA (see Table 6.1). This figure has to be set against an overall demand for Fund assistance of 1,900 million EUA, thus necessitating a more rigorous application of selection criteria.[5] Whereas, in the past, country allocations were made by a nearly automatic process based on the efficiency with which member governments filed applications, recent allocations have begun to reflect more clearly a sense of Community policy priorities. Thus, in 1980, some 32 per cent assistance was for Italy, 23 per cent for the United Kingdom, 19 per cent for France, and only some 11 per cent for Germany. Ireland on a per capita basis fared generously, with some 8 per cent (see Table 6.2).

As of 1980, and following a further reappraisal in 1977, the Social Fund's work emphasizes eight priority areas.

Regional Development

The amended Social Fund Regulation, adopted in December 1977, provides that at least 50 per cent of all aid granted has to be channelled into the 'less-favoured regions' (defined as those regions eligible for assistance from the European Regional Development Fund), and that shared-cost rates of Social Fund grants to five priority regions (Mezzogiorno, Ireland, Northern Ireland, Greenland, and the French Overseas Departments) could reach a ceiling of 55 per cent from 50 per cent. Grants for the 'less-favoured regions', as a proportion of overall Social Fund aid, in fact increased from 73 per cent in 1976 to 85 per cent in 1979.[6] The emphasis of the Fund has been on the provision of a wider training to those seeking jobs. It is estimateed that some 235,000 people in 1978 found jobs in the five priority regions, helped by Social Fund aided projects.[7]

Young People

Almost 40 per cent of the total unemployed people in the Community are under 25 years of age, even though they constitute less than 20 per cent of the working population. The Fund therefore supports numerous vocational training programmes directed at this age group. The selection criteria adopted give priority to requests affecting small- and medium-sized companies as well as those benefiting young girls and women in occupations from which they have been traditionally excluded. New job creation programmes for the unemployed under 25 are also now in process.[8]

Handicapped

Programmes of a wide variety have been helped by the Social Fund, although preference is given to efforts to employ or re-employ handicapped people in competitive industry, especially in zones where such activities are least developed.[9]

Migrant Workers

It is estimated that over 20 per cent of the 6 million migrant workers living in the Community were unemployed in 1978. Often they lack even rudimentary training, and the Fund participated (1978) in organizing language and vocational training courses for some 130,000 adults and some 100,000 of their children (school enrichment programmes). Some 4,000 teachers and social workers were also given specialist training under the Fund in 1978.[10]

Women

The Fund covered both traditional vocational training activities and measures specifically designed to give women access to employment. Two categories of women benefit from this latter interventionary approach: those who wish to start work again after a long gap — usually due to family reasons (about 70 per cent of the cases in 1978), and those who have lost their jobs.[11]

Technical Progress and Groups of Companies

Numerous training programmes, for both workers and managers, have been supported, particularly linked to the application of modernized processes and approaches.[12]

Textiles

The majority of Fund-assisted work, in this problem area, has been aimed at giving additional qualifications to workers wishing to stay in the most viable segments of the industry. Only 15 per cent of the requests for Fund help in 1978 concerned people ready to take jobs in other sectors.[13]

Agriculture

The main purpose of Fund-assisted interventions, in this sector, has been to train people for leaving the land, though allowances to help relocate families in rural areas and to provide farmers with complementary activities (such as in rural parks and nature reserves) have been supported.[14]

Pilot Projects

A substantial number of quite varied pilot projects and studies have been undertaken in the above sectors. Their results are distributed among the member states as a means of sharing project and policy information and of improving the quality of national and non-governmental agency programmes.[15]

The Fund as Catalyst

Table 6.1 shows the manner in which the European Social Fund was allocated for 1980. The allocations to these sectoral (e.g., agricultural and textile industry) and target groups (e.g., young people and migrant workers) fit within the overall guide-lines of providing at least 50 per cent of all aid to the 'less-favoured regions'. However, the European Social Fund does not operate within the rigid quota system (country by country) framework of the European Regional Development Fund, a point viewed as being in the Social Fund's favour by one of its former directors, Michael Shanks.[16] In the review of the European Regional Development Fund in the previous chapter, it can be seen that this writer is convinced of the merits of the quota system in that case. In the case of the Social Fund, it is felt that Shank's view is substantially coloured by his years of administrative problems, during which he saw the merits of the greater flexibility of the Social Fund. It should be noted that such a view is also quite widespread among officials of the ERDF, for much the same mix of reasons. However, the advantage of the quota system is that it forces member states to identify their regional priorities — as a Community. Having said that, it is believed that the case for a quota system is somewhat less strong for the Social Fund than for the ERDF, because of the different goals of the Social Fund and because of the merits of some extra flexibility to focus on such problems as migrant workers, moving from poorer to more prosperous regions.

The European Social Fund has, after a very modest start, grown fairly substantially: 1980 allocations were some 909 million EUA, compared with 1,165 million EUA for the European Regional Development Fund and loans made by the European Investment Bank of some 2,950 million EUA, for the same year.

As has already been said of the ERDF, the Social Fund is relatively small, given the scale of social programmes financed by the member states and given also the dimensions of the social problems faced by many parts of the European Community. Thus, even with the increased size of the Social Fund, it can only be expected to have a very marginal impact as an instrument for social policy, on the one hand, and as an instrument more particularly of regional adjustment, on the other hand.

As is the case with the ERDF, aid from the European Social Fund has not been intended to substitute for usual government expenditures in its areas of priority, but rather it is intended to encourage the relevant authorities to increase efforts. It is similarly unclear to what extent this actually occurs.

As also in the case of the ERDF, it can be asked whether the Social Fund is really needed, given its relatively small size. The primary case for the Fund rests on its role as a catalyst. To some degree it is the 'social conscience' of the Community. It has played a harmonizing role, for example, in helping migrant workers from within Common Market countries to carry over benefits in various ways. Through its studies and the so-called 'Social Budget', which is an effort to specify the social budgets of the nation members in a consistent and comparable manner, the Fund has performed a 'gap identification' role. By communicating details of country programmes to each other, it has provided a much needed basis for the exchange of lessons.

Finally, like the other agencies of the European Commission, the Social Fund should not be assessed in isolation. It is simply one part of a fabric of activities that make for a binding, rather than a divisive, process of European development and planning.

IV. The Fund as an Instrument of Regional Adjustment: Points for Canadian Review

As an instrument of regional adjustment, the European Social Fund has allocated a high proportion of its assistance to the less-developed areas of the Community, with a focus on the five priority regions (Greenland, the French Overseas Departments, Ireland, Northern Ireland, and the Mezzogiorno in Italy). The average amount of aid per capita of active population in these five areas from the Fund for 1978 has been calculated as 34 EUA as distinct from an average of 7 EUA for the Community as a whole.[17]

The main point is that the Fund is viewed as having a substantial regional adjustment mandate, and while it has developed criteria for priorities according to main target groups, the onus of policy and programme design and development is firmly with the member-state governments. Thus it does not impose homogeneous programmes across the Community as a whole, but aids the individualized programmes within each member state, at the same time acting as an information and lesson-sharing catalyst.

There is no comparable agency to the Social Fund in Canada. Its far from clearly defined role is somewhat diffused in a number of federal and provincial programmes, such as those of the Employment and Immigration Commission and the Department of Labour. The importance of emphasizing the social problems of people in depressed regions, and the need for coherent social programmes to facilitate regional adjustment (for example, for migrant workers), is a main underpinning of the Social Fund. The need to identify and focus assistance to specific categories of people as target groups for benefits, and not merely to pour financial incentives into somewhat abstract areas of land, is clearly one of the Social Fund's biggest challenges in defining its goals. This is an aspect of federal regional planning, in Canada, that has possibly not been given the same degree of 'programming focus', but has been approached — in other respects more logically — through the fiscal-equalization transfer arrangements. The latter kind of programme is not available to the EEC at this time.

The manner in which the Fund has developed criteria for the priority interventions (such as migrant workers), and the manner in which it has related (in more recent years) to regional programmes, is somewhat reminiscent of the rather faltering efforts in similar directions under the Canadian fund for rural/regional economic development (FRED) programmes — particularly those in Prince Edward Island, the Interlake, and the Gaspé.

While it is apparent that the Fund does provide useful comparative background for reviewing policy options for Canadian social and regional adjustment, it is not clear that any such Fund is appropriate to the Canadian context.

Notes

[1] European Documentation, *The European Community and Vocational Training* (Luxembourg: June 1980), p. 27.

[2] Commission of the European Communities, *The Community Today* (Brussels: 1979), p. 116.

[3] European Documentation, *The European Community's Social Policy* (Luxembourg: February 1978), p. ii.

[4] For example, P.N. Lemerle, 'Le Fonds social européen', *Reflets et perspectives de la vie économique* (no. 2, 1970).

[5] Commission of the European Communities, *Fourteenth General Report on the Activities of the European Communities in 1980* (Brussels: 1981), p. 133.

[6] European Regional Development Fund, *Fourth Annual Report* (Brussels: 1979), pp. 58–59. See also Commission of the European Communities, *Eighth Report on the Activities of the European Social Fund, Financial Year 1979* (Brussels: July 1980).

[7] *The European Social Fund*, European File (Luxembourg: Nov/Dec 1979), p. 4.

[8] *Ibid.*, pp. 4–5.

[9] *Ibid.*, p. 5.

[10] *Ibid.*, p. 5.

11 *Ibid.*, p. 6.

12 *Ibid.*, p. 6.

13 *Ibid.*, p. 6.

14 *Ibid.*, p. 6.

15 *Ibid.*, p. 7.

16 Michael Shanks, *European Social Policy, Today and Tomorrow* (Oxford: Pergamon Press, 1977), p. 26.

17 For further details, see Commission of the European Communities, *Seventh Report on the Activities of the European Social Fund, Financial Year 1978* (Brussels: June 1979).

The Common Agricultural Policy and Regional Development

7

I. Introduction

Regional development has never been a central thrust of Community agricultural policy. Indeed it is quite likely that the more prosperous farmers, in the richer regions (largely in the North), have been the main beneficiaries of the Common Agricultural Policy (CAP) and not the farmers in the poorer (more peripheral) areas.[1] This is illustrated in Map 7.1. However, it is quite clear that CAP is by default, if not design, an EEC instrument of major significance for regional development. In part, this is because many of the poorer regions do have a relatively large proportion of labour in the agricultural sector. In part, this stems from the fact that some 75 per cent of the Community budget has traditionally been allocated to agricultural policy.

It is apparent that somewhat more weight is now being placed on defining the regional development role of the Common Agricultural Policy. For example, on 22 March 1971, the Council resolved that "from 1972 onwards the European Agricultural Guidance and Guarantee Fund (EAGGF) may be used for measures to foster regional development."[2]

More recently, in June 1977, the Commission emphasized that it was indispensable "to introduce henceforth into the underlying ideas and application of the principal Community policies an assessment and consideration of the territorial dimension of those policies. This will allow policies to be adopted taking account of their impact on the regions and, in the event, to adopt the measures needed to implement those policies fully and to correct possible negative effects in the regions."[3]

It is also apparent that it has been "difficult to conciliate the aims of an agricultural sectoral policy seeming to help competition between regions with a view to increasing European productivity and those of regional policy designed to remove the handicaps of regions where development is less than the Community average."[4]

Map 7.1
REGIONAL INDICATOR OF CAP SUPPORT INTENSITY*

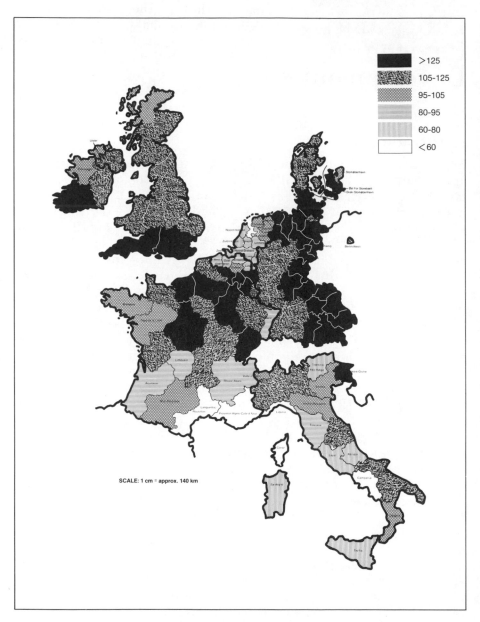

Legend:

- >125
- 105-125
- 95-105
- 80-95
- 60-80
- <60

SCALE: 1 cm = approx. 140 km

Source: Commission of the European Communities, *The Regions of Europe* (Brussels: January 1981), p. 74 (and pp. 184–89 for methodology).

Note: Data used are for a two-year average — 1976/77.

   * EUR=100.

II. Agricultural Change in the EEC

Backcloth to the Treaty of Rome

The shape of the Treaty of Rome and the way the Common Agricultural Policy evolved have to be viewed in a broad historical context if one is to appreciate why some 75 per cent of the Community budget has been allocated solely to one sector, agriculture. Also, the budget has to be viewed as only one indicator of EEC priorities. The dismantling of trade obstacles within the Community and the European Investment Bank's role obviously impacted heavily on the manufacturing sectors and also (in the EIB case) on energy, transport and, quite broadly defined, infrastructure.

When the Treaty of Rome was signed, agriculture was undergoing traumatic changes that were reaching deeply into the societies of Europe.

The 1930s, in Europe, had seen a considerable expansion of agricultural capacity and actual production, coincident with a shrinking of effective demand. Hence there came a slump in world market prices for food and, as a countermeasure, an increase in protection for farmers by West European governments. Inter-country specialization tended to be reduced.

The 1940s saw a quite different situation — a concern to ensure adequate supplies of food during, and in the aftermath of, the Second World War. West European agricultural capacity was severely damaged. Government involvement extended from protection (by way of, for example, tariffs, quotas, and price subsidies) to more direct management involvement (for example, with the introduction of systems of price controls and guarantees).[5]

By the late 1950s, a new situation was on hand, namely a revolution in the use of applied agricultural technology, not merely with the use of increased capital equipment, but also with the application of improved pesticides, seed stocks, and animal husbandry. Despite a growing shift of labour from rural to urban societies, from agriculture to the service sector and to a far lesser degree to industry, the increases in productivity (combined with the depressing drag of home market elasticities of demand for food) were resulting in downward pressures on food prices. The liberal use of various price support systems resulted in growing food surpluses. This situation was made more extreme by the huge food stocks being developed in the United States, for the same general reasons.

The pressures on Western governments, at the time of the Treaty of Rome, were therefore of the following kinds:

- Concern for the protection of incomes for farmers, many of whom were quite heavily in debt as they were financing capital equipment.

- Concern for the maintenance of some degree of rural-urban balance, in the face of pressures on the congested towns.

- Concern for long-term, secure access to food supply. This produced a somewhat mixed view about the gains from specialization when that could mean depending on food supplies from more distant regions of the Community (and the globe). The problems of the Second World War years were not readily forgotten.

Post−Treaty of Rome Era

The post−Treaty of Rome era continued to witness a substantial movement away from agricultural employment. Without the mish-mash of national programmes and the evolving Community Agricul-tural Policy, the adjustment might well have been yet more extreme. The trade-off between efficiency, measured in somewhat narrow terms, and social dislocation would have been more starkly evident, even though the periodic mountains of surplus food presumably would have been avoided.

In 1958, in the nine member countries, some 19 million people were employed in agriculture;[6] by 1980, this had fallen to some 8 million, and recent estimates suggest that the decline will be of the order of 3 per cent per year to 1990, resulting in an agricultural labour force, in 1990, of some 5.6 million.[7] At least some of this decline, it is suggested, will be as a result of the retirement of present farmers; more than 25 per cent of the agricultural labour force (for 1980) was over 55 years of age.

Between 1960 and 1975, the number of farms fell by an average of 2.3 per cent per year, a trend that is forecast to continue.[8] Thus it is estimated that the (approximately) 5.1 million farms in the nine-member Community in 1975 will fall to about 3.6 million by 1990. A similar trend is forecast for Greece, Spain, and Portugal, from some 4.8 million farms in 1975 to some 3 million by 1990.[9] Part-time farming now occurs in some 60.0 per cent of the farms in the ten-member Community, a trend that is likely to increase.

Although the size of farms varies considerably among European Community members, the average size of farms has tended to grow. Future estimates suggest an increase of average farm size from some 17 hectares in 1977 to some 24 hectares by 1990. The present spread between countries is substantial; thus (in 1976) the United Kingdom was at the top of the list with an average farm size of 64 hectares, and Italy at the bottom with 7.5 hectares. Such numbers have to be interpreted cautiously, particularly when viewing countries such as Ireland and France (above the average) and Germany (below the average), given differences of climate, terrain, and soil conditions, and efficiencies of different forms of agricultural production. Figure 7.1

Figure 7.1
NINE MEMBER STATES' SHARE IN FINAL
AGRICULTURAL PRODUCTION, BY PRODUCT, 1976
(percentage)

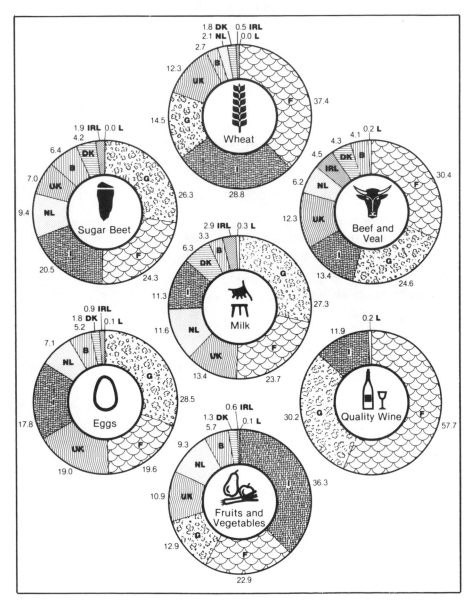

Source: European Documentation, *The Agricultural Policy of the European Community* (Luxembourg: 1979), p. 11.

illustrates the different shares in a number of main agricultural outputs between the member countries.

III. Common Agricultural Policy

Goals and Principles

Four main objectives had been laid down in the Treaty of Rome (Article 39) for the Common Agricultural Policy.

- Increased agricultural productivity

- A 'fair standard of living' for the agricultural community

- Stable markets

- The ensurance that supplies reach consumers at reasonable prices.

Each one of these goals has required substantial interpretation and each has been the subject of often acrimonious debate. Essentially three principles have been laid down as the 'golden rule of the CAP':[10]

- The single-market principle for agricultural output, which implies internal trade liberalization and also the harmonization of administrative, health, and other such regulations

- The Community preference principle, whereby EEC agricultural products are protected from imports from outside the Community and Community farmers are also effectively paid an export subsidy in circumstances when world prices are below (artificially protected) EEC prices (see Figure 7.2)

- The financial solidarity principle, which is operationalized through the EAGGF, which finances the CAP.

The market organizations to pursue these objectives and principles have been progressively developed, until in 1981 virtually all agricultural production was covered. There are four main categories of agricultural protection:[11]

- The support price, which covers 70 per cent of production (including most cereals, milk, beef, some fruit and vegetables)

- External protection, which covers some 25 per cent of production (items considered of 'secondary necessity', such as flowers, some wines, rice, some fruit, eggs, and poultry)

- Additional product aid, which covers some 2.5 per cent of production (being a 'deficiency' gap between market prices and government guaranteed floor prices, for a few items such as durum wheat, olive oil, and tobacco)

Figure 7.2
LEVY AND REFUND SYSTEM FOR WHEAT

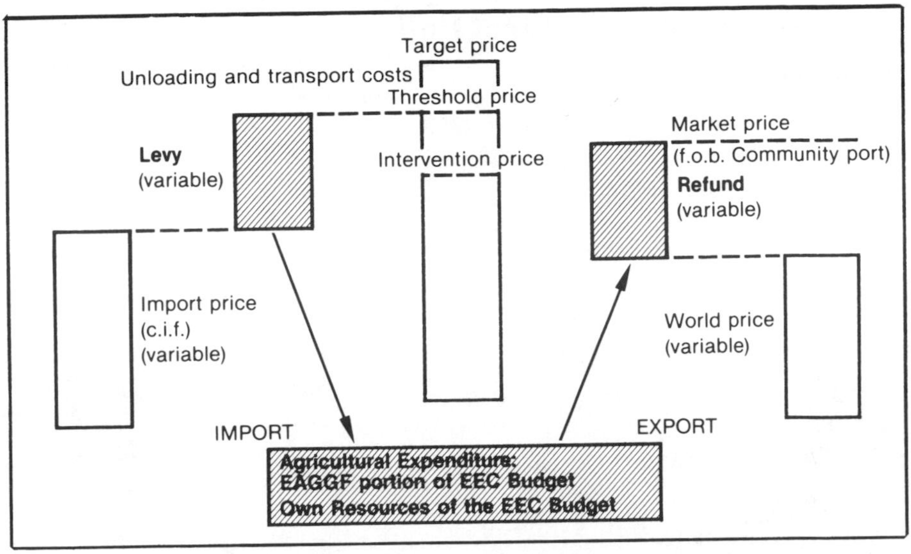

Source: European Documentation, *The Agricultural Policy of the European Community* (Luxembourg: 1979), p. 13.

- Flat rate aid, which applies to less than 1 per cent of total agricultural production (e.g., to cotton-seed, flax and hemp, hops, silkworms).

The EAGGF

The mechanism through which CAP is financed is the European Agricultural Guidance and Guarantee Fund (EAGGF). It is an integral part of the Community budget. The Fund was set up in 1962 and detailed operational regulations were spelled out in 1964.[12] The Fund has accounted for the largest share of European Community expenditures (consistently in the range of 75 to 80 per cent of the total EEC budget). It has two sections: guarantee and guidance.

1. The Guarantee Section

The lion's share of the EAGGF has been spent through its price Guarantee Section — largely on price compensatory measures and on refunds. Milk products have dominated the appropriations, followed by cereals and sugar. While it has served to raise agricultural earnings by artificially protecting the price levels of agricultural products within the framework, the Guarantee Section has had no particular regional development focus — albeit the poorer regions do

Table 7.1
EAGGF GUARANTEE SECTION APPROPRIATIONS 1980
AND DRAFT BUDGET 1981

	1980 appropriations	1981 draft budget[b]
Cereals and rice	1666.4	2267.7
Milk and milk products	4929.6	4313.0
Oils and fats	787.0	976.1
Sugar	696.5	739.9
Beef and veal	1178.0	1353.4
Pigmeat, sheepmeat, eggs and poultrymeat	244.0	488.0
Fruit and vegetables	659.0	730.1
Wine, tobacco	632.0	789.9
Other[a]	163.0	220.5
Refunds on processed products	275.0	294.0
Accession compensatory amounts	1.0	24.5
Monetary compensatory amounts	276.0	250.9
Total	11507.5	12448.0
Provisional appropriations EAGGF Guarantee Section	—	254.5
Grand Total	11507.5	12702.5

Source: Commission of the European Communities, *Fourteenth General Report on the Activities of the European Communities in 1980* (Brussels: 1981), p. 178.
[a] Including fisheries.
[b] Not including Chapter 10.0 appropriations (195 million EUA).

frequently depend more heavily on agricultural income than do many of their richer neighbours.

Table 7.1 illustrates the scale of Community support for agricultural prices for 1980. The scale of subsidies for milk and milk products, cereals, and beef is particularly notable, much of this going to the richer, more developed, and industrialized regions. Inasmuch as the total payments made, during 1980, by the European Regional Development Fund were some 726 million EUA , it can be seen that the subsidies *on milk alone* (under the EAGGF programme) were almost seven times as large.

2. The Guidance Section

The other main element of the EAGGF is the Guidance Section. While originally (Regulation 25/64) the Guidance Section was to correspond to some one third of the expenditures of the Guarantee Section, it has generally ranged between one fifteenth and one twentieth the size of the Guarantee Section. The general purpose of this section is to support structural measures, by the member states, to increase agricultural productivity and to upgrade the quality of the rural environment.

At the end of 1980, the Commission estimates the annual commitment appropriations for indirect measures to be about 325 million EUA — mainly for aid to hill farming and farming in selected, less-advantaged areas, for the non-marketing of milk and milk products, for the eradication of certain cattle diseases, and for drainage operations in less-favoured areas of Ireland.

Some 300 million EUA will have been granted as well to finance direct measures, in the form of 813 projects, over 1980. They include projects to improve processing and marketing conditions for some agricultural products, upgrading of public services in some rural areas, a common measure for forestry in some Mediterranean areas, and further help for irrigation projects in the Mezzogiorno.[13]

Historically, the richer regions presented more projects to the Fund than the poorer areas, creating a "bias in the operation of the [very modest] Guidance Section in favour of the richer agricultural regions."[14]

Broad Results

The European Commission assesses the broad results in terms of the main objectives of the Treaty of Rome regarding CAP. The following is a summary of their argument:[15]

1. Agricultural productivity has increased rapidly, on average by 6.7 per cent per year from 1968 to 1973 and by 2.5 per cent thereafter. Technical improvements, farm rationalization, and a reduction of the number of farmers by one third are given as major factors.

2. Agricultural incomes have risen by some 3 per cent between 1968 and 1979, but there are still many discrepancies between farm groups and also between sectors.

3. Market stability, in overall agricultural terms, has generally been accomplished over the past fifteen years — but not without many repercussions such as massive product surpluses at times (e.g., milk products have been especially problematic).

4. Supply security has generally been attained and reasonable consumer prices, for most products, have been achieved. On

average, prices paid to agricultural producers have increased by 8.5 per cent per year between 1973 and 1979, while the prices for food produce have increased by more than 11 per cent (as have general price levels).

The relationship of these broad indicators to the performance of CAP is not discussed in any detail, but given the relative size of EEC expenditures on agriculture, it would be unreasonable to suggest CAP has not had a fairly large impact. However, the trade-offs between 'efficiency' and 'cautious adjustment', with particular concern for social difficulties, has meant that CAP has supported a variety of directions, policies, and activities — many of which (from the vantage point of several objectives) lacked consistency in any purist sense.

In a review of 'directions for the future', the Commission highlights two main approaches. First, "the pursuit of a market balancing policy" requires "the regularization of the sectors in surplus." Secondly, Europe "must also step up agricultural specialization based on differing national conditions and promote the production of quality products. . . . the socio-structural policy must be strengthened by introducing new measures to accelerate the modernization of agriculture, to reduce income disparities and to promote the development of regions in specific difficulties."[16] Such broad statements, however, sweep grandly over the regional dimension, some of which are raised in a recent study by Henry.[17]

The Regional Impact of CAP

The recent study group report on the regional impact of CAP (headed by P. Henry) is far from adequately comprehensive or detailed. However, it does represent a significant step by the Commission to examine the regional implications of sectoral policies, in a *public* fashion. Some of the main conclusions are therefore of importance and merit citing.

- The . . . group . . . thought more detailed reflection necessary taking account of existing regional situations, to define *the regional aims to which the CAP should contribute in regions* while respecting community limitations. . . .[18]

- [Over the period 1964–1977] the regions most oriented towards a particular [type of agricultural] production have increased that production; regions where the output of this product has been low have abandoned it by degrees. The phenomenon is especially noticeable for cereals, pigs and poultry; it is less noticeable for milk and beef. For instance in 1976–1977 more than half the European regions featured an agricultural product representing alone between 30 and 50% of regional turnover; this emphasizes the present degree of regional sensitivity to market organisation mechanisms per product.[19]

- It is certain that the observed trends of regional specialisation correspond largely to the use of advantages, which are either natural (cereal producing areas close to ports) or structural and technical, existing prior to the CAP. It is no less true that the creation of a large market in agricultural products and the establishment of a common market organisation per product has accentuated these trends.[20]

- ... in view of substantial EAGGF expenditure on milk and cereals, producing regions principally located in northern regions obtain higher indicators [of CAP aid] than the southern regions where fruit, vegetable and wine predominate.[21]

- [The analysis also shows] the low productivity per hectare of Irish regions and the French South West and the small size of Italian structures and how these lead to expenditure per worker two or three times less than in areas of the Paris region or Northern Germany.[22]

- In consequence, within the current functioning of the financial mechanisms . . . , expenditure of the EAGGF is closely related to levels of agricultural output per worker and therefore to some extent to regional wealth level(s).[23]

- Without [the] possibility of attributing a decisive role to the CAP in aggravating growth imbalances in regional agricultural in-comes, one cannot avoid noting that the combination of these two mechanisms: proportional supports for volumes produced with higher supports for milk, cereals and sugar have accompanied growth in northern Community regions whereas the inverse process of weak social structural policy has affected the develop-ment of farm and holding structures and smaller support for products like fruit, vegetables and wines has been unable to correct the relative decline of regions in the south of the Community.[24]

- [The study group concludes that] if the CAP should contribute to regional policy aims it should: first *avoid increasing previous regional imbalances*, and to some extent *play a specific role in mitigating these imbalances*.[25]

They further state that "it seems indispensable for prices and market policies mechanisms to take more account of different situations in agricultural regions (regional specialisation, structural, technological and income levels) which even if unable to improve the situation of

Community regional agricultural imbalances in income at the present time might at least avoid the current continuing aggravation of these imbalances."[26]

IV. CAP and Canadian Regional Policy Issues

Two main conclusions, of relevance to Canadian regional policy, are drawn from the Common Agricultural Policy experience.

First, with due appreciation of the situation faced by the Community in 1957, nevertheless expenditures on agricultural policy lost all semblance of due proportion — given the many alternatives available within the broad Treaty of Rome mandate, and its subsequent appendages. For milk product subsidies alone to warrant seven times the entire allocation to the European Regional Development Fund (1980) indicates just how out of balance agricultural subsidies have become.

Secondly, any broad regional framework for agricultural policy has been more notable for its absence than for any moderating influence it may have contributed to the weighting given sectoral and regional priorities for CAP. Inasmuch as yardsticks of 'efficiency' have played their role, they apparently have been prescribed somewhat narrowly and, in many cases, in favour of sectors focused in the more prosperous farming regions (particularly in the North). The specific regional aids, linked particularly to the Guidance Section of the EAGGF, have been relatively trivial in the context of the problems of the poorer regions and when set beside the massive allocations to such industries as milk, under the Guarantee Section.

From a Canadian regional policy vantage point, such extreme parallels are hard, if not impossible, to find; CAP so dwarfs the rest of the EEC budget. However, three main points are raised.

1. Without broad regional development frameworks, with both generalized goals and (of great importance) systematic monitoring reviews, sectoral programmes and policies can readily become 'out of line'. It is not a tradition, in Canada, to review the regional impact and implications of federal sectoral policies — albeit piecemeal efforts are periodically made (often not for public consumption); broad regional goals appear still a gap in federal policy directions.

2. The Guidance Section of the EAGGF, in particular, has many points of similarity with the Canadian Agricultural and Rural/Regional Development Act (ARDA). Both are 'fleas on the elephant', when set beside the major, respective agricultural policies, and both work considerably in the extremely difficult milieu of less-advantaged rural areas that may require sustained aid until they can compete (using productivity yardsticks) with more prosperous regions. At the same time, such rural areas frequently have not been party to the (often massive) infrastructure investments that have frequently

reinforced (and often helped develop) the comparative advantage of the more prosperous regions. Lessons and insights are to be found for ARDA and similar Canadian programmes from the Guidance Section of the EAGGF, and also, it would appear, vice versa.

3. CAP might have prevented a social revolution among some EEC member countries and reduced the degree of tension between town and country. Such a judgement is virtually impossible to make. At the same time, the experiences of CAP (relevant to a wide spectrum of Canadian programmes) are that before the government starts to interfere with the 'three-legged stool' of demand, supply, and price, the package as a whole has to be understood and the likely impacts of interference carefully assessed. In the case of CAP, the emphasis has rather tended to focus on one 'leg of the stool' at a time, hence the lurching extremes.

Notes

[1] This is based on discussions with officials, less than adequate data, and an interpretation of the findings of P. Henry, *Study on the Regional Impact of the Common Agricultural Policy*, XVI/44/81-EN (Brussels: European Commission, Directorate General for Regional Policy, December 1980).

[2] *Official Journal of the European Communities*, No. C38 (18 April 1972).

[3] *Official Journal of the European Communities*, No. C36 (9 February 1979) — an updated version of Council Regulation (EEC) No. 724/75 (18 March 1975), establishing the European Regional Development Fund; supplemented by discussions with EEC officials.

[4] Henry, *op. cit.*, p. 80.

[5] For further discussion, see Rosemary Fennell, *The Common Agricultural Policy of the European Community* (London: Granada, 1979), Chapter 1.

[6] European Documentation, *The Agricultural Policy of the European Community* (Luxembourg: 1979), p. 6.

[7] European Commission, *The Agricultural Situation in the Community*, 1979 Report (Brussels/Luxembourg: 1980), pp. 143–60 for outlook estimates cited.

[8] *Official Journal of the European Communities*, No. C38 (18 April 1972), p. 8.

[9] European Commission, *The Agricultural Situation in the Community*, 1979 Report pp. 143–60 for outlook estimates cited.

[10] For further details, see European Documentation, *The Agricultural Policy of the European Community*, pp. 12–14.

[11] *Ibid.*, pp. 13–14.

[12] Regulation No. 17/64/EEC of the Council, 5 February 1964, "on the conditions for granting aid from the European Agricultural Guidance and Guarantee Fund." See *Official Journal of the European Communities, 1963–1964* (Luxembourg: November 1972), pp. 103–11.

[13] Commission of the European Communities, *Fourteenth General Report on the Activities of the European Communities in 1980* (Luxembourg: 1981), pp. 178–80.

[14] Norbert Vanhove and Leo H. Klaassen, *Regional Policy: A European Approach* (Farnborough: Saxon House, 1980), p. 421.

[15] This section draws upon Commission of the European Communities, *Europe's Common Agricultural Policy*, European File (Luxembourg: February 1981).

[16] *Ibid.*, p. 7.

[17] Henry, *op. cit.*

[18] *Ibid.*, p. 80.

[19] *Ibid.*, p. 7.

[20] *Ibid.*, p. 13.

[21] *Ibid.*, p. 30.

[22] *Ibid.*, p. 30.

[23] *Ibid.*, p. 30.

[24] *Ibid.*, p. 73.

[25] *Ibid.*, p. 80.

[26] *Ibid.*, p. 86.

Conclusions for Canadian Policy Review

8

I. Introduction

Four main points have emerged from this review of regional development experience within the EEC.

1. Many of the regional problems and issues are remarkably similar to those found in Canada, despite the differences of history, geography, culture, average population density, and governmental structures. The scope for comparative assessment of the manner in which EEC problems are perceived, and then approached by government regional policies, was found to be considerable. Moreover, considerations drawn from failure were often viewed to be every bit as useful as were the experiences drawn from more successful policies and programmes.

2. The more 'explicit' instruments of EEC regional policy were accorded, it is concluded, an exaggerated degree of importance in their role as contributors to more balanced regional development. This was at the expense of paying due concern to the regional implications of broader fiscal, monetary, social, and sectoral policies and activities. Examples include the national tax structures, external trade arrangements, the investment strategies and decisions of many state corporations, national social programmes such as unemployment insurance, and major sector policy approaches for energy, agriculture, and transportation. A similar fixation with 'explicit' regional instruments seems to have occurred in Canada, without due effort to grapple with the regional development roles of broader, national policies and activities.

3. The range of national level, regional development policies, approaches, and programmes is somewhat bewildering in scope. Yet a number of patterns do emerge, many of which merit serious review by Canadian federal, provincial and, quite frequently, municipal levels of government. Some main approaches are identified in Section IV of this chapter (more details are presented in Chapter Two).

4. The European Community's 'supranational' structure of government does not equate tidily with the Canadian federal level of government. Although the European Parliament appears to be gathering strength, and despite the existence of a large variety of

Community-level directorates and policy instruments (such as the Common Agricultural Policy and the European Regional Development Fund), the EEC is still far from having any federal government in the Canadian sense. The total Community budget, for example, while large in absolute terms, still only accounts for some 1 per cent of the Community GNP; the Canadian federal budget accounts for some 16 per cent of the Canadian GNP.

Notwithstanding these differences, indeed in some ways because of them, the Community-level experience of regional policy formulation and programming (as distinct from the national levels) contains a large number of points of very current value to the strained Canadian federation. In the context of remarkably similar regional problem situations, the European Community has often taken quite different approaches to those found in Canada, or, on occasion, has developed the same kind of policy instrument, but then has proceeded to operate it with substantial modifications to the most similar Canadian counterpart.

In particular, the experiences of two EEC regional development instruments are noted — those of the European Investment Bank and of the European Regional Development Fund. Section V of this chapter highlights some of the conclusions (details of which are given in Chapters Three to Seven).

II. The Definition of Regional Issues

In the European Community, as in Canada, the very delineation of regional development problems, priorities, and options has not proven a straightforward task. Neither the Community nor Canada can point to accomplishments, on any grand scale, as an obvious outcome of their regional development efforts. Even the appropriate yardsticks to measure the performance of regional policies are still far from agreed upon. In large part, this reflects the complexity of many of the issues, as well as the political difficulties inherent in approaching many regional problems head on.

Since 1958, and more particularly over the past decade, there has been a proliferation of efforts to measure the characteristics and to diagnose the causes of regional differences within the Community. Such work has extended considerably beyond the analysis of demographic and economic data — to seek to embrace a plethora of social, cultural, and environmental features. Particularly as the wealthier members of the European Community continue to view the actual and potential costs to their treasuries of regional policies for their less prosperous partners, interest in finding appropriate methods of diagnosing and tackling regional development is likely to grow.

Despite the efforts by the member governments of the EEC and by the European Community instruments, there are indications that any slight narrowing of regional disparities in the Community, over the 1960s, was reversed in the 1970s. This is raising serious questions about the kind of regional balance to be sought within the Community as a whole, and consequently of the appropriateness of the goals and scale of programmes of both the member governments and the Community instruments. The formation of the European Regional Development Fund has served to provide extra focus for such questions.

There are many parallels in the Canadian situation — both in terms of the willingness of the wealthier provinces to continue to subsidize their less prosperous neighbours and of the relevance and scale of federal programmes such as those embodied in the Department of Regional Economic Expansion (until January 1982).

Despite a growing body of information on regional characteristics within the European Community as a whole, public perceptions (and most analysis) of regional problems and issues are focused within the framework of individual states. The same tends to be true in Canada — in this case within the framework of individual provincial boundaries.

III. Main Problem Categories

Many of the regional problems and issues facing the European Community fall into the following seven categories (see Chapter One for details).

1. Peripheral areas of the Community with a high proportion of the labour force in agriculture and low agricultural productivity. These areas are characterized by low income levels, high unemployment and underemployment, and relatively inadequate infrastructure.

2. Old industrial areas facing problems in adjusting to sweeping structural and technological change. In addition to high unemployment levels and the run-down character of much of the industrial plant, these areas usually suffer from environmental degradation and poor-quality social infrastructure.

3. Urban growth problems, where the cities are dominating very broad areas yet have failed to digest effectively the influx of people — often on a commuter basis from outlying communities. Many such communities have been swollen not only by people from the rural areas of their own country, but also (especially in the 1960s) by migrant workers from other parts of the Community and from outside. In turn, many of these communities have themselves become enmeshed in the urban sprawl.

4. Environmental destruction. This is clearly a problem of major proportions that is being treated radically differently by the various member countries. West Germany, France, and the Netherlands have quite successfully attempted to integrate environmental guide-lines into regional development planning.

5. Ethnic divisions often linked to economic circumstances. Affected groups often perceive themselves to be ignored by their national governments and believe, not unreasonably, that they are eligible for additional regional development aid and improved representation.

6. Frontier regions abutting the East European bloc. West Germany has developed incentives to encourage greater development along these borders.

7. Mountain village areas where inadequate infrastructure compounds the problems of isolation and terrain. This applies particularly to Italy and Greece.

All but two of the above categories also fit the Canadian situation, and even those two (items 6 and 7) bear some comparison. For example, while Canada's northern proximity to the USSR has not been viewed as a regional development priority (in the manner of item 6), considerable interest has been shown in its resource potential and the matter of territorial rights, not to mention the defence aspects. Similarly, (in the case of item 7), while mountain areas are no great regional problem in Canada, isolated coastal and northern communities are and share a number of the same problems as mountain villages.

IV. National Programmes for Regional Development

The second chapter of this review sought to delineate the main regional policy approaches and experiences of the EEC member governments, as distinct from the instruments of the European Community. The following points might be highlighted (without attempting to repeat the detail) as meriting consideration in any reappraisal of Canadian regional policy.

1. The quality of regional development planning, and the capacity to rationalize and execute regional policies, has varied very substantially at the national levels of government in the European Community. Quite often the regions with the most severe problems have appeared to have governments that are the least equipped to tackle them. While in part financial and administrative capacity is an obvious factor, in considerable part the problem is a direct reflection of political and broader social will.

2. In the European Community, regional development theories and philosophies have played some role in providing frameworks to EEC national level, regional policies and programmes — though the degree to which they have been 'engines behind the policies' or 'crutches' to give them 'respectability' has varied from country to country. Two particular examples were noted — 'balanced' as distinct from 'unbalanced' growth, and 'growth centres'/'pôles de croissance'.

In the Canadian situation, greater attention might usefully be paid to the logic behind much of the regional development effort. Jargon seems often to have replaced clear strategy. A motley set of aids to specific sectors has almost hopelessly complicated the task of spelling out the overall goals of Canadian regional policies.

3. The national governments in the EEC have developed a large number of regional instruments, many of which have their counterparts in Canada. Some European governments appear to have done considerably better than Canada in the emphasis on the need for close integration of *national* regional policies with *national* development priorities as a whole (the Netherlands and France might be cited). However, whereas in the case of those two examples — a fairly strong, centralized planning process is at the core — the German experience (with great emphasis on harmonization of the efforts of the Länder) is of possibly greater relevance to the present Canadian setting. Both approaches merit careful assessment.

4. A few EEC member governments have very successfully integrated regional planning with physical (both urban and rural) and environmental planning. In such cases, geographers (land-use planning specialists in particular) have worked closely with sociologists, engineers, architects, economists, and representatives of other disciplines. The Netherlands and the Federal Republic of Germany might particularly be noted. In Canada, such an integration is far less evident, but should be seriously explored.

5. Industrial parks, linked to towns of various sizes, have been a main framework for a galaxy of incentives offered by most national (EEC) governments. Overall this appears to have been a useful approach to broad economic development and specifically to urban and rural land-use planning. The quality of industrial parks in the Federal Republic of Germany and southern France is particularly impressive and might be carefully studied for regions as southern Ontario and the Lower Fraser Valley in British Columbia.

In Italy, as a main cautionary example, the social infrastructure and planning regulations (including environmental) have often not kept pace with industrial growth, while a combination of lack of political stability and the form of tax aids may have resulted in somewhat lower standards of industrial plant, on many sites.

Industrial parks have also played a role in regional development programming in Canada. The standards vary quite markedly across the country, as in the European Community. There appears to be considerable scope for comparative review at an operational level of industrial park planning and management.

6. Containment of urban growth is a pressing issue for regional development policy both in Europe and Canada. France and the United Kingdom have applied controls to the expansion of their major cities. The use of 'green belts' around London and the control of ribbon development in West Germany, the Netherlands, and southeastern

France are also particularly notable. Many federal, provincial, and municipal planning agencies could usefully examine such activities more closely.

7. All EEC member governments appreciate the importance of education to regional and national development, but their approaches are far from uniform. For example, at the vocational training level, some place more weight on an apprenticeship approach (e.g., West Germany and Denmark), others place more emphasis on full-time vocational education (e.g., France, Belgium, and Italy). Luxembourg, the United Kingdom, the Netherlands, and Ireland employ a mix of the two approaches.

One overriding point was made — while the mobility and training instruments, on balance, appear to be in general support of 'bringing work to the workers', they are viewed also as 'safety valves'. If work does not materialize, in sufficient quantity, in the poorer regions, then would-be migrants should not be trapped there because of inadequate education, training, and mobility aids. Research and education are both a vehicle for regional development and a mechanism to facilitate mobility if adequate jobs do not materialize.

No obvious implications for agencies such as the federal Employment and Immigration Commission emerged from this, except that many of the problems are strikingly similar.

8. Particularly in France and Italy, state corporations have provided considerable leadership in the development of some poorer regions. There is scope for a review of the potential role of both federal and provincial Crown corporations as instruments for Canadian and provincial-level regional development.

9. The members of the European Community have agreed to impose ceilings on the amount of direct aid that can be given — as regional incentives — to industry locating in various parts of the country. This is differentiated, depending on the particular government's perceptions of where the main problem areas lie. At the present juncture of federal-provincial relationships, it is unlikely that such an approach would be acceptable for the Canadian setting, albeit the logic is clear.

10. Regional development instruments — without reasonably clear regional policy frameworks — can be shown to be 'busy', in terms of impact on such indicators as direct employment or income generation; but the recital of changes in such data can often serve to obscure rather than to focus on the reasons for major regional problems. Symptoms may get treated but the root causes of problems can be neglected. That conclusion can be gleaned from the experiences of most member countries at one stage or other in the post-1945 era. It is particularly clear in the cases of Italy and the United Kingdom. A review of many speeches by Canadian provincial and federal ministers will show that this country has not been immune to such 'window dressing'.

V. The European Community and Its Instruments of Regional Development

The Setting

The European Economic Community faces many of the same issues as the Canadian federal government (see Chapters Three to Seven on the various instruments for regional development). Energy, North-South relations, inflation, unemployment, and substantial regional disparities are on both lists. Three particular differences, however, should be noted at the outset.

1. The European Community is expanding territorially, with a waiting list of would-be entrants. On the other hand, the Canadian debate has focused on constitutional reform and redivision of powers, always with the threat of Quebec (at least) reducing the size of that federation. This appears to have resulted in a somewhat 'inward-looking' process in Canada, while the converse has been the situation in the EEC.

2. The European Parliament, while developing more political muscle, is still at a far more embryonic stage than that of the Canadian federal government. The Council of Ministers and the European Council (despite the latter's 'loose' relationship) also contribute important political direction. In the Canadian sense, the EEC level of supranational government does not equate neatly to a federal level of government, nor is its budget (as a proportion of GNP) nearly as large.

3. Geographically and in terms of population, the Comunity is far more concentrated than Canada, containing about ten times the population in about one tenth the land mass. Moreover, if Canada is apprehensive about the 'fickleness' of United States political directions, the EEC has the far graver concern about its proximity to the military strength of the East European bloc and of its internal strains, which could spill over into the West.

European Community Becoming More Involved in European-Level Regional Policies

The European Community has become increasingly concerned about the degree and persistence of regional disparities, in a context of wider considerations about energy, unemployment, and economic malaise. By its actions, as well as its words, the Community has become somewhat more 'interventionist' in its approach to regional development, especially over the past six years. The national governments, on the other hand, have become somewhat more cautious since 1973. Hence, after an initial period (1958–1975) of almost exclusive reliance on the regional activities of the European Investment Bank (with its focus on lending, at quasi-commercial rates, in less-prosperous regions), the Community has now broadened its attack both by establishing, in 1975, a grant agency (the European Regional Development Fund) and also by directing all EEC policy instruments to take explicit account of regional imbalances, within the framework of the Community. The framework of European Community-level regional policy and programming is still far from comprehensive and suffers from several major drawbacks. These include the following:

1. An absence of agreement, and definition, of what are really the goals of regional policy at the level of the European Community. A series of sub-goals are noted, without adequate attention to the overall framework. The extent to which jobs are merely to be propped up in poorer regions as distinct from the seriousness with which real effort is to be made to foster reasonably self-sustained economic growth, in currently less prosperous regions, is still far from obvious.

2. Many of the Community's own sector policies, not to mention those of the national governments, may actually be aggravating regional disparities rather than ameliorating them. This is particularly relevant, for example, in the case of the major expenditure instrument of the Community, the Common Agricultural Policy.

3. An absence of agreement, and definition, as to just how far transfers are to be made from the wealthier to the poorer members of the Community, for the purposes of regional development, and just where a fund such as the ERDF is expected to fit. For example, while the problems of the Italian Mezzogiorno are well appreciated, virtually nothing is being done (by such instruments as the ERDF) for northern Italian regional development, large areas of which are far less developed than other regions of the Community (in wealthier countries) that are receiving regional aid. This, in turn, also raises questions about the appropriate size of the ERDF budget. Should it really only be about one seventh the size of the subsidies paid out for milk production under the EAGGF? Indeed, what is viewed as an appropriate scale of endeavour for such a fund?

Exactly these same kinds of issues are pertinent regarding Canadian federal and provincial regional goals, frameworks, and policy instruments.

Conclusions from EEC Instruments

Four EEC instruments were examined in some detail, because of their roles in regional development at the Community level. The main conclusions, on each, are as follows.

The European Investment Bank

1. One main principle is fundamental to the EIB: it is essentially a development bank — displaying many of the strengths and disadvantages of a bank's approach to projects. On the one hand, it seeks to

safeguard project viability; on the other hand, it is conspicuous for its failure to broaden lending criteria to take fuller account of social benefits and costs.

2. Over two thirds of the EIB loans have been for projects in less-developed regions of the Community — at quasi-commercial rates. Projects have been assessed in terms of their 'bankability', and the Bank has successfully funded some 17,264 million EUA/ECU worth of projects since 1958.

Canada has no comparable agency, and it is argued that there may be scope for a Canadian Development Bank, somewhat along the EIB lines, with a clear regional development mandate and with direct provincial government participation, including a sharing of financial responsibility with the federal government.

3. Some 40 per cent of EIB loans have been for projects of common interest to more than one member state, and the EIB has used this as a mechanism for binding the Community more closely together in a concrete manner. The EIB indeed has been something of a 'flagship' of the EEC.

4. There are a very large number of ideas of relevance to Canadian regional policy from the EIB experience, as well as for the closest Canadian federal agency, the Federal Business Development Bank. The global loan arrangement is one such example, as is the manner in which the EIB links its programme to those of national governments, enabling them often to avoid the duplication of separate lending agencies.

The European Regional Development Fund

1. The ERDF represents concrete recognition that the European Community should play a more dynamic role in fostering less-unbalanced regional development across the Community. Essentially the ERDF is a grant-allocating agency, although, in the process, it is also playing an important catalytic role, as it seeks to define the logic for allocating its budget.

2. Two key principles underpin ERDF grants:

- The grants are viewed as supplemental to the regional development assistance given by member governments, hence are tied to their own regional development programmes.

- ERDF aid is limited to designated areas, the criteria for designation being determined largely by the respective national governments.

3. The ERDF does not have as broad a range of powers as were given to the federal Department of Regional Economic Expansion, but it does operate under one distinctly different framework — that of a national quota system.

It is concluded that a quota system also has substantial merit for Canadian regional policy, as a mechanism to bring greater logic and clarity to regional goals, as a way to screen regional priorities and to rationalize the appropriate level of federal funding involvement as distinct from provincial responsibilities. It is suggested, in the Canadian case, that the federal government should confine its grant-giving regional development role to the 'poorer' provinces. Even though many wealthier provinces have pockets of depressed areas, they also have the resources to resolve the problems.

4. The ERDF does not 'run its own programmes', but supplements various national programmes according to increasingly clear frameworks, with specific criteria as a basis for project approval. This places more onus on the member government to design programmes to fit its own specific regional needs and averts pressure on the European Community to develop homogeneous programmes regardless of different regional circumstances and priority sets.

5. The ERDF has particularly encouraged industrial estates as a developmental focal point.

6. Some 30 per cent of ERDF aid has gone to projects in the industrial and service sectors (as distinct from infrastructure), the larger proportion being in the form of subsidies to projects of more than 10 million EUA capital investment.

7. In Canada, the Department of Regional Economic Expansion became far more directly involved in regional programme management than is the case of the ERDF. Indeed, despite the scope for DREE project direction under the General Development Agreements with the provinces, even greater DREE involvement was apparently being sought prior to DREE's closure, largely to give additional federal visibility for such work. The ERDF approach presents a study in contrast to that of the DREE direction, with many distinctive advantages.

The new Canadian Ministry of State for Economic and Regional Development appears designed to give broader policy direction to federal agencies responsible for aspects of regional development. The manner it proposes to relate with provincial government programming is not clear at the time of writing.

A major, as yet unresolved, question (given ERDF's short life) is whether the ERDF will succeed in making its programme framework work (as described in Chapter Five).

The European Social Fund

1. The European Social Fund has served to emphasize the importance of social programming, as a deliberate adjunct to regional economic development policy, and, in addition, has served as a catalyst for comparing and helping shape regional social programmes. There

are a number of comparative policy ideas for Canadian review as a result of this aspect of the Fund's work; for example, the value of identifying target groups in areas, as distinct from the land mass as a whole as if the inhabitants are uniform, is really emphasized by the Social Fund.

2. It is not at all clear that the equivalent of a Social Fund would be appropriate to the Canadian situation, given the existence of federal agencies as the Employment and Immigration Commission. However, the Social Fund's role as a catalyst of regional social policies is not replicated in Canada and that aspect, at least, merits serious consideration.

The Common Agricultural Policy

1. The main conclusions, for Canadian regional policy review, from the CAP experience are of a cautionary nature. Compared to other programmes, CAP has grown disproportionately large and has also failed to pursue any coherent 'regional development balance' in its sector programming. The regional adjustment programmes (under the Guidance Sector of the EAGGF) have been of an almost 'token' nature (in comparison with the Grant Sector aid to the richer areas producing, in particular, milk and cereals).

2. The CAP experience demonstrates how, without broad regional development frameworks (with both generalized goals and systematic monitoring reviews), sectoral programmes and policies can readily become 'out of line'. In Canada it has not been a tradition to review routinely the regional impact and implications of federal sectoral policies. Such a process is recommended. The regional dimensions and implications of many Canadian programmes (such as price support) could usefully be compared with the lessons of CAP.

3. There are a number of operational-level, 'programme-specific' benefits to be gained from a comparison of CAP experiences with those of Canadian programmes, for example, the lessons for the Agricultural and Rural/Regional Development Act (ARDA) from the Guidance Section of the EAGGF.

VI. Conclusion

The European Community experience suggests no panacea for Canadian regional development problems. There is scope for greatly improved logic and performance of both the Community's regional policy and practice and Canada's. By presenting the experiences, as gleaned from this study, in a 'non-prescriptive' manner at the start of each section, it is hoped that readers may find the comparative information and ideas useful, even if they may disagree with some of the policy/programme application suggestions.

It is concluded that there would be substantial benefits to Canada from an ongoing monitoring of EEC regional policies and practices. There has been a widespread tendency to view Canadian problems as if they are unique, when, quite frequently, they have close parallels in the EEC.

The EEC and Canada have both encountered great difficulty in defining, let alone gaining consensus on, goals and frameworks for regional policy action. In both settings, regional development agencies have been established with relatively hazy targets and have proceeded to carve themselves niches in the halls of bureaucracy. Over time, many such agencies have compiled thoughtful documents recommending guide-lines, not only for their own programmes and projects, but also quite often for the regional activities of other agencies and levels of government. Useful comparative ideas can be gleaned from such work.

In both the EEC and Canada, the level of transfer payments necessary to contribute to greater regional development balance is at serious issue. In both situations, also, sector policies have walked a tight-rope between narrowly circumscribed economic efficiency and more broadly defined social concerns. In neither setting have sector policies been particularly responsive to regional considerations (especially from a longer-term, strategy vantage point, as distinct from shorter-term, *ad hoc* efforts). The recent work by the European Commission to study and publish the regional implications of sectoral policies is one step forward. A similar practice is suggested for routine application by the Canadian federal government.

It is clear, from this review of the European Community's experience, that regional disparities are frequently not just a product of differences in resource and other factor endowments. Often they are a mirror of the long-standing views of national and regional societies about their own order of priorities.

Conclusions pour un examen de la politique canadienne

8

I. Introduction

Quatre grandes lignes se dégagent de cet examen du développement régional au sein de la CEE :

1. Beaucoup des questions et des problèmes régionaux ressemblent de façon remarquable à ceux que l'on retrouve au Canada malgré les différences d'histoire, de géographie, de culture, de densité moyenne de la population et de structures gouvernementales. Les possibilités d'évaluation comparative de la façon dont les problèmes de la CEE sont perçus et traités dans le cadre des politiques de développement régional des gouvernements ont été jugées considérables. En outre, on a souvent considéré aussi valables les conclusions à tirer des échecs que celles à tirer des politiques des programmes plus réussis.

2. On a conclu que l'on avait accordé une importance démesurée aux instruments les plus « explicites » de la politique régionale de la CEE quant à leur rôle comme agents d'un développement régional plus équilibré. Cela s'est fait aux dépens d'une attention raisonnable aux implications régionales des politiques et des activités fiscales, monétaires, sociales et sectorielles globales. On peut citer en exemple les structures d'imposition nationale, les dispositions pour le commerce extérieur, les stratégies d'investissement et les décisions de plusieurs sociétés d'État, les programmes sociaux nationaux, tels que l'assurance-chômage, et les grandes politiques sectorielles en matière d'énergie, d'agriculture et de transport. Une fixation analogue sur les instruments régionaux « explicites » semble s'être produite au Canada sans que l'on fasse les efforts nécessaires pour saisir les rôles des politiques et des activités d'ensemble nationales dans le développement régional.

3. L'envergure et la portée des politiques, des approches et des programmes de développement régional à l'échelon national est quelque peu déconcertante. Pourtant, il est possible de dégager certaines lignes de force dont plusieurs mériteraient d'être étudiées sérieusement par les gouvernements fédéral, provinciaux et, assez souvent, municipaux. Dans la quatrième section de ce chapitre, on

définira certaines des approches principales (le chapitre deux renferme plus de détails).

4. La structure de gouvernement « supranational » de la Communauté européenne n'est pas réellement l'équivalent du gouvernement fédéral au Canada. Même s'il semble que le parlement européen prend des forces, et malgré l'existence d'une grande variété de directions et d'instruments d'orientation à l'échelon de la Communauté (tels que la politique agricole commune et le Fonds européen de développement régional), la CEE est encore loin d'être dotée d'un gouvernement fédéral au sens canadien. Le budget global de la Communauté, par exemple, bien qu'assez élevé en termes absolus, ne représente quand même que 1 % du PNB de la communauté; le budget fédéral canadien représente par contre près de 16 % du PNB canadien.

Nonobstant ces différences et, à vrai dire, en partie à cause d'elles, l'expérience, à l'échelon de la Communauté, de l'élaboration et de l'exécution d'une politique régionale (par opposition à l'échelon national) renferme plusieurs éléments qui peuvent intéresser notre fédération canadienne déchirée. Face à des problèmes régionaux étonnamment semblables, la Communauté européenne a souvent adopté des approches fort différentes de celles du Canada ou, à l'occasion, a élaboré le même genre de politiques qu'elle a cependant mis en oeuvre avec de fortes variantes par rapport à une politique analogue au Canada.

On remarque en particulier les expériences de deux instruments de développement régional de la CEE — celles de la Banque européenne d'investissement et celle du Fonds européen de développement régional. La section V de ce chapitre souligne certaines des conclusions (dont les détails se trouvent aux chapitres trois à sept).

II. La définition des questions régionales

Au sein de la Communauté européenne, tout comme au Canada, la définition même des problèmes, des priorités et des options de développement régional ne s'est pas faite sans détours. Ni la Communauté ni le Canada ne peuvent se vanter de grandes réalisations qui seraient une illustration évidente de leurs efforts en matière de développement régional. On est même encore loin de s'entendre sur les critères de mesure du rendement des politiques régionales. Cela témoigne en grande partie de la complexité de plusieurs des questions ainsi que des difficultés politiques soulevées par une approche directe de plusieurs problèmes régionaux.

Depuis 1958, et plus particulièrement au cours de la dernière décennie, on a vu proliférer les efforts en vue de mesurer les caractéristiques et de diagnostiquer les causes des différences régionales au sein de la Communauté. Un tel travail a débordé considérablement l'analyse des données démographiques et économiques — et a cherché à englober un vaste éventail de traits sociaux, culturels et environnementaux. À mesure surtout que les membres les plus riches de la Communauté européenne continuent de songer aux coûts actuels et éventuels des politiques régionales destinées à leurs partenaires moins prospères, on risque de voir s'accroître l'intérêt pour la recherche de méthodes pertinentes de diagnostic et de solutions du développement régional.

Malgré les efforts consentis par les gouvernements membres de la CEE et par les instruments de la Communauté européenne, certains indices montrent que la légère diminution de la disparité régionale qui a pu survenir dans la Communauté au cours des années 1960 a été annulée dans les années 1970. Cette situation soulève de graves questions au sujet du genre d'équilibre régional à viser au sein de la Communauté dans son ensemble, et, du fait même, sur la pertinence des buts et de l'échelle des programmes tant des gouvernements membres que des instruments de la Communauté. La formation du Fonds européen de développement régional a servi à mettre davantage en relief de telles questions.

On peut établir de nombreux parallèles avec la situation au Canada, à la fois quant à la volonté des provinces les plus riches de continuer à subventionner leurs voisins moins prospères et quant à la pertinence et à l'ampleur des programmes du fédéral, tels que ceux mis en oeuvre (jusqu'en janvier 1982) par le ministère de l'Expansion économique régionale.

Malgré une masse grandissante d'informations sur les caractéristiques régionales au sein de la Communauté européenne dans son ensemble, les perceptions du public (et la plupart des analyses) des questions et des problèmes régionaux se situent dans le cadre des États individuels. La situation tend à être la même au Canada, le cadre étant ici composé par les provinces individuelles.

III. Les principales catégories de problèmes

Plusieurs des questions et des problèmes régionaux avec lesquels la Communauté européenne est aux prises se rangent dans une des sept catégories suivantes :

1. Les régions périphériques de la Communauté, avec une forte proportion de la population active dans l'agriculture et une faible productivité agricole. Ces régions se caractérisent par des faibles niveaux de revenus, un chômage élevé et un sous-emploi ainsi qu'une infrastructure relativement insuffisante.

2. Les vieilles régions industrielles aux prises avec des problèmes d'adaptation aux changements structurels et technologiques d'envergure. Outre les forts taux de chômage et le caractère désuet d'une bonne part des équipements, ces régions souffrent habituellement d'une dégradation de l'environnement et d'une infrastructure sociale de piètre qualité.

3. Les problèmes de croissance urbaine, où les villes dominent de très grandes régions sans avoir réussi à intégrer de façon efficace l'influx de personnes — qui sont souvent des banlieusards en provenance des communautés avoisinantes. Beaucoup de ces communautés ont grossi non seulement en raison de l'arrivée de personnes en provenance des régions rurales de leur propre pays, mais aussi (particulièrement dans les années 1960) suite à l'arrivée de travailleurs migrants des autres parties de la Communauté et de l'extérieur. Plusieurs de ces communautés ont à leur tour été livrées au développement tentaculaire des villes.

4. La destruction de l'environnement. Cela est de toute évidence un problème de grande importance que les différents pays membres abordent de façon radicalement différente. L'Allemagne de l'Ouest, la France et les Pays-Bas ont tenté, non sans succès, d'intégrer des normes sur l'environnement à la planification du développement régional.

5. Les divisions ethniques découlant souvent de circonstances économiques. Les groupes en cause jugent souvent que leurs gouvernements nationaux les ignorent, et croient, non sans raison, qu'ils sont éligibles à de l'aide supplémentaire au titre du développement régional et à une représentation améliorée.

6. Les régions frontières voisines de l'Europe de l'Est. L'Allemagne de l'Ouest a mis au point des encouragements pour le développement de ces régions frontalières.

7. Les villages de montagnes où une infrastructure inadéquate vient s'ajouter aux problèmes d'isolement et de topographie. Cela vaut particulièrement pour l'Italie et la Grèce.

Toutes ces catégories, sauf deux, s'appliquent aussi à la situation canadienne, et même ces deux catégories (les articles 6 et 7) sont comparables à certains titres. Par exemple, bien qu'au nord la proximité du Canada et de l'URSS n'a pas été perçue comme une priorité en matière de développement régional (un peu comme l'article 6), on s'est intéressé considérablement à ses possibilités en matière de ressources et à la question des droits territoriaux, sans oublier les questions de défense. De même (dans le cas de l'article 7), bien que les régions montagneuses ne présentent pas de grand problème régional au Canada, les communautés isolées de la côte et des régions nordiques en présentent et partagent un certain nombre de problèmes avec les villages de montagne.

IV. Les programmes nationaux pour le développement régional

Le deuxième chapitre de cet examen cherchait à cerner les principales approches de la politique régionale et l'expérience des gouvernements membres de la CEE, en autant qu'elles se distinguent des instruments de la Communauté européenne. On pourrait faire valoir (sans entrer à nouveau dans les détails) que les points qui suivent méritent d'être étudiés dans toute réévaluation de la politique régionale canadienne.

1. La qualité de la planification du développement régional, et l'aptitude à rationaliser et à exécuter une politique régionale ont varié très substantiellement à l'échelon des gouvernements nationaux de la Communauté européenne. Il est apparu assez souvent que les régions aux prises avec les problèmes les plus graves aient semblé être dotées des gouvernements les moins capables d'y faire face. Bien que les possibilités financières et administratives constituent un facteur évident, le problème témoigne pour une bonne part d'une volonté politique et sociale plus générale.

2. Dans la Communauté européenne, les théories et les philosophies de développement régional ont eu un certain rôle à jouer dans l'établissement de cadres pour les politiques et les programmes régionaux de la CEE à l'échelon national, bien que la mesure dans laquelle elles ont servi de « moteur des politiques » ou de «béquilles » devant leur donner une certaine « respectabilité » ait varié d'un pays à l'autre. On a remarqué deux exemples en particulier — la croissance « équilibrée » par rapport à la croissance « déséquilibrée » et les « pôles de croissance » / « *growth centres* ».

Dans le cas du Canada, il pourrait être utile d'accorder une plus grande attention à la logique qui sous-tend une bonne part des tentatives de développement régional. Il semble qu'une stratégie bien définie ait souvent cédé la place au jargon. Un mélange disparate de programmes d'aide à certains secteurs bien précis a compliqué presque irrémédiablement le travail d'élaboration d'objectifs globaux pour la politique régionale canadienne.

3. Les gouvernements nationaux, au sein de la CEE, ont mis au point un grand nombre d'instruments régionaux dont plusieurs ont leur équivalent au Canada. Certains gouvernements européens semblent avoir beaucoup mieux réussi que le Canada à faire valoir le besoin d'intégrer intimement les politiques régionales nationales et les priorités de développement nationales dans leur ensemble (on pourrait mentionner à ce titre les Pays-Bas et la France). Cependant, tandis que, dans ces deux exemples, on retrouve un processus de planification centralisé assez fort, l'expérience allemande (qui insiste beaucoup sur l'harmonisation des efforts des *länder*) est peut-être plus pertinente à la situation canadienne actuelle. Les deux approches méritent d'être étudiées sérieusement.

4. Quelques-uns des gouvernements membres de la CEE ont intégré avec grand succès la planification régionale et la planification physique (tant urbaine que rurale) et environnementale. Dans de tels cas, les géographes (en particulier les spécialistes de la planification de l'utilisation des sols) ont travaillé intimement avec les sociologues,

les ingénieurs, les architectes, les économistes et les représentants des autres disciplines. On pourrait mentionner en particulier les Pays-Bas et la République fédérale allemande. Au Canada, une telle intégration est beaucoup moins évidente, mais devrait être étudiée sérieusement.

5. Les parcs industriels, reliés à des villes de diverses grandeurs, ont constitué un des principaux cadres d'une vaste gamme d'encouragements offerts par la plupart des gouvernements nationaux (CEE). Dans l'ensemble, cela semble s'être avéré une approche utile au développement économique global et, en particulier, à la planification des sols en milieu urbain et rural. La qualité des parcs industriels dans la République fédérale allemande et dans le sud de la France est particulièrement impressionnante, et mériterait d'être étudiée de près en regard de régions comme le sud de l'Ontario et la basse vallée de la rivière Fraser en Colombie-Britannique.

À titre d'avertissement, et l'Italie offre un exemple de choix en cette matière, on pourrait mentionner que l'infrastructure sociale et les règlements en matière de planification (y compris les règlements sur l'environnement) ont souvent traîné de l'arrière par rapport à la croissance industrielle — tandis qu'un mélange d'instabilité politique et d'allégements fiscaux d'un genre particulier pourrait avoir abaissé quelque peu les normes d'équipement industriel en plusieurs endroits.

Les parcs industriels ont aussi joué un rôle dans la programmation du développement régional au Canada. Les normes varient très sensiblement d'une région du pays à l'autre, tout comme au sein de la Communauté européenne. Il semble exister de grandes possibilités d'études comparatives, à l'échelon opérationnel, de la planification et de la gestion des parcs industriels.

6. L'endiguement de la croissance urbaine constitue une dimension brûlante de la politique de développement régional tant en Europe qu'au Canada. La France et la Grande-Bretagne ont imposé des limites à l'expansion de leurs plus grandes villes. Le recours aux ceintures vertes autour de Londres, et le contrôle de l'extension urbaine en bordure des routes en Allemagne de l'Ouest, aux Pays-Bas et dans le sud-est de la France méritent d'être mentionnés. Plusieurs organismes de planification fédéraux, provinciaux et municipaux pourraient étudier avec profit de telles activités.

7. Tous les gouvernements membres de la CEE se rendent compte de l'importance de l'éducation pour le développement régional et national, mais leurs approches sont loin d'être uniformes. Par exemple, sur le plan de la formation professionnelle, certains insistent davantage sur l'apprentissage (par exemple l'Allemagne de l'Ouest et le Danemark), tandis que d'autres privilégient la formation professionnelle à temps plein (par exemple la France, la Belgique et l'Italie). Le Luxembourg, la Grande-Bretagne, les Pays-Bas et l'Irlande ont recours à un mélange des deux approches.

On a fait valoir un point capital, à savoir que, bien que les instruments de mobilité et de formation semblent viser, à tout prendre, à « apporter le travail aux travailleurs », ils sont aussi considérés comme « soupape de sûreté ». Si le travail ne se concrétise pas en quantité suffisante dans les régions les plus pauvres, les migrants éventuels ne devraient pas y être pris au piège en raison d'une éducation, d'une formation ou d'une aide à la mobilité insuffisantes. La recherche et l'éducation sont à la fois un véhicule du développement régional et un mécanisme pour faciliter la mobilité si les emplois ne se concrétisent pas en quantité suffisante.

Aucun enseignement évident ne se dégage de cela pour des organismes telle la Commission de l'emploi et de l'immigration, si ce n'est que plusieurs des problèmes sont remarquablement semblables.

8. Les sociétés d'État, particulièrement en France et en Italie, ont fourni un leadership considérable pour le développement de certaines régions plus pauvres. Il y a place pour un examen du rôle éventuel des sociétés d'État tant fédérales que provinciales comme instruments du développement régional à l'échelon canadien et à l'échelon provincial.

9. Les membres de la Communauté européenne se sont entendus pour imposer des plafonds à la quantité d'aide directe qui peut être accordée — comme encouragements régionaux — aux industries qui s'établissent dans diverses régions du pays. Ces limites varient selon la perception de chaque gouvernement des secteurs problématiques. Même si sa logique est claire, il est peu probable qu'une telle approche soit acceptable dans la situation canadienne, compte tenu de l'état actuel des relations fédérales-provinciales.

10. Il est possible de démontrer le lourd fardeau des instruments de développement régional — sans encadrement raisonnablement bien défini de la politique régionale — quant à leur incidence sur des indicateurs tels l'emploi direct ou la génération des revenus; mais l'énumération de changements dans de telles données peu souvent servir à voiler les raisons des principaux problèmes régionaux plutôt que les mettre en relief. Il arrive que l'on traite les symptômes au détriment des causes profondes. Les expériences de la plupart des pays membres, à un moment donné ou l'autre depuis 1945, permettent de tirer une telle conclusion. Elle est particulièrement évidente dans les cas de l'Italie et de la Grande-Bretagne. Un recensement des nombreux discours des ministres canadiens, tant à l'échelon provincial que fédéral, révélera que ce pays n'a pas échappé à un tel « maquillage ».

V. La Communauté européenne et ses instruments de développement régional

La toile de fond

La Communauté économique européenne est aux prises avec plusieurs des mêmes problèmes que le gouvernement fédéral canadien. L'énergie, les relations Nord-Sud, l'inflation, le chômage et les importantes disparités régionales figurent sur les listes des deux parties. Il importe toutefois de remarquer d'emblée trois différences particulières :

1. La Communauté européenne accroît son territoire, et certains pays attendent pour y adhérer. Par contre, le débat canadien a porté avant tout sur la réforme constitutionnelle et un nouveau partage des pouvoirs, avec en arrière-plan la menace du Québec (à tout le moins) de réduire la taille de la fédération. Cela semble avoir entraîné un certain processus d'introspection au Canada, tandis que la situation de la CEE était à l'opposé.

2. Le parlement européen, tout en acquérant plus de force politique, est encore à un état beaucoup plus embryonnaire que celui du gouvernement fédéral canadien. Le Conseil des ministres et le Conseil européen (malgré des rapports « éloignés » de ce dernier) fournissent aussi une importante orientation politique. Au sens canadien, le niveau de gouvernement supranational de la CEE n'est pas parfaitement analogue à un niveau de gouvernement fédéral, et son budget est loin d'être aussi important (comme proportion du PNB).

3. Du point de vue de la géographie et de la population, la Communauté est beaucoup plus concentrée que le Canada : elle renferme environ dix fois la population dans environ un dixième de la superficie. En outre, tandis que le Canada se méfie de l'inconstance des orientations politiques américaines, la CEE s'inquiète bien davantage de la proximité de la force militaire du bloc européen de l'Est et de ses tensions internes qui pourraient déborder vers l'Ouest.

La participation grandissante de la Communauté européenne aux politiques régionales à l'échelon européen

Dans le contexte des considérations d'ensemble sur l'énergie, le chômage et le malaise économique, la Communauté européenne s'est de plus en plus préoccupée du degré et de la persistence des disparités régionales. Tant par ses actions que par ses paroles, la Communauté est devenue un peu plus « interventionniste » dans son approche du développement régional, surtout depuis six ans. Les gouvernements nationaux, par contre, sont devenus quelque peu plus prudents depuis 1973. Ainsi, après une période initiale (1958–1975) de recours quasi exclusif aux activités régionales de la Banque européenne d'investissement (qui privilégiait les prêts, à des taux quasi commerciaux, dans des régions moins prospères), la Communauté a élargi ses visées en établissant, en 1975, un organisme de subvention (le Fonds européen de développement régional) (FEDR) et en ordonnant à tous les organes de politique de la CEE de tenir compte explicitement des déséquilibres régionaux au sein de la Communauté. Le cadre de la politique et de la programmation régionale à l'échelon de la Communauté européenne est encore loin d'être complet et souffre de plusieurs inconvénients d'importance. Ceux-ci comprennent :

1. Un manque de définition de ce que sont réellement les objectifs de la politique régionale à l'échelon de la Communauté européenne et d'accords à ce sujet. On a établi une série de sous-objectifs sans accorder une attention suffisante au cadre global. Il est encore loin d'être évident dans quelle mesure on ne fait que pallier le chômage dans les régions les plus pauvres plutôt que de consacrer de réels efforts à l'établissement d'une croissance économique raisonnablement autosuffisante.

2. Plusieurs des politiques sectorielles de la Communauté, sans compter celles des gouvernements nationaux, sont peut-être en train d'aggraver les disparités régionales au lieu de les éliminer. Cela vaut particulièrement, par exemple, dans le cas du principal outil de défense de la Communauté, la politique agricole commune.

3. Un manque d'accords et de définitions quant à la portée du transfert des pays plus riches aux pays pauvres de la Communauté à des fins de développement régional, et sur la place d'un fonds tel le FEDR dans cet ensemble. Tandis que, par exemple, on connaît bien les problèmes du Mezzogiorno italien, on ne fait presque rien (au moyen d'instruments tel le FEDR) pour le développement régional dans le nord de l'Italie, dont plusieurs régions sont beaucoup moins développées que d'autres régions de la Communauté (dans des pays plus riches) qui reçoivent de l'aide au titre du développement régional. Cela provoque des questions sur la taille du budget du FEDR. Devrait-il réellement n'être que le septième des sommes versées en subsides à la production de lait en vertu du Fonds européen d'orientation et de garantie agricole (FEOGA)? À vrai dire, quelle est la taille convenable à fixer pour un tel fonds?

Ce sont là exactement les mêmes questions qui se posent dans le cadre des objectifs, des cadres et des instruments de politique du développement régional au Canada, tant à l'échelon fédéral que provincial.

Les conclusions à tirer des instruments de la CEE

En raison de leurs rôles de développement régional à l'échelon de la Communauté, nous avons étudié en quelque détail quatre instruments de la CEE. Voici les principales conclusions que nous avons tirées de l'étude de chacun :

La Banque européenne d'investissement

1. Dans le cas de la BEI, un principe est fondamental : il s'agit essentiellement d'une banque de développement — elle manifeste plusieurs des forces et des désavantages d'une approche bancaire des projets. D'une part, elle cherche à protéger la viabilité des projets; d'autre part, elle brille par son refus d'élargir les critères de prêts en vue de tenir davantage compte des coûts et avantages sociaux.

2. Plus des deux tiers des prêts de la BEI sont allés à des projets dans les régions moins développées de la Communauté — à des taux quasi commerciaux. Les projets ont été évalués en fonction de leurs possibilités « bancaires » — et la banque a financé avec succès l'équivalent de quelques 17 264 millions uc/ECU de projets depuis 1958.

Le Canada ne compte aucun organisme comparable, et l'on prétend qu'il peut y avoir de la place pour une banque de développement canadienne qui s'apparenterait quelque peu à la BEI, qui disposerait d'un mandat précis en matière de développement régional et à laquelle les gouvernements provinciaux participeraient directement, tout en partageant une part des responsabilités financières avec le gouvernement fédéral.

3. Près de 40 % des prêts de la BEI sont allés à des projets qui intéressaient plus d'un État membre, et la BEI a utilisé ces prêts comme mécanisme pour créer des liens plus intimes au sein de la Communauté. La BEI a été à vrai dire un des éléments moteurs de la CEE.

4. L'expérience de la BEI recèle un très grand nombre d'idées pertinentes à la politique régionale canadienne ainsi qu'à l'organisme fédéral canadien le plus apparenté, la Banque fédérale de développement. Les accords de prêts globaux en sont un exemple ainsi que la façon dont la BEI rattache son programme à ceux des gouvernements nationaux en leur permettant souvent d'éviter le chevauchement des organismes de prêts.

Le Fonds européen de développement régional

1. Le FEDR représente une reconnaissance concrète du rôle plus dynamique que devrait jouer la Communauté européenne pour encourager un développement régional plus équilibré au sein de la Communauté. Le FEDR est essentiellement un organisme de subvention bien que, ce faisant, il joue également un important rôle de catalyseur en cherchant à préciser la logique de la répartition de ses argents.

2. Deux grands principes sous-tendent les subventions du FEDR :
• Les subventions sont jugées comme des suppléments à l'aide au développement régional accordé par les gouvernements membres et

sont donc liées à leurs propres programmes de développement régional;

• L'aide du FEDR est restreinte à certaines régions désignées, les critères de désignation étant déterminés en grande partie par les gouvernements nationaux respectifs.

3. Le FEDR ne jouit pas de pouvoirs aussi étendus que le ministère fédéral de l'Expansion économique régionale; il fonctionne cependant en vertu d'un cadre fort différent, soit un régime national de contingentement.

On a conclu qu'un régime de contingentement pourrait avoir un grand mérite pour la politique régionale canadienne en tant que mécanisme destiné à apporter une plus grande clarté et une plus grande logique aux objectifs régionaux, et en tant que moyen de trier les priorités régionales et de rationaliser le niveau approprié de participation du gouvernement fédéral au financement, par rapport aux responsabilités provinciales. On suggère, dans le cas du Canada, que le gouvernement fédéral limite son rôle de subvention du développement régional aux provinces « plus pauvres ». Même si plusieurs des provinces les plus riches ont des îlots de pauvreté, elles ont également les ressources pour résoudre les problèmes.

4. Le FEDR ne « gère pas ses propres programmes », mais complète les divers programmes nationaux en vertu de cadres de plus en plus clairs et en fonction de critères bien précis pour l'approbation des projets. Cela fait porter plus de responsabilité, sur les gouvernements membres, pour la conception de programmes adaptés à leurs propres besoins régionaux, et évite à la Communauté européenne d'avoir à mettre au point des programmes homogènes indépendamment des différentes circonstances et d'ensembles distincts de priorités régionales.

5. Le FEDR a encouragé plus particulièrement, comme point de mire du développement, le domaine industriel.

6. Près de 30 % de l'aide du FEDR a été affectée à des projets dans les secteurs de l'industrie et des services (plutôt que l'infrastructure), la plus forte proportion ayant été versée sous forme de subsides à des projets exigeant plus de 10 millions uc d'investissements de capital.

7. Au Canada, le ministère d'Expansion économique régionale s'est engagé beaucoup plus directement dans la gestion des programmes régionaux que ne l'a fait le FEDR. À vrai dire, malgré l'envergure de la direction des projets du MEER en vertu des accords généraux de développement des provinces, on appelait apparamment à une participation encore plus grande du MEER avant sa fermeture — surtout pour mettre en relief davantage l'apport du fédéral à de tels travaux. L'approche du FEDR contraste avec l'orientation du MEER et présente de nombreux avantages. Le nouveau ministère d'État canadien au Développement économique régional semble avoir été créé afin de

mieux guider les agences fédérales responsables de certains aspects du développement régional. Il n'était pas clair, au moment d'aller sous presse, de quelle façon le ministère envisageait la coordination avec les programmes provinciaux. Il reste cependant toujours à savoir (compte tenu de la nouveauté du FEDR) si le FEDR réussira à faire fonctionner le cadre de ses programmes (tel qu'il a été décrit au chapitre cinq).

Le Fonds social européen

1. Le Fonds social européen a servi à accentuer l'importance de la programmation sociale comme auxiliaire intentionnel de la politique de développement économique régional et, de plus, a servi de catalyseur pour la comparaison des programmes socio-régionaux et leur élaboration. Cette dimension du travail du Fonds offre un certain nombre d'idées comparatives en matière de politique pour l'étude des Canadiens; par exemple, le Fonds social insiste beaucoup sur l'importance d'identifier des groupes cibles dans les régions, plutôt que de traiter le territoire dans son ensemble comme si tous les habitants étaient pareils.

2. Il n'est pas du tout évident qu'un organisme analogue au Fonds social conviendrait à la situation canadienne, compte tenu de l'existence d'organismes fédéraux telle la Commission de l'emploi et de l'immigration. Toutefois, le rôle du Fonds social comme catalyseur des politiques sociales régionales ne se retrouve pas au Canada, et cet aspect, au moins, mérite d'être étudié sérieusement.

La politique agricole commune

1. C'est surtout à titre d'avertissement que l'on peut tirer des conclusions de la PAC pour l'étude de la politique régionale canadienne. La PAC a grandi de façon disproportionnée par rapport aux autres programmes et n'a pas réussi à maintenir un « équilibre de développement régional » cohérent dans sa programmation sectorielle. Les programmes de rajustement régional (qui relèvent du secteur d'orientation du FEOGA) ont eu un caractère presque symbolique (par rapport à l'aide accordée par le secteur de subvention aux régions les plus riches produisant, en particulier, du lait et des céréales).

2. L'expérience de la PAC démontre combien, sans des cadres globaux de développement régional (dotés à la fois d'objectifs généraux et de contrôles thématiques), des programmes et des politiques sectorielles peuvent facilement sortir du rang. Au Canada, on n'a pas l'habitude d'examiner régulièrement les répercussions régionales et les implications des politiques sectorielles fédérales. On recommande l'adoption d'un tel processus. Les dimensions et les implications

régionales de plusieurs programmes canadiens (tels que le soutien des prix) pourraient utilement être comparées aux leçons de la PAC.

3. La comparaison de certaines expériences de la PAC avec celle des programmes canadiens peut procurer certains avantages à l'échelon opérationnel ou à celui de programmes précis, comme, par exemple, les leçons de la section d'orientation du FEOGA pour la Loi sur l'aménagement rural et le développement agricole (ARDA).

VI. Conclusion

L'expérience de la Communauté européenne n'offre pas de solution miracle aux problèmes de développement régional au Canada. Il y a place pour une grande amélioration de la logique et du rendement à la fois de la politique et de l'exercice du développement régional dans la Communauté et au Canada. En présentant les expériences tirées de cette étude de façon non prescriptive au début de chaque section, on espère que le lecteur pourra trouver utiles l'information et les idées comparatives même s'il n'est pas d'accord avec certaines des suggestions d'application des politiques et des programmes.

On conclut que le Canada tirerait d'importants avantages d'une étude permanente des politiques régionales de la CEE et de leur application. On a eu trop tendance, dans l'ensemble, à percevoir les problèmes du Canada comme étant uniques alors que, très souvent, ils s'apparentent de près à ceux de la CEE.

La CEE et le Canada ont tous deux éprouvé d'énormes difficultés à définir des objectifs et des cadres des activités en matière de développement régional, et encore plus à obtenir le consensus à ce sujet. Chez les deux, on a créé des organismes de développement régional avec des objectifs plutôt vagues qui se sont employés à se tailler une place au sein de la bureaucratie. Avec le temps, de nombreux organismes du genre ont accumulé des documents bien réfléchis recommandant les lignes directrices non seulement pour leurs propres programmes et projets, mais aussi, assez souvent, pour les activités régionales des divers organismes et des autres niveaux de gouvernement. On peut glaner des idées comparatives utiles de tels travaux.

Tant dans la CEE qu'au Canada, le niveau de transfert des paiements nécessaires pour aider à un plus grand équilibre dans le développement régional est sérieusement remis en question. Dans les deux situations aussi, les politiques sectorielles ont chevauché la frontière entre une efficacité économique au sens restreint et des préoccupations sociales plus globales. Nulle part les politiques sectorielles ont-elles été particulièrement sensibles aux considérations régionales (notamment du point de vue d'une stratégie à long terme, par opposition à des efforts spéciaux à court terme). Les récents travaux de la Commission européenne en vue d'étudier et de publier les implications régionales des politiques sectorielles constituent un pas en avant. On suggère au gouvernement fédéral d'avoir recours régulièrement à une pratique du genre.

Cette étude de l'expérience de la Communauté européenne fait ressortir clairement que les disparités régionales ne sont souvent pas seulement qu'un produit des différences en matière de ressources ou d'autres facteurs. Elles sont souvent le reflet des opinions traditionnelles des sociétés nationales et régionales au sujet de leurs propres priorités.

Glossary

ARDA	Agricultural Rehabilitation and Development Act (Canada), 1960-61, Elizabeth II, Chapter 30. 'Rehabilitation' was later changed to 'and Rural'.
BLEU	The Belgo-Luxembourg Economic Union. This Economic and Customs Union was founded in 1921 and involves a pooling of foreign currency and combining balance-of-payments and foreign trade statistics.
CAP	Common Agricultural Policy of the Community.
Casa per il Mezzogiorno	This is the major regional development agency for southern Italy.
CDB	Canadian Development Bank. No such organization exists at this time, but it is proposed for future consideration by this review.
CET	Common External Tariff.
CIDA	Canadian International Development Agency.
Commission	The fourteen commissioners, under their President, Gaston Thorn, collectively propose legislation to the Council.
COREPER	The Committee of Permanent Representatives. It prepares the work of the Council of Ministers. Each country is a member through its representative in Brussels who is effectively ambassador to the Community.
Council of Ministers	Ministers of the ten member states meeting to agree on Community legislation proposed by the Commission.

Community Currency

u.a.   Unit of account. The value of the u.a.
                                  was defined by reference to a given
                                  weight of fine gold.

EUA   European unit of account introduced in
                                  1974.

ECU   European currency unit introduced on
                                  13 March 1979. The value of the ECU
                                  and EUA is determined on a day-to-day
                                  basis among the various currencies on
                                  the foreign exchange market. In both
                                  cases, the unit is defined by reference to
                                  a sum of fixed amounts of member
                                  states' currencies. The value of the
                                  EUA/ECU, at the ECU introduction
                                  date on 13 March 1979, was equal to the
                                  sum of the following amounts of member
                                  states' currencies:

Deutsche Mark	0.828
Pound Sterling	0.0885
French Franc	1.15
Italian Lira	109
Dutch Guilder	0.286
Belgian Franc	3.66
Danish Krone	0.217
Irish Pound	0.00759
Luxembourg Franc	0.14

The changes of name reflect a gradual movement in the direction of
monetary union with a single European currency. However, while the
formation of the European Monetary System is a substantial step in
that direction, it is still far from a complete union and the ECU's role
is limited.

In the use of comparative economic and financial data, this book
refers to the unit of account precisely as used in the source from which
the information is taken. Thus u.a.'s, EUA's, and ECU's are all to be
found. The exception to this is Chapter Four on the European
Investment Bank. At the suggestion of the EIB, the term ECU has
been used for all data concerning the Bank. Not all instruments of the
EEC historically used the same weighting system when defining the
u.a. (e.g., the currency weighting of agricultural units of account
differed from that of the EIB). As national currencies have changed
their relationships both with each other and with external currencies
(such as the US dollar), the value of the EUA (and ECU) has also
changed over time. Caution must be exercised, therefore, in comparing
data over time. Until 1971, the u. a. was equivalent to the US dollar,

but with the international monetary changes of that year, the u. a. and then the EUA and ECU have varied in relation to the US dollar. Thus on 31 December 1977, the EUA was equal to US$1.225. In the first quarter of 1979, the EUA and its successor, the ECU, were valued at US$1.3. On 30 June 1981, the ECU was valued at US$1.055.

Increasingly the ECU is being used to describe the entire EEC period from 1958 to the present (e.g., this convention was followed in Chapter One when citing EEC statistics). However, it was not used systematically in some of the later chapters, in order to maintain the policy of using the precise definitions of the data source and to alert the reader to the process.

Country Abbreviations		
	B	Belgium
	DK	Denmark
	F	France
	G	West Germany
	I	Italy
	IRL	Ireland
	NL	Netherlands
	UK	United Kingdom

Customs Union

A group of countries that have abolished internal customs duties and introduced a common customs tariff. To be fully effective members of the union, they must harmonize their customs legislation. The difference between a free-trade area and a customs union is that a free-trade area has no common customs tariff.

DATAR

Délégation à l'aménagement du territoire et à l'action régionale (France).

Decisions

Community decrees addressed to a state, a company, or an individual.

Directives

Community legislation binding on member states but leaving them free to decide how to carry them out.

DREE

Department of Regional Economic Expansion, the Canadian federal government agency with a regional development responsibility. It operated between 1969 and January 1982, when its functions were largely absorbed by a new Ministry of State for Economic and Regional Development, and a restructured department, now called the De-

	partment of Regional Industrial Expansion.
EAGGF	The European Agricultural Guidance and Guarantee Fund, which finances the CAP. The Fund was set up in 1962.
EC	The European Community — probably the name by which the EEC will be known in the future.
ECOSOC or ESC	The Economic and Social Committee that gives opinions on Commission proposals.
ECSC	The European Coal and Steel Community. Established in 1951, its considerable responsibilities have now been taken over by the Commission.
EEC	The European Economic Community. It was established by a Treaty of Rome in 1957.
EIB	The European Investment Bank. It makes loans and guarantees that facilitate the financing of Community projects. It was established in 1958 under a Treaty of Rome.
EMA (EMS)	European Monetary Arrangement. The new European monetary proposals put forward initially at the Bremen European Council in 1978. It is now known as the European Monetary System (EMS).
EMU	Economic and Monetary Union. The Council decided to establish this in 1971. It remains a long-term goal.
ERDF	The European Regional Development Fund. It was set up in 1975.
Euratom	The European Atomic Energy Community. It was established in 1958 under a Treaty of Rome.
European Council	A meeting several times a year of the EEC heads of government. Possibly the most powerful body influencing the future developments of the Community, its relationship with the European Parliament is still evolving.
European Parliament	Directly elected Parliament from June 1979. It will probably influence the

	Commission and Council of Ministers, in an increasing way, after a somewhat slow start.
European Social Fund	It provides retraining and resettlement assistance to facilitate re-employment for workers as well as financial assistance to workers temporaily displaced by industrial conversion. Established under a Treaty of Rome, it began very modestly before substantial expansion in recent years.
FBDB	Federal Business Development Bank. This is a Canadian industrial development banking agency of the federal government.
FRED	Fund for Rural/Regional Economic Development (Canada). Established in 1966, its functions were absorbed by DREE.
Fund Committee	It is responsbile for formulating opinions on draft decisions to grant aid from the ERDF.
GDP	Gross domestic product.
GNP	Gross national product.
ILO	International Labour Organization. The ILO is a specialized United Nations agency dealing with matters relating to employment.
NCI	New Community Instrument (described in Appendix 4.2).
OECD	Organisation for Economic Co-operation and Development. This is the economic club of twenty-three of the world's industrialized nations.
OPEC	Organization of Petroleum Exporting Countries.
Recommendations	Suggestions by the Commission or the Council but with no binding force.
Regional Policy Committee	It is responsible for studying the development of the regions of the Community and advising the European Commission on projects for which ERDF assistance is being sought.
Regulations	A form of Community law binding and directly applicable in all member states.

Safeguard Clause

A clause permitting a member state to request a temporary dispensation from its obligations towards its Community partners. The Commission judges whether the request is justified. On 23 August 1968, France was authorized to take safeguard measures reintroducing exchange controls, export aid, and import quotas.

Treaties of Rome

These Treaties, which were signed in the spring of 1957 and put into effect in early 1958, established the European Economic Community and the European Atomic Energy Community. All quotations in this review are from the *Encyclopedia of European Community Law, Vol. BII, European Community Treaties* (Andover: Sweet and Maxwell).

UN

United Nations.

VAT

Value added tax. A tax charged on the value added to goods at each stage in the production and distribution chain.

Selected Bibliography

I. An Introduction to the European Economic Community

Brugmans, Henri. *L'Idée européenne, 1920–1970*. Bruges: De Tempel, 1970.

Cairncross, A.; Giersch, H.; Lanfalussy, A.; Petrilli, G.; and Uri, P. *Economic Policy for the European Community*. London: Macmillan, 1974.

Coffey, Peter, ed. *Economic Policies of the Common Market*. London: Macmillan, 1979.

Commission of the European Communities. *The Community Today*. Brussels: 1979.

Commission of the European Communities. *The European Community in the 1980's*. Brussels: 1980.

Commission of the European Communities. *European Economy — Special Issue*. Brussels: 1979.

Drew, John. *Doing Business in the European Community*. London: Butterworths, 1979.

Hallstein, Walter. *Europe in the Making*. New York: W.W. Norton, 1972.

Meade, J.E. *The Theory of Customs Unions*. Amsterdam: North Holland, 1955.

Monnett, Jean. *Les États-Unis d'Europe ont commencé. Discours et allocutions 1952–1954*. Paris: Robert Laffont, 1955.

Morgan, E. Victor and Harrington, Richard. *Capital Markets in the European Community*. London: Wilton House, 1977.

Parker, Geoffrey. *The Countries of Community Europe*. London: Macmillan, 1979.

Swann, Dennis. *The Economics of the Common Market*, 4th ed. Harmondsworth: Penguin Books, 1978.

Wellenstein, Edmund. *25 Years of European Community External Relations*. Luxembourg: European Documentation, 1979.

II. Regional Issues, Theories, and Statistics

Balassa, B., ed. *European Economic Integration*. Amsterdam: North Holland, 1975.

Brown, A.J. and Burrows, E.M. *Regional Economic Problems*. London: Allen and Unwin, 1977.

Clout, Hugh, ed. *Regional Development in Western Europe*. London: John Wiley, 1975.

Clout, Hugh. *The Regional Problem in Western Europe*. Cambridge: Cambridge University Press, 1976.

Colot, M. *Métropoles d'équilibre et avies métropolitaines*. Paris: La Documentation Française, 1969.

Commission of the European Communities. *Europeans and Their Regions*. Brussels: 1980.

Commission of the European Communities. *European Economy — Short Term Economic Trends and Prospects: Adaptation of Working Time*. Luxembourg: 1980.

Commission of the European Communities. *Regional Development Atlas*. Brussels: 1979.

Commission of the European Communities. *The Regions of Europe*. Brussels: 1981.

Commission of the European Communities. *Report on the Regional Problems in the Enlarged Community*. Brussels: 1973.

Eurostat. *Regional Statistics: Community's Financial Participation in Investments 1978*. Luxembourg: 1980.

Friedman, J. and Alonso, W., eds. *Regional Development and Planning*. Cambridge, Mass.: MIT Press, 1964.

Gravier, J.F. *Paris et le desert français en 1972*. Paris: Flammarion, 1972.

Hirshman, A.O. *The Strategy of Economic Development*. New Haven: Yale University Press, 1958.

Holland, Stuart. *Capital versus the Regions*. London: Macmillan, 1976.

Klaassen, L.H. *Location of Industries in Depressed Areas*. Paris: OECD, 1968.

Kuklinski, A.R., ed. *Growth Poles and Growth Centres in Regional Planning*. The Hague: Mouton, 1972.

McKee, D.L.; Dean, R.O.; and Leahy, W.H. *Regional Economics: Theory and Practice*. New York: Free Press, 1970.

Molle, William, with Bas van Holst and Hans Smit. *Regional Disparity and Economic Development in the European Community*. Farnborough: Saxon House, 1980.

Myrdal, G.M. *Economic Theory and Underdeveloped Regions*. London: Duckworth, 1957.

Nurkse, R. *Problems of Capital Formation in Underdeveloped Countries*. Oxford: Blackwells, 1953.

Organisation de Coopération et de Développement Économiques. *Les Politiques régionales, perspectives actuelles*. Paris: 1977.

Organisation for Economic Co-operation and Development. *The Regional Factor in Economic Development*. Paris: 1971.

Petrella, R. *La renaissance des cultures régionales en Europe*. Paris: Éditions Entente, 1978.

Richardson, H.W. *The Economics of Urban Size*. Farnborough: Saxon House, 1973.

Robinson, E.A.G. *Backward Areas in Advanced Countries*. London: Macmillan, 1969.

Romus, Paul. *L'Europe et les régions*. Paris: Fernand Nathan, 1979.

Shoup, Carl S., ed. *Fiscal Harmonization in Common Markets, Vol. I*. New York: Columbia University Press, 1967.

Stilwell, F.J.B. *Regional Economic Policy*. London: Macmillan, 1972.

III. National Policies for Regional Development in the EEC

Allen, K. and MacLennan, M.C. *Regional Problems and Policies in Italy and France*. London: Allen and Unwin, 1970.

Brown, A.J. *The Framework of Regional Economics in the United Kingdom*. Cambridge: Cambridge University Press, 1972.

Clout, H.D., ed. *Regional Development in Western Europe*. London: John Wiley, 1975.

Europe. Amsterdam: North Holland, 1975.

Fitzgerald, G. *Planning in Ireland*. Dublin: Institute of Public Administration and Economic Planning, 1968.

Hansen, Niles M. *Public Policy and Regional Economic Development*. Cambridge, Mass.: Ballinger, 1974.

Kuklinski, A. *Social Issues in Regional Policy and Regional Planning*. The Hague: Mouton, 1977.

MacLennan, D. and Parr, John B. *Regional Policy: Past Experience and New Directions*. Glasgow: Martin Robertson, 1979.

McCrone, G. *Regional Policy in Britain*. London: Allen and Unwin, 1969.

Organisation for Economic Co-operation and Development. *Reappraisal of Regional Policies in OECD Countries*. Paris: 1975.

Organisation for Economic Co-operation and Development. *Regional Problems and Policies in OECD Countries*. Paris: 1976.

Pagé, J.-P., ed. *Profil économique de la France*. Paris: La Documentation Française, 1975.

Petrella, R., ed. *Le développement régional en Europe*. The Hague: Mouton, 1971.

Seers, D.; Schaffer, B.; and Kiljunen, M.L. *Underdeveloped Europe*. Sussex: The Harvester Press for the Institute of Development Studies, 1979.

Strong, A.L. *Planned Urban Environments*. Baltimore: Johns Hopkins University Press, 1971.

Vanhove, Norbert and Klaassen, Leo H. *Regional Policy — A European Approach*. Farnborough: Saxon House, 1980.

Yuill, Douglas; Allen, Kevin; and Hull, Chris, eds. *Regional Policy in the European Community*. London: Croom Helm, 1980.

IV. EEC Policies and Instruments for Regional Development

Commission of the European Communities. *The Agricultural Policy of the European Community*. Luxembourg: European Documentation, 1979.

Commission of the European Communities. *The Agricultural Situation in the Commmunity, 1979 Report*. Brussels/Luxembourg: 1980.

Commission of the European Communities. *Eighth Report on the Activities of the European Social Fund, Financial Year 1979*. Brussels: 1980.

Commission of the European Communities. *Energy Policy*, COM/(80)130 final. Brussels: 20 March 1980.

Commission of the European Communities. *The European Community and Vocational Training*. Luxembourg: European Documentation, Periodical 6, 1980.

Commission of the European Communities, *The European Community's Social Policy*. Luxembourg: European Documentation, Periodicals, 1978−2.

Commission of the European Communities. *European Regional Development Fund — Annual Reports*. Brussels: especially those for 1978 and 1979.

Commission of the European Communities. *The European Social Fund*. Brussels/Luxembourg: European File, November-December 1979.

Commission of the European Communities. *Principal Regulations and Decisions of the Council of the European Communities on Regional Policy*. Brussels: 1979.

Commission of the European Communities. *The Regional Development Programmes*. Regional Policy Series No. 17. Brussels: May 1979. Also the Programmes, published under the same series, for each member state.

Commission of the European Communities. *Report of the Study Group on the Role of Public Finance in European Integration*, chairman D. MacDougall. Brussels: 1977.

Commission of the European Communities. *Young People in the European Community*. Brussels/Luxembourg: European File, February 1981.

European Investment Bank. *Annual Reports*. Luxembourg.

European Investment Bank. *EIB Information*. Luxembourg (a series of excellent publications available in six languages).

European Investment Bank. *Press Releases*. Luxembourg (many of which provide useful current data on the Bank's activities).

European Investment Bank. *Statute and Other Provisions*. Luxembourg: 1 January 1981.

European Investment Bank. *Twenty Years, 1958−1978*. Luxembourg: 1978.

Fennell, Rosemary. *The Common Agricultural Policy of the European Community*. London: Granada, 1979.

Hayek, F.A. *Denationalisation of Money*. Hobart Paper Special, 70. London: The Institute of Economic Affairs, 1976.

Henry, P. *Study on the Regional Impact of the Common Agricultural Policy*. XVI/44/81-EN. Brussels: European Commission: Directorate General for Regional Policy, December 1980.

Lucas, N.J.D. *Energy and the European Community*. London: Europa Publications, 1977.

McAllister, Ian. "Regional Policy in the European Community." *Policy Options* 2 (March/April 1981): 48–53.

McLachlan, D.L. and Swann, D. *Competition Policy in the European Community*. London: Oxford University Press, 1967.

Romus, Paul. *L'Europe et les régions*. Paris: Fernand Nathan, 1979.

Shanks, Michael. *European Social Policy, Today and Tomorrow*. Oxford: Pergamon Press, 1977 (also contains useful bibliography for more specialized reference purposes).

Vanhove, Norbert and Klaassen, Leo H. *Regional Policy — A European Approach*. Farnborough: Saxon House, 1980.

Wilkinson, C. "Recent Developments in ECSC Policies." *Three Banks Review*, vol. 113.

V. Regional Development in Canada

This review is on regional development experiences in the EEC, with reference to possible Canadian application. It is not a review of the Canadian regional development experience. However, for readers who may be unfamiliar with Canadian regional problems and approaches, the following selected bibliography is provided.

Brewis, T.N. *Regional Economic Policies in Canada*. Toronto: Macmillan, 1969.

Canada. Parliamentary Task Force on Federal-Provincial Fiscal Arrangements. *Fiscal Federation in Canada*. Ottawa: Minister of Supply and Services Canada, 1981.

Economic Council of Canada. *Living Together*. Ottawa: Minister of Supply and Services Canada, 1977.

Green, Alan G. *Regional Aspects of Canada's Economic Growth*. Toronto: University of Toronto Press, 1971.

Lithwick, N.H. *Regional Economic Policy: The Canadian Experience*. Toronto. McGraw-Hill Ryerson, 1978.

Mackintosh, W.A. *The Economic Background of Dominion-Provincial Relations*. Reprinted in the Carleton Library Series. Toronto: McClelland and Stewart, 1964.

Pomfret, Richard. *The Economic Development of Canada*. Toronto: Methuen, 1981.

Savoie, Donald J. *Federal-Provincial Collaboration*. Montreal: McGill-Queen's University Press, 1981.

Smiley, D.V. *Canada in Question: Federalism in the Eighties*. Toronto: McGraw-Hill Ryerson, 1980.

Zukowsky, Ronald James. *Intergovernmental Relations in Canada: The Year in Review 1980*. Volume I. *Policy and Politics*. Kingston: Queen's University, Institute of Intergovernmental Relations, 1981.

Starting with its first edition, March 1980, *Policy Options* (The Institute for Research on Public Policy) has published a number of articles on contemporary regional development issues in Canada.

The Members of the Institute

Institute Management

Gordon Robertson	President
Louis Vagianos	Executive Director
John M. Curtis	Director, International Economics Program
Ian McAllister	Director, Regional Employment Opportunities Program
Zavis P. Zeman	Director, Technology and Society Program
Donald Wilson	Director, Conferences and Seminars Program
Dana Phillip Doiron	Director, Communications Services
Ann C. McCoomb	Associate Director, Communications Services
Tom Kent	Editor, *Policy Options Politiques*

The Institute for Research on Public Policy
Publications Available*
March 1982

Books

Leroy O. Stone &
Claude Marceau
Canadian Population Trends and Public Policy Through the 1980s. 1977 $4.00

Raymond Breton
The Canadian Condition: A Guide to Research in Public Policy. 1977 $2.95

Raymond Breton
Une orientation de la recherche politique dans le contexte canadien. 1978 $2.95

J.W. Rowley &
W.T. Stanbury, eds.
Competition Policy in Canada: Stage II, Bill C-13. 1978 $12.95

C.F. Smart &
W.T. Stanbury, eds.
Studies on Crisis Management. 1978 $9.95

W.T. Stanbury, ed.
Studies on Regulation in Canada. 1978 $9.95

Michael Hudson
Canada in the New Monetary Order: Borrow? Devalue? Restructure! 1978 $6.95

W.A.W. Neilson &
J.C. MacPherson, eds.
The Legislative Process in Canada: The Need for Reform. 1978 $12.95

David K. Foot, ed.
Public Employment and Compensation in Canada: Myths and Realities. 1978 $10.95

W.E. Cundiff &
Mado Reid, eds.
Issues in Canada/U.S. Transborder Computer Data Flows. 1979 $6.50

David K. Foot
Public Employment in Canada: Statistical Series. 1979 $15.00

Meyer W. Bucovetsky, ed.
Studies on Public Employment and Compensation in Canada. 1979 $14.95

Richard French &
André Béliveau
The RCMP and the Management of National Security. 1979 $6.95

---

* Order Address: The Institute for Research on Public Policy
                   P.O. Box 9300, Station A
                   TORONTO, Ontario
                   M5W 2C7

Richard French &   *La GRC et la gestion de la sécurité nationale*. 1979
André Béliveau $6.95

Leroy O. Stone &   *Future Income Prospects for Canada's Senior*
Michael J. MacLean   *Citizens*. 1979 $7.95

Richard Bird (in collaboration   *The Growth of Public Employment in Canada*. 1979
with Bucovetsky & Foot) $12.95

G. Bruce Doern &   *The Public Evaluation of Government Spending*.
Allan M. Maslove, eds.   1979 $10.95

Richard Price, ed.   *The Spirit of the Alberta Indian Treaties*. 1979
                            $8.95

Richard J. Schultz   *Federalism and the Regulatory Process*. 1979
                            $1.50

Richard J. Schultz   *Le fédéralisme et le processus de réglementation*.
                            1979 $1.50

Lionel D. Feldman &   *Bargaining for Cities. Municipalities and*
Katherine A. Graham   *Intergovernmental Relations: An Assessment*. 1979
                            $10.95

Elliot J. Feldman &   *The Future of North America: Canada, the United*
Neil Nevitte, eds.   *States, and Quebec Nationalism*. 1979 $7.95

Maximo Halty-Carrere   *Technological Development Strategies for*
                            Developing Countries. 1979 $12.95

G.B. Reschenthaler   *Occupational Health and Safety in Canada: The*
                            Economics and Three Case Studies. 1979 $5.00

David R. Protheroe   *Imports and Politics: Trade Decision-Making in*
                            Canada, 1968–1979. 1980 $8.95

G. Bruce Doern   *Government Intervention in the Canadian Nuclear*
                            Industry. 1980 $8.95

G. Bruce Doern &   *Canadian Nuclear Policies*. 1980 $14.95
R.W. Morrison, eds.

Yoshi Tsurumi with   *Sogoshosha: Engines of Export-Based Growth*.
Rebecca R. Tsurumi   1980 $8.95

Allan M. Maslove &   *Wage Controls in Canada, 1975–78: A Study of*
Gene Swimmer   *Public Decision Making*. 1980 $11.95

T. Gregory Kane

Consumers and the Regulators: Intervention in the Federal Regulatory Process. 1980 $10.95

Albert Breton &
Anthony Scott

The Design of Federations. 1980 $6.95

A.R. Bailey &
D.G. Hull

The Way Out: A More Revenue-Dependent Public Sector and How It Might Revitalize the Process of Governing. 1980 $6.95

Réjean Lachapelle &
Jacques Henripin

La situation démolinguistique au Canada : évolution passée et prospective. 1980 $24.95

Raymond Breton,
Jeffrey G. Reitz &
Victor F. Valentine

Cultural Boundaries and the Cohesion of Canada. 1980 $18.95

David R. Harvey

Christmas Turkey or Prairie Vulture? An Economic Analysis of the Crow's Nest Pass Grain Rates. 1980 $10.95

Stuart McFadyen,
Colin Hoskins &
David Gillen

Canadian Broadcasting: Market Structure and Economic Performance. 1980 $15.95

Richard M. Bird

Taxing Corporations. 1980 $6.95

Albert Breton &
Raymond Breton

Why Disunity? An Analysis of Linguistic and Regional Cleavages in Canada. 1980 $6.95

Leroy O. Stone &
Susan Fletcher

A Profile of Canada's Older Population. 1980 $7.95

Peter N. Nemetz, ed.

Resource Policy: International Perspectives. 1980 $18.95

Keith A.J. Hay, ed.

Canadian Perspectives on Economic Relations with Japan. 1980 $18.95

Raymond Breton &
Gail Grant

La langue de travail au Québec : synthèse de la recherche sur la rencontre de deux langues. 1981 $10.95

Diane Vanasse

L'évolution de la population scolaire du Québec. 1981 $12.95

Raymond Breton,
Jeffrey G. Reitz &
Victor F. Valentine

Les frontières culturelles et la cohésion du Canada. 1981 $18.95

H.V. Kroeker, ed.   *Sovereign People or Sovereign Governments.*
                                 1981 $12.95

Peter Aucoin, ed.   *The Politics and Management of Restraint in*
                                 Government. 1981 $17.95

David M. Cameron, ed.   *Regionalism and Supranationalism: Challenges*
                                 and Alternatives to the Nation-State in Canada and
                                 Europe. 1981 $9.95

Heather Menzies   *Women and the Chip.* 1981 $6.95

Nicole S. Morgan   *Nowhere to Go? Possible Consequences of the*
                                 Demographic Imbalance in Decision-Making
                                 Groups of the Federal Public Service. 1981 $8.95

Nicole S. Morgan   *Où aller? Les conséquences prévisibles des*
                                 déséquilibres démographiques chez les groupes de
                                 décision de la fonction publique fédérale.
                                 1981 $8.95

Peter N. Nemetz, ed.   *Energy Crisis: Policy Response.* 1981 $10.95

Allan Tupper &   *Public Corporations and Public Policy in Canada.*
G. Bruce Doern, eds.   1981 $16.95

James Gillies   *Where Business Fails.* 1981 $9.95

Réjean Lachapelle &   *The Demolinguistic Situation in Canada: Past*
Jacques Henripin   *Trends and Future Prospects.* 1982 $24.95

Ian McAllister   *Regional Development and the European*
                                 Community: A Canadian Perspective. 1982 $13.95

Occasional Papers
W.E. Cundiff   *Nodule Shock? Seabed Mining and the Future of the*
(No. 1)   *Canadian Nickel Industry.* 1978 $3.00

IRPP/Brookings   *Conference on Canadian-U.S. Economic Relations.*
(No. 2)   1978 $3.00

Robert A. Russel   *The Electronic Briefcase: The Office of the Future.*
(No. 3)   1978 $3.00

C.C. Gotlieb   *Computers in the Home: What They Can Do for*
(No. 4)   *Us—And to Us.* 1978 $3.00

Raymond Breton &   *Urban Institutions and People of Indian Ancestry.*
Gail Grant Akian   1978 $3.00
(No. 5)

K.A. Hay   *Friends or Acquaintances? Canada and Japan's*
(No. 6)   *Other Trading Partners in the Early 1980s.*
                                  1979 $3.00

T. Atkinson   *Trends in Life Satisfaction Among Canadians,*
(No. 7)   *1968 – 1977.* 1979 $3.00

Fred Thompson &   *The Political Economy of Interest Groups in the*
W.T. Stanbury   *Legislative Process in Canada.* 1979 $3.00
(No. 9)

Pierre Sormany   *Les micro-esclaves : vers une bio-industrie*
(No. 11)   *canadienne.* 1979 $3.00

Zavis P. Zeman &   *The Dynamics of the Technological Leadership of*
David Hoffman, eds.   *the World.* 1980 $3.00
(No. 13)

Russell Wilkins   *Health Status in Canada, 1926 – 1976.* 1980 $3.00
(No. 13*a*)

Russell Wilkins   *L'état de santé au Canada, 1926 – 1976.*
(No. 13*b*)   1980 $3.00

P. Pergler   *The Automated Citizen: Social and Political Impact*
(No. 14)   *of Interactive Broadcasting.* 1980 $4.95

Donald G. Cartwright   *Official Language Populations in Canada:*
(No. 16)   *Patterns and Contacts.* 1980 $4.95

Report
Dhiru Patel   *Dealing With Interracial Conflict: Policy*
                                  Alternatives. 1980 $5.95

Robert A. Russel   *Office Automation: Key to the Information Society.*
                                  1981 $3.00

Irving Brecher   *Canada's Competition Policy Revisited: Some New*
                                  Thoughts on an Old Story. 1982 $3.00